DO *YOU!*

RUSSELL SIMMONS

with Chris Morrow

DO *YOU!*

12 LAWS TO ACCESS
THE POWER IN *YOU*
TO ACHIEVE HAPPINESS
AND SUCCESS

GOTHAM
BOOKS

GOTHAM BOOKS
Published by Penguin Group (USA) Inc.
375 Hudson Street, New York, New York 10014, U.S.A.
Penguin Group (Canada), 90 Eglinton Avenue East, Suite 700, Toronto, Ontario M4P 2Y3,
Canada (a division of Pearson Penguin Canada Inc.); Penguin Books Ltd, 80 Strand, London
WC2R 0RL, England; Penguin Ireland, 25 St Stephen's Green, Dublin 2, Ireland (a division
of Penguin Books Ltd); Penguin Group (Australia), 250 Camberwell Road, Camberwell,
Victoria 3124, Australia (a division of Pearson Australia Group Pty Ltd); Penguin Books India
Pvt Ltd, 11 Community Centre, Panchsheel Park, New Delhi – 110 017, India;
Penguin Group (NZ), 67 Apollo Drive, Mairangi Bay, Auckland 1311, New Zealand (a division
of Pearson New Zealand Ltd.); Penguin Books (South Africa) (Pty) Ltd, 24 Sturdee Avenue,
Rosebank, Johannesburg 2196, South Africa

Penguin Books Ltd, Registered Offices: 80 Strand, London WC2R 0RL, England

Published by Gotham Books, a division of Penguin Group (USA) Inc.

First printing, May 2007
1   3   5   7   9   10   8   6   4   2

Gotham Books and the skyscraper logo are trademarks of Penguin Group (USA) Inc.

LIBRARY OF CONGRESS CATALOGING-IN-PUBLICATION DATA HAS BEEN APPLIED FOR

ISBN 978-1-592-40293-9

Printed in the United States of America
Set in ITC Galliard with Dicot
Designed by Sabrina Bowers

CONTENTS

FOREWORD

DONALD TRUMP

IF YOU'VE SPENT ANY TIME following my own career, you know success is a subject I take very seriously. I not only work very hard to be successful in my own life, but to help other people become successful as well. From my books to my university to my TV show, I want to help people understand what it takes to be successful. Even my buildings are designed to inspire people and remind them to always follow their dreams. So endorsing someone else's views on success is not something that I do lightly. Yet when Russell asked me to write the foreword for this book, I said yes without any hesitation. Because if there's one person I believe can show you a path toward true success, it's Russell Simmons.

Russell is one of the great entrepreneurs out there today. I've always been astounded by his ability to see where the world is going and then move in that direction. That ability to follow a vision, even if it means leaving his comfort zone, is just one of the qualities that make Russell such a fabulous businessman.

As you'll read, he also understands the importance of surrounding yourself with the right people; people who are competent, but not complacent. Russell and I might get the credit for our respective successes, but we also both know that we'd never reach those heights without a strong home team. Similarly, we both realize how important it is to never quit. If there is a concrete wall in front of you, you have to go through it. You can never, ever give up or even think in terms of giving up.

And of course, we both appreciate the importance of building strong brands. Just as I've always tried to ensure that the Trump name connotes luxury and quality, for over twenty years Russell's stamp on a product means that it's an authentic reflection of the best in popular culture.

But while I could talk about Russell's entrepreneurial acumen all day, this book is about so much more than just making money. That's because Russell understands that the true definition of success can never be measured in dollars and cents. This concept might not seem to be something I would normally promote, but I couldn't agree with it more. In fact, I've always said that while success is good, success with significance is even better. And I think you'll find that the kind of success that Russell is promoting in this book is very, very significant indeed.

That's because it's a success that's based on sharing instead of hoarding. On staying open to new ideas, even ones that might seem strange at first. On making the right choices, even when they don't seem to be in your best interests. It's the kind of success that we should all strive for.

Russell and I have been friends for over twenty years and he's always been kind enough to call me a mentor and an inspiration. But I'd be lying if I didn't say that I've learned so much from Russell over the years as well. That's why I encourage you to open up not only your eyes, but your heart as well, and really let the messages in this book sink in. I believe that if you can even absorb just a small portion of the laws Russell shares in this book, it won't be long before you'll find the success you've always been after.

DONALD TRUMP
2007

INTRODUCTION

WHY LAWS?

The seed that eventually blossomed into this book was planted several years ago when I was asked to create a radio series based on the strategies for success that I had developed and observed in over twenty-five years in the entertainment business. While I was flattered that people were interested in my observations, I'll also admit to being slightly intimidated by the prospect of sharing them with the world in such a structured manner. The strategies I wanted to share were derived from the struggles and experiences that had transformed me over a considerable period of time. And since I am still learning and growing every day, it seemed slightly premature to set them down in such a definitive manner.

But I also knew that I had come to a place where, when reflecting on my life's journey, I could see that there were particular laws and principles that had guided my professional and personal success. And more importantly, I had only been able to learn those principles because individuals from a variety of cultures had been willing to share the lessons that they had learned across the lines of global divisions and inspire me. Reflecting on how much knowledge I had gained through the gifts of others is what ultimately committed me to sharing the changes I've made in my own life. While some people might have preconceived notions about which sort of principles power a "hip-hop" mogul, I wanted to make it clear that my purpose is defined by the power of giving back and sharing. Whereas earlier in my career I admittedly might have been focused on consumption, now I'm focused on giving. It's more about "us" and less about "me." And I'm not the only one who's changing. Hip-hop isn't just kids anymore—there are literally millions of people thirty-five, forty, even fifty, who have spent half their lives or more listening to hip-hop. And they're becoming more aware of their duty to give back to their community. It's not that I'm ashamed of the first part of my career. In fact I wouldn't change a thing even if I could. But I know I'm truly happier with my success now than I was with it then. And true happiness is all that anyone wants.

From speaking at colleges and the Hip-Hop Summits, I realized there was a genuine interest from people about my approach to success. The hip-hop nation is nothing if not aspirational, and everywhere I go, people ask me for advice on how to improve their lives. A lot of times it's stuff like "Yo, Russell, my brother is the next Jay-Z. Lemme hit you with a demo," or, "Hey, Russell, let me get a job at Phat Farm!" But I also get deeper questions about my philosophies on business and spirituality. It's always a little surprising, but a lot of people seem genuinely interested in my message.

So with some prodding, I decided to focus on sharing these laws. Since the interest was there, I realized it was more important for me to serve than to be self-conscious. We started with the radio series, which people really responded to. And after a couple years of sharing through that medium, it only seemed natural to put it all down in a book. I've made plenty of mistakes in my career and I'll make plenty more. But I don't think this book is one of them. This is a sincere effort on my part to help people find an easier way to live based on what I've found works for me. It took me a while to figure out what works, but like most people who feel like they're starting to put the puzzle together, now I want to share those skills with the world.

I'm not suggesting that my approach is in any way novel or revolutionary, only that maybe reading about these laws will help them sink in for you. That's why people go to church (or in my case, go to yoga), to help the laws sink in. I need to hear these laws over and over again to remind myself how to operate under them. The laws are simple, but it's still a struggle to follow them. Personally, I have a hard time practicing everything I preach. I try to stay focused on my higher self, but sometimes I slip. I break these laws every day, but I'm dedicated to trying to do better every day too. Just as, I know, everyone out there is already struggling to do the best they can.

Or maybe you're not struggling. Maybe you're reading this because you're already doing well and you just want to sharpen your skills. Or maybe you're an executive who's never listened to rap but want to learn more about the hip-hop game and what makes it tick. That's fine, because this book is designed to be a reminder to those already living under these laws, or living in close proximity to them, to simply become more conscious of them. That way, they can build on the success they've already achieved. No matter what your motivation is, I'm happy you're here, because I'm trying to speak to everyone who can hear me.

Of course, if you try to speak to everyone at once, sometimes you just end up making a lot of noise. But I'm someone who's always tried to connect with as many people as possible. I want to be able to chop it up with folks in the Hamptons just like I chop it up with folks in Harlem. One of the first things I noticed when I got in the game was that hip-hop was gravitating downtown. I saw that people loved hip-hop in punk-rock bars, or dance clubs like Danceteria, just like they were loving it in the streets of Harlem. So while some people saw a white group like the Beastie Boys as exploitive, to me that was natural. And while I've been credited with creating a common ground in hip-hop, I don't deserve it. The common ground was already there. I just tried to build something lasting on it. And of course, in the case of the Beastie Boys and Run DMC, they ended up being superstars who laid the foundation not only for much of my subsequent personal success, but for hip-hop's subsequent success as well.

I also want to mention that while all of these rules are rooted in spirituality, I don't make any distinction between Christian law, Muslim law, Buddhist law, Jewish law, the yoga sutras (the most basic yogic scripture), et cetera. That's because the most fundamental law is a belief in the oneness of humanity. And that law is at the heart of all these religions and philosophies. None of these rules stands alone, either on a personal or collective basis. They're all interwoven. So while we've broken these laws down into different categories, at the end of the day, all these laws fall under one basic unbreakable law—and that's God's law.

In fact, I'll let you in on a secret, though my publisher probably won't like it: I'm not saying anything in this book that hasn't already been said before. These are the exact same laws that Jesus Christ, Moses, Muhammad, Lord Buddha, Patanjali, Mother Teresa, and countless other inspirational people all shared in their own lifetimes. Which is not to say that I'm in any way comparing myself to those incredible individuals. I'm just pointing out that all these truth-telling scriptures run parallel to each other. They might have been written down at different times, or in different languages, but they're all explaining God's law.

Everything that I'm promoting in this book should already sound familiar to you from your church, or your synagogue, or your mosque, or wherever you go for spiritual dialogue. Or maybe you've already heard it in a family or academic setting from your parents and teachers. This book is designed to help you *remember to remember* (a phrase I'll use a lot in this book) those lessons. If this book has any value, it will be as a reminder of what you *already* know. Because what I'm trying to do here is help some of these ancient, ancient laws sink in for you. I didn't create any of them, but maybe by hearing these laws from me, you'll be able to unlock the potential for success that's already inside you.

Now that I've spoken a bit about what my book will be about, let me say a few words about what this book *isn't* about. It isn't about my life story. That story has already been told several times, in different settings. If you're still not familiar with my story, let me rehash it very quickly so that there is some context for the references I'll make later in the book.

I grew up in Hollis, Queens, and as a young man found myself falling into the same traps that ensnare so many other young people growing up in the streets of urban America. I began to get caught up with drugs and gangs—not because I was a bad person at heart, but because they seemed to be the most powerful ways for me to express myself in that environment. And like so many others, I would have probably continued to make empty investments in that type of expression if I hadn't come in contact with a new force on the streets, a force that was even more powerful than drugs or gangs. And that presence was called hip-hop. The very first time I heard hip-hop, I knew my life would never be the same. I knew that I had found a better avenue to express myself and pursue a better relationship with the world. In hip-hop's powerful beats and rhymes, I heard the truth. And I heard it loudly.

I could never really rap myself, so that love affair led to me promoting artists who could, including my brother Joey's group Run DMC. Later, I founded Def Jam Records with my friend Rick Rubin and was able to introduce the world to incredible artists like Public Enemy, the Beastie Boys, LL Cool J, DMX, and Jay-Z before eventually selling the label. I also started a clothing company called Phat Farm and started dabbling in film, where I produced *The Nutty Professor,* and television, where I've been fortunate to find some success with shows such as *Def Comedy Jam, Def Poetry Jam,* and *Run's House.* Between all those projects, I married the incredible and inspirational Kimora Lee Simmons. In addition to bringing two beautiful young girls into the world, we also started a successful women's clothing line, Baby Phat. And in addition to those commercial pursuits, I've also been heavily involved in social change initiatives like the Hip-Hop Summit Action Network, the Rush Philanthropic organization, and the Foundation for Ethnic Understanding.

There's been plenty more written about me than that, some good, some bad, some true, some dead wrong. But those are some of the facts that are useful for this book. So now let me touch on some more things this book *isn't* about. It isn't about behind-the-scenes stories and gossip from the rap game—so if you're looking for lots of wild anecdotes from the record business, then this book isn't for you. If you want to read stories about my struggles with drugs, or the decadent lifestyle I used to live, then this isn't the book for you either. Yes, I will use examples from my own life to try to illustrate how some of these laws work, but, frankly, my stories aren't the main focus. I want to state for the record that this book is about the message more than the messenger. I freely admit that I struggle to practice much of what I preach (though I'll try not to be too preachy), so I don't want my personal weaknesses to overshadow the strength and validity of these laws. What I'm really asking is that you come into this book with an open mind. Not for my sake, but for your own. The last thing I would want is for anyone's feelings about me personally to be an obstacle between their life and these laws.

This book also isn't about surefire ways you can get rich. I understand that when you pick up a book by a "music mogul," that might be the type of information you're expecting, but again, this isn't that book. You're not going to hear me say, "This is the particular management style I advocate." My approach is much too instinctual. But my instincts *are* based on a set of spiritual rules. I promise that if you really explore the ideas I'm promoting, you'll see that getting rich is just one of the many benefits that come from living under them. Instead of financial advice, some of you might be expecting the types of laws promoted by a Machiavelli or a Sun Tzu, the "power at all costs" philosophies that have been popular within hip-hop over the years. While I'm not criticizing those philosophies, or the people who follow them, mentalities that promote self-preservation are not what I'm promoting. Instead of *The Prince* or *The Art of War*, these laws are rooted in books like *Autobiography of a Yogi* or *The Yoga Sutras of Patanjali* (particularly the version with commentary by Sri Swami Satchidananda).

If I were to heavily promote how to grab power, or how to make a lot of money, that would be a dishonest book. That's not me. Because when I stand up at financial summits, these are the truths I talk about. When I'm speaking at colleges, these are the truths I talk about. When I'm hanging out in St. Barts with Puffy and Ron Perelman, these are the truths I talk about. When I'm meeting with a young rapper looking for advice on how to get his career started, these are the truths I talk about. When I talk to my staff, or my friends, or my family, these are the truths I talk about. When I'm sitting on a train, or riding in a plane, or walking down the street and people approach me, these are the truths I end up talking to them about. So I won't switch messages now, just because a hip-hop nigga is supposed to be talking about power and money instead of God and spirituality and giving. It's the message of finding a sustainable happiness. This book might seem too "intellectual," or too "spiritual," or too "New Age," for some, but for better or for worse, these are the truths I believe in. I've found success promoting the truth a lot of times in my career, but I've rarely found it when I've tried to create a commercial for what people expect from me instead of what I truly feel and believe.

Of course the laws in this book can help you make more money, achieve more influence, make more friends, or improve your career.

But if those transformations do take place, hopefully they'll be part of a larger and ultimately, I believe, more rewarding metamorphosis, which is the change you'll feel as you move closer to God.

Besides, we all already live under these laws, even if we aren't completely aware of it. I can say that, because I lived under these laws for many years without being fully conscious of them. I now recognize that these are the same laws that helped propel hip-hop out of the struggle and into a space where it continues to shape the world in incredible ways. So for those of you who have been conditioned to only hear hip-hop's low notes, perhaps this book can clean off your lenses so that you can clearly see hip-hop's tremendous achievements and potential. I've already heard the high notes from hip-hop, so I know it's a cultural *and* spiritual force.

And please don't get hung up on the term *laws*. A lot of people, especially people in the struggle, think rules are meant to tell you what you *can't* do. But rules are really the process through which we realize our dreams. These laws are just a way of reminding you of what you *can* do.

My hope is that after reading this book, you'll be more focused on what you need to do to get to a better place in life, both financially and spiritually. But you have to remember that there's no end of the road when it comes to being successful. That's because success is a journey, not a destination. Thank you for letting me take part of that journey with you.

Last but not least, I want to say that while I've spent many years trying to articulate these laws on my radio show, at lectures, Hip-Hop Summits, speeches, fund-raisers, or the many other venues where I've been blessed to share my thoughts with an audience, until now I've never been able to present them in such a cohesive structure. That's why I want to take this opportunity to thank my friend and coauthor, Chris Morrow, for helping me gather all these ideas together and express them in a succinct voice. Chris reminds me of some of the rappers I've worked with, in that he has a gift for observing a specific environment (in this case, the ideas that I've been babbling about all these years) and then sharing it in a way that makes sense to the larger world. That gift will serve him well in the future—Chris possesses one of the most compelling voices in hip-hop culture and it's been a pleasure to collaborate with him.

RUSSELL SIMMONS
2007

Degrees are helpful, but they won't guarantee you success in the business world. Only faith and dedication to your vision can do that.

LAW NUMBER ONE:

SEE YOUR VISION AND STICK WITH IT

I dream my painting and paint my dream.
—VINCENT VAN GOGH

BEING AN ENTREPRENEUR can be nerve-wracking, largely because there's no by-the-book way to do it. Some people think they'll get the blueprint at business school, but that degree alone definitely won't guarantee success. In fact, out of all the degrees you can get, a business degree might be the *least* valuable.

Think about it—if you go to medical school, when you come out, you'll know how to help sick people. Just like when you get out of law school, you'll know how to sue people. But an MBA doesn't mean you'll have the skills to actually run a business. They probably don't want to hear that up at Wharton or Harvard, but it's the truth. And I'm a living example. I might run multimillion-dollar companies, but I didn't graduate from college, let alone get an MBA. I don't know how to write a business plan. Truth is, I've never even read the ones I pay people with MBAs to write *for* me. Now, don't get me wrong—a business degree can open up a lot of doors for you. But it should always complement, instead of compensate for, an entrepreneurial spirit that's born in your imagination. That's because, in my experience, there's only one thing that will *always* steer you toward success: That's to have a vision and to stick with it.

Once I have a vision for a new venture, I'm going to ride that vision until the wheels come off. There are always going to be bumps in the road, but I try not to let them faze me. In fact, my greatest successes started as visions that very few other people believed in. No one in the music industry, and I mean *no one,* believed in Def Jam Records at first. Just like how fifteen years later, no one thought a hip-hop clothing company called Phat Fashions would be able to make it. But in both cases, I was able to ignore the naysayers because my vision for those companies was so strong. And it's not just me. From Microsoft to CNN to Roc-A-Fella Records, many successful businesses started as a vision in the mind of a dreamer. Of course, we all have dreams. The difference is that Bill Gates, Ted Turner, Jay-Z, and Dame Dash believed in their dreams so strongly that they refused to quit until those dreams became reality. Those guys didn't win because they had an MBA, or wrote the best business plan, or read *The Wall Street Journal* with their coffee every morning. They won because they had the strongest visions. I'm not going to make too many absolute statements in this book, but I will promise you that following your vision will always lead to success.

When sailors used to get lost in a storm, they'd always look for the North Star for guidance. They could use that star to help them get their bearings because it never moved in the sky. You have to use your vision the same way. Whenever you face obstacles or hurdles in life, look to your vision. As long as you've frozen it in your mind and it never moves, you'll know which direction to go in. As long as you never lose sight of your vision, you'll never lose sight of success either.

CREATING CLASSIC AMERICAN FLAVA

Following my vision has paid off many times in my career, but the example that really stands out is my clothing company Phat Farm. Today, the concept of a hip-hop clothing company seems as natural as air. But when I started telling people about my vision for such a company back in 1992, *nobody* was feeling it. Even people I had enjoyed success with in the record business didn't believe in my vision. But I was convinced that it was time for hip-hop to make clothes *for* hip-hop. I knew we could build and maintain our own companies, just like we had done in the record industry. And once I locked in on that vision, I was going to pursue it no matter what sort of negativity or skepticism I encountered.

I first envisioned the high-end fashion company that would become Phat Farm back in 1991 at a couture fashion show in New York City (I can't remember who the exact designer was, but I'm hazy on a lot of details from those days). I was going to a lot of shows back then, not because I was particularly into fashion, but because I was single and very much into beautiful women. Still, I had never been to a show like this before. Instead of the "normal" couture I had seen at shows, the designer had these models wearing clothes inspired by the latest hip-hop styles, like door-knocker earrings and crazy gold chains. I knew he or she was trying to copy what the kids were rocking back in the hood, but it felt fake. The designs were inspired by hip-hop, but in the same way a designer would go to Africa, see what the "natives" were wearing, fly back to New York, and put it on the runway. This show had a similar vibe. Nothing was authentic. The way the models walked, the way they tilted their Kangols, their attitude—everything was bogus. It was almost like watching the fashion version of a minstrel show. I'm sure that's not what the designer intended, but that's how it came off, to me anyway.

I was laughing when they first came down the runway, but the more I thought about it, the situation didn't seem so funny. I began to ask myself, why should this designer, who obviously has no real connection to hip-hop culture, get paid off of ideas that we cherished and believed in? Why should he or she receive the credit for styles that we were already invested in?

It's important to inject a little history lesson here—hip-hop had always been a collage of styles and influences. Our rappers borrowed the "toasting" of Jamaican DJs and the rhymes of James Brown, Frankie Crocker, and Dolemite and turned it into MCing. Our DJs took the music of rock 'n' rollers like the Steve Miller

Band and the Rolling Stones, funk acts like the Bar-Kays and Jimmy Castor, old-school legends like Joe Tex and Otis Redding, and turned their music into break beats. Our dancers took the moves of the Lindy Hop, of salsa, and even martial arts films and turned them into break dancing. And it was the same with fashion. We took hats that were meant for old men in England and made Kangols that everyone wanted to rock on the street. We took glasses from Europe and made them so hot that stores couldn't keep Cazals in stock. Whenever we saw, or heard, or felt elements that seemed authentic or inspirational, we took them and turned them into hip-hop.

But creating that collage was very hard work, especially when it came to clothes. Getting the right clothes back then was no joke. You would go to a store and look through three racks of Ralph Lauren shirts until you found one that spoke to you. Or you would have to try on ten pairs of Nikes until you found one with the right flavor. You were looking for something that was subtle but had edge at the same time. Because Ralph wasn't designing with the streets in mind, he was designing clothes that would look cool at a prep school in Connecticut. Just like Phil Knight wasn't making sneakers for kids in the ghetto. He was making Nikes for white guys running mountain trails in Oregon. And we accepted it, because we thought those images represented our American Dream.

And it has always been like that for African-Americans in this country. If you wanted to look fashionable while you were strolling down Lenox Avenue during the Harlem Renaissance, then you needed to have on a dress by Jeanne Lanvin. But that dress wouldn't have been designed with you in mind—it was made for rich white women in New York and Paris. Just like if you were a jazz musician during the 1960s and you wanted to look fly, you had to wear a Brooks Brothers suit. But that was a suit that was made for a white businessman. Guys like Miles Davis and John Coltrane took that style and made it their own, but it was never intended for them. The streets have never been on the radar when it comes to designing clothes.

That's because the mainstream's mindset has always been: How could some poor black kid from the streets represent what people aspire to? In the 1980s, it seemed only Calvin Klein or Ralph Lauren or Tommy Hilfiger could represent the American Dream. (Of course, Ralph Lauren's real name is Ralph Lipschitz. The truth is, a lot of people thought Jews couldn't reflect the American Dream either.) It's a sad fact, but the older fashion gods could never conceive that mainstream America would aspire to be anything other than blond-haired and blue-eyed. It made perfect sense to them that black people might want to dress like a Polo model, but there was no way that the opposite could be true. They couldn't get their heads around the idea that a white kid in the suburbs might want to dress like a rapper. If clothes make the man, then what man would want to make himself black? In a nutshell, they believed that the American Dream could never be black.

I do want to pause here for a moment and make it clear that I'm not suggesting Ralph or Tommy weren't making great clothes. In fact, just the opposite. At the time there were things about Ralph or Tommy that were so cool to hip-hop. It's just that they were totally unaware of it.

Getting back to Phat Farm, these issues had been troubling me even before the couture show, but that was what really crystallized my belief that something needed to be done. Because while before hip-hop had been borrowing from these other mainstream cultures, now the mainstream was borrowing from us. But while they were getting paid off it, they weren't getting it right. So instead of shaking my head while other people got it wrong, I could do something that made sense for us. I realized that instead of letting other people interpret us, let's take what we do know, what we do love, and make the entire collection ourselves. Essentially, let's exploit ourselves. Not in a negative way, but in the sense that now *every* stock keeping unit (SKU), instead of every fifth jacket or third pair of jeans, will speak to our culture. I envisioned a collection that would allow us to finally realize that we deserved to be the American Dream. A line that said we could actually buy into ourselves. A line that would allow us get over our self-hate.

Those were very big issues. So I knew that I had to deliver these clothes on a very big scale as well. I wasn't dreaming about making a few T-shirts and then calling it a day. I envisioned an institution, something that was classic and would last. I could envision shirts and pants and sneakers and hats rolling out of the factories and into stores all over America. I was determined to make it happen.

For the first few months after the couture show, I had to tell everyone I knew about my idea. But the more people I spoke with, the more I began to realize that not everyone could see my vision. At first, I took it personally. I figured maybe they doubted me because my background was in music instead of fashion. Fair enough. I knew fashion was an insular world that wasn't easy to break into. So I decided to surround myself with the best fashion people I could find, hoping that would satisfy the skeptics. But finding those people was difficult. Very few established designers were willing to work for a company where they couldn't see the vision. I did manage to find several young people who understood the vision, but the more established people in the industry still weren't jumping on board. And I began to realize that it wasn't that the industry people didn't believe in *Russell Simmons* so much as they didn't believe in *hip-hop*. And even more painfully, *hip-hop* didn't believe in hip-hop. I could feel it in the way the cool people only wanted Ralph Lauren or Tommy because they thought that's what represented success. I knew it would be very hard to get people to believe in themselves after they'd been told they were worthless for so long.

Those hurdles were very difficult to get over. And I won't lie, there were many times I felt like the naysayers were right and I should forget the whole idea. I was at the crossroads. But I couldn't let go of my vision. It was so clear, I could see the end result in my mind before I even started to work. There was no way I was going to turn around or change paths.

Instead, I became even more focused on making Phat Farm a reality. I knew it was unrealistic to think I could build an institution overnight. But if I took baby steps, eventually it would happen. One of those first steps was hooking up with a friend named Mark Regev, who owned a store in SoHo called Bagutta, where I used to buy clothes for the women I was dating. It wasn't hip-hop stuff, but high-end clothes like Hervé Léger and Azzedine Alaïa. One day we got to talking about my idea for a hip-hop clothing line and Mark said he wanted to get involved. We decided to open a store in SoHo that would sell the clothes and really articulate this vision. Mark put up half the money and I put up the other half.

But after we sank our money in, we started hemorrhaging. There were orders that never got shipped. There were designs that didn't work, shirts that didn't sell. I didn't understand how the industry worked and manufactured clothes too late. I didn't realize that clothes for the fall season actually have to get delivered in July. I thought we could deliver our fall clothes at the end of August and it would all be good. That was very basic information, but my ignorance of it was costly. I was losing money like crazy and struggling to pay the rent. It felt like this beautiful vision I had been carrying around in my head was shattering into a million pieces (while costing me millions of dollars).

Almost overnight (notice how success never happens overnight, but what you perceive to be failure can), we were half a million dollars in the hole, with no profit in sight. Mark's reaction was "Hey, let's shut this down before we lose even more." Which only made sense. Mark understood *my* vision, but it wasn't *his* vision. Hip-hop was something he knew from the outside looking in. So when the money started disappearing, it was hard for him to have faith that there was still this incredible market right around the corner. He didn't want to keep pushing, he just wanted his money back. (I think it was in the neighborhood of $50K.)

I found myself at yet another crossroads. But I still wasn't ready to turn around. Even though everyone thought that Mark was smart and I was crazy for not cutting my losses, I decided to buy Mark out. I wrote Mark his check, because my vision for what Phat Farm could become was still very strong. And in retrospect, I'm sure that Mark wishes he had stayed in a little longer, because that initial investment would have been worth in excess of $30 million when I eventually sold the company. But when you aren't passionate about a vision, it's hard to have faith in it.

That's why you can never go by the bottom line alone when you're following your vision. According to the bottom line, our little store was a failure. But the bottom line couldn't see what I saw. The bottom line couldn't see how hip-hoppers were coming in off the street and getting excited about our clothes. How they would talk to me, telling me the things I could do to make the clothes even better. I could feel their energy. I could see that with the exception of Karl Kani, who was doing big things first with Cross Colours and then on his own, there still wasn't anyone else who was speaking to the streets correctly. I could sense there was an appreciation of the brand developing. I remember the first year we went to the MAGIC trade show in Las Vegas, which is the industry's biggest annual trade event, we were the only hip-hop line there. If you go to MAGIC today, it looks like a rap concert. Puffy, Jay-Z, 50 Cent, The Game, Nelly, and every other rapper with a clothing line are there trying to meet buyers and convince them to pick up their lines. But back in the early nineties, there was not one other African-American-owned clothing company at that show. Still, I was happy to be in the house. Instead of feeling locked out, I was inspired to stand there on the floor and look at all the booths and buyers. I saw opportunity and I was determined to make the most out of it.

Ultimately, it took me a long time to make Phat Farm profitable. I lost money for six straight years, to the tune of $10 million. Not someone else's money—my money. Remember, I hadn't sold my stake in Def Jam yet, which meant that my investment in Phat Farm represented all the equity I had in the world. As they say in poker, I went "all in." I spent six years busting my ass while I could hear people on the sidelines laughing at me, saying I was going to fail. But eventually, after all the struggles, we started to find our groove. In time, we progressed from a small boutique to a line that was carried in department stores. Almost seven years after I started it, Phat Farm finally turned a profit. But when I was finally making money, I learned that my vision was still in danger.

As soon as Phat Farm raised its profile a bit, people were knocking on my door, begging me to change our look. Retail chains like Champs were begging me to make hockey jerseys and extra-baggy pants. Styles that were very juvenile and trendy. But as tempting as the money was, I couldn't do those things. My original tag line for Phat Farm was "Classic American Flava." And jerseys and extra-baggy pants aren't classic flavor. History has proven that. Those things were hot at the moment and a lot of people had success making them. But they did not meet my vision for classic American flava. So I turned down every offer.

Never forget that trends change. That's why your vision has to stay firm. If Phat Farm had tried to move with the trends, it would have damaged the company terribly in the long run. We would have ridden that wave for a second and then wiped out. But we resisted the temptation, and fifteen years later, we're still bringing the Classic American Flava. We still haven't compromised that original tagline.

And by maintaining its integrity, the Phat Farm brand has been able to keep growing. After ten years in the game, we were grossing close to $300 million a year and I had taken the brand as far as I could with my resources. So I sold Phat Farm (in a deal that still gives me day-to-day control of the company) to Kellwood for $115 million, plus back-end participation. And I really believe that with Kellwood's resources behind it, almost fifteen years after I started, Phat Farm is even closer than ever to becoming the institution of my dreams.

Turning Phat Farm into a profitable business was great, but the money isn't what makes me so proud of the company. I like to think that hip-hop has its own images in fashion partly because I was so persistent and resilient in following my dream back in the day. That's what's important to me. Now people like myself, Jay-Z, P. Diddy, Nelly, 50 Cent, and Marc Ecko can articulate the new American Dream, instead of having someone else tell us what it looks like. Maybe if we keep promoting these types of businesses, people will take stock in the beauty of diversity. Because I'm not just talking about African-American designers. I hope we've opened up the game for everybody. Maybe now Ralph Lauren will come out with a Lipschitz line. Wouldn't that be something? And I'm not knocking Ralph, as he's a friend of mine. I just want everybody to be comfortable wearing themselves.

VISIONS ARE SPIRITUAL

Selling Phat Farm for $120 million might have made headlines in the business pages, but I really saw it as more of a spiritual victory. You might wonder what's so spiritual about getting a big check like that, but if that's what following my vision got me, then it was a spiritual reward.

I say that because I don't believe that people create their own visions. Rather, I believe that visions are actually God's way of communicating with us. I know that sounds dramatic, but it's a belief that's fundamental to many faiths. I first understood it myself after reading Paramhansa Yogananda's *Autobiography of a Yogi*. Yogananda was a great spiritual leader from India and when he wrote, "Your imagination is God itself," that really rang true to me. And if you think about it, that message is echoed in most of the great scriptures. In Proverbs, it says, "Where there is no *vision,* the people perish." In Islam, Muhammad didn't sit down and write the Koran—he received it in a *vision.* Just like how it was in a *vision* that Buddha was finally shown the path to enlightenment. I'm certainly not a scholar when it comes to religion (or many subjects, for that matter), but I think you'll find that no matter what religion you practice, vision is a very big part of it.

I think all these great prophets lived in order to demonstrate the potential of our vision. If you have the faith that Jesus Christ had, or Lord Buddha had, or Yogananda had, then you're a miracle. If you're like the rest of us, you're just trying to realize some of that potential for greatness. Remember, Jesus or Lord Buddha didn't share their visions to teach you who *they* were. They shared their vision to help teach you who *you* are. To help you understand the power God has already blessed you with. Most of us are very far away from that, but that's the goal.

That's why I really believe the imagination of God is the collective imagination of man. And I believe that's why people who listen to their imagination, instead of ignoring it, have a much more fulfilling life.

Your Ear Is Like an Embryo

Another thing I believe is that every single person has been blessed by God with unique ideas. Notice the plural tense. That includes you. There are no exceptions. The problem is that only a small number of us actually follow through on those ideas. What holds most people back isn't the quality of their ideas, but a lack of faith in themselves. Whatever dream you're following, people will always tell you, "You can't do this," or "You'll never be able to do that." But you *can* do it. The world belongs to people who say, "I can."

That's why you can't let negativity get in your ear. Your ear is like an embryo. Negative ideas will grow in there if you're not careful. There are always going to be critics trying to dull your dreams. But you can't let them. Back in the day, my brother Reverend Run used to say, "The critics can get the didick." Of course, he'd say it differently now, but the message is still the same: Don't listen to the haters. Listen to your dreams. As soon as you hear that negativity in your ear, try to block it out. Instead, focus on what made you so excited about your dream in the first place. Let that excitement drown out the negativity.

It hurts my heart when I think about all the people who have had incredible ideas, but give up because things don't pop off right away. Try to remember that nothing worthwhile is ever going to just pop off. If you want a very big example, consider that even God didn't make the Earth the same day he envisioned it. He imagined it on the first page of Genesis but didn't actually *create* the world until four chapters later. So even God needed a little time to make things happen! What makes you think you're going to get a deal the first time you spit a rhyme for a label? What makes you think you'll get into medical school the first time you apply? What makes you think that beautiful girl is going to go out with you the first time you ask? Anything worthwhile is going to take time to manifest itself. And a lot of perseverance.

Whatever obstacles appear in your path, put your head down and get past them. Those obstacles aren't real. They're just God's way of testing you. He's asking you, "Do you want to make it or not?" That's what God was asking me when I had trouble finding investors for Phat Farm. That's what God was asking me when we spent all that money designing and manufacturing a fall line but delivered it to the stores too late. That's even what God was asking me later on down the road, when those distributors wanted me to make a hockey jersey that would have made money but compromised our basic vision.

Those kinds of tests are given to you *from* God to see if you believe *in* God. Don't fail your test. Focus on your vision and keep going until you hit the finish line. Don't be one of the people who believe in their vision at first but then give up. See it through, no matter how long that takes. Understand that obstacles are just part of the game. Whatever you imagine, you can achieve. Once you realize this truth, no one is going to be able to stop you.

THE VISION OF HIP-HOP

It's true that prophets like Yogananda and Jesus and Muhammad have played a tremendous role in shaping my personal belief in the power of vision. But they haven't been alone. Because I've also learned about the power of vision from many rappers. I'm not comparing rappers to Jesus (though I do believe he would be hanging out with rappers if he were walking the earth today—they both love poor people and love to tell the truth), but I will say that rappers are living, breathing testaments to the power of vision.

Hip-hop is all about believing in your vision. In its original form, hip-hop was about one person grabbing a microphone and telling the world how great he or she was. It was about a poor kid who probably didn't have much creating an all-powerful vision of himself in his mind and then sharing it with his friends, his block, his borough, his city, and then ultimately the world.

That's how hip-hop started—poor kids with nothing, rhyming about having everything. But over the years it's evolved to the point where that artistic attitude has transformed into a very successful business model. No one can argue that hip-hop hasn't created a new way of doing business in the country. It's proven that a bunch of kids who didn't go to business school, who don't have MBAs, and who don't speak "proper" English can still make a lot of money. Despite their apparent lack of sophistication and training, they can still create thriving businesses, companies that leave the rest of corporate America playing catch-up. So while every one else is struggling, cutting back, and trying to downsize, how are these kids from the ghetto rolling up in brand-new Bentleys and building new companies every week? It's really very simple: They believe in their vision.

There are plenty of examples of this mindset, but one that I think really illustrates it is Brian "Baby" Williams, the cofounder (along with his brother Ronald "Slim" Williams) of Cash Money Records. When a lot of people in the industry first met Baby, they almost automatically assumed that he wasn't the best business-man. He's got a deep New Orleans drawl, tattoos on his face, and more than a few paychecks hanging around his neck. After all, this is the man who helped coin the phrase *bling-bling*. Not the kind of guy industry suits are usually comfortable around. But Baby got a better deal for Cash Money than any of the suits from Harvard or Howard could have ever gotten. The distribution deal he set up with Universal Records was one of the most favorable I've ever seen. It's become the standard that everyone in the music industry aspires to. What was his secret?

The answer is that Baby wouldn't compromise his vision. When he and Slim started selling records independently in the early nineties, they learned how to distribute their own product and make their own margins. They became so good at doing it regionally that they started plotting how to do it on a national level. Of course, once the major record labels heard about these two brothers moving thousands of units in the Big Easy, they all wanted to sign them. But they wanted to sign them to the stan-dard industry contract, one that gave the label most of the profits for very little risk. But Baby wasn't going for it. He wasn't edu-cated in the industry norms and frankly wasn't interested in being educated about something that didn't make sense financially to him. Instead, he had a vision of what he and his brother could do and refused to compromise that vision.

I felt the power of Baby's faith firsthand, because Lyor Cohen and I unsuccessfully tried to negotiate a deal with him at Def Jam. The way it went down was so gangster, he just refused to budge. He told us, "I'll pay you a little fee to distribute my records, but I want to keep the rights to my masters. Plus loan me a little money while you're at it." It was so outrageous, but he literally didn't know any better. In some way, his ignorance was his strength. Someone with a business degree would have never dared ask for those terms. But Baby didn't know, or care, how the industry worked. He had a vision and he refused to lose sight of it.

Baby's confidence in his vision became contagious. Because after watching him turn down deal after deal, the industry started to think, "This guy must really be holding a strong hand." So eventually some guys very high up at Universal got involved and gave him the deal he was looking for. It was unprecedented. And it took someone from the streets to make it happen. Because for Baby and Slim, following their dreams gave them better direction than any textbook or diploma could have.

Now, I want to be very clear here, because in no way am I knocking a formal education. School is so critical and I'm sure even Baby and Slim would tell you that themselves. They would probably admit that as lucrative as their deal was, it would have been worth even more with a little more education under their belts. And even though I never graduated from college, I still put a tremendous emphasis on education. In fact, when young people come to me for help, the first thing I insist they do is get more schooling. I'm happy to help them follow their dreams, but I want them to get some education first. In fact, I was paying for the education of someone in my family until I found out he was taking the money I was sending him for school and putting it into a business venture he was trying to start instead. And when I found out, I cut him off—refused to speak to him, refused to see him—until he went back to school. Not because I didn't love him, but rather because I loved him so much. I knew he could be great, but I also knew that with an education he could be even greater. And even though he thought I was being too harsh at the time, now he understands that I was trying to save him from having to needlessly bang his head against the wall.

So if I'm knocking anything, it's not education itself, but more the rigidity that takes over some people once they become educated. The goal is not to become educated and set in your ways but to be educated while staying childlike in your imagination. Because as much as education can teach you what the possibilities are, it can also teach you not to dream.

Education in America today has become very much about rules, about passing a standardized test rather than exploiting the talent you have inside of you. Our youth spend so much time studying the established model that gradually they begin to believe that anything outside that model can't have real value. That's why I might hire Ivy Leaguers, but I won't follow them blindly. They're in this mindset where if you can pass the tests and get the degrees, you're smart. If you can't, you must be stupid. But life isn't black and white. Some people get those degrees and then go on cruise control. But you have to be willing to learn new things every day, every second. You can't just depend on what you've already been taught. That's why sometimes education can hold you down instead of lift you up. One of the beautiful things about this country is that it affords you the freedom to do whatever you imagine. Both as an art form and a business model, hip-hop has helped rekindle some of that imagination.

I think the challenge for hip-hop now is to bridge these two realities. It's great that we've taught people that you can overcome the struggle by following your vision. But I'd also like to see those visions applied with the benefit of a formal education. Because as much as I promote following your own vision, the truth is that it is extremely rare to get a project going without a professional business plan. Right now, hip-hop has a void in education as a means to set up entrepreneurial aspirations. If you look at companies like GE or IBM, they have recruiters at all the top schools, making sure every year there's a pipeline bringing new energy out of the schools and into their staffs. I want to see hip-hop companies do the same thing. Let's be a presence at Howard or Spelman and recruit all these students who share a great education and a love of hip-hop. I don't think doing that will compromise people's vision. I think it will actually make those visions stronger. I love that this generation has an eye toward ownership. Now it's up to the people who are already established to help them.

HOW TO HARNESS YOUR VISION

You can see just how strongly I believe in the power of vision. That's why I want to break down the various steps you can take to harness it. Separately, they're all useful. And if you can master just a few of them, you'll see an incredible improvement in your life. But if you can draw upon the faith, dedication, and focus to bring all of these steps together, you'll be in control of how you see the world and how the world sees you. And that's a beautiful way to live.

Which Vision?

Everybody dreams. You dream every night when you go to sleep, and if you're like me, you spend lot of time dreaming during the day too. So the first question to ask is, out of all these dreams and visions, which is the one you should follow? A lot of people spend their entire lives dreaming but never pursue any of their dreams to their conclusion. That's understandable—it's very scary to dedicate yourself to one dream. To take all of your eggs and put them in one basket, you need to be very confident in that vision. That's why I believe you can be sure you're making the right choice when you let your passion pick your vision.

When you have an idea that you find yourself feeling very passionate about, then that's the one you need to go after. If you feel lukewarm about an idea, or lose interest in it after a few days, it probably wasn't the one you were meant to pursue. But when you have a dream that you can't get out of your mind and your heart beats faster every time you think about it, then that's the one.

But make sure it's *your* vision you're following. It has to be *your* vision for *your* life. Don't go to medical school because that's what your parents want you to do. Don't play basketball because you're seven feet tall and people always assume you're a baller. You'll just end up as one of these centers who everyone thinks is lazy and unskilled but really just doesn't have a true love for the game. Don't decide to be a model because every time you go to a club, some photographer gives you his card. Pursue those careers because you love *them,* not because you think people will love *you* for pursuing them. If you only do something because it's what other people want you to do or it seems like the easy way out, you'll never have a passion for it. And without passion for what you're doing, you'll never, ever be successful at it.

Because my own work is often about creating, I admit that sometimes I get too hung up on the creative process. I'll get so excited by a new record or a new show or a new poet that I'll forget that not everyone shares the passion to assist the creative process. It's important to remember that not everyone is a Lauryn Hill or an Andy Warhol or a Miles Davis. Some people aren't creative, but they are tremendous businesspeople. For them, the art of buying and selling is just as rewarding as creating. As my friend Donald Trump put it, "Deals are my art form. Other people paint beautifully on canvas or write wonderful poetry. I like making deals, preferably big deals. That's how I get my kicks." So while Donald might not be an artist per se, he's still a great visionary in his own field.

If you're struggling to come up with a truly unique idea, it's OK. You can start by building on someone else's foundation and keep adding your own flavor and your own twists, until eventually it becomes something that's uniquely you. There are many roads to success, even within one industry. Never forget that. That's very important.

Freeze Your Vision

Once you've picked a vision that you feel passionate about, the next step is to freeze it. I can't stress this enough. When a vision begins to resonate with you, you can't let it slip away. Do whatever you can to freeze it. Even a powerful vision can get lost quickly among the distractions of the world. I know, because I've forgotten visions and ideas that I thought would stick with me forever. That's why you must freeze a powerful vision in your mind *immediately*.

The safest way to freeze a vision is by articulating it as soon as you have it. If you're a writer and you dream the plot to a novel, write it down the second you wake up. Don't get up and brush your teeth or get a cup of coffee (you should be drinking green juice or tea anyway). Write it down before you do anything else. If you're a painter and you see an incredible landscape in your mind, freeze that vision by drawing it immediately. Don't wait to get to your studio. Use your kids' crayons if that's all that's around. Maybe you're a singer and an amazing melody comes into your head while you're in your car. Don't assume you'll remember it later. Pull over and sing that melody into your answering machine. No matter who you are or what you do, freeze your vision so that you can never lose it. Freeze it in your mind and meditate on it every day. Because you have to be able to call on that vision whenever you need it.

It's also very important to try to always see the details in your vision. Freeze the big picture first. But then keep working on the details. For instance, it's not enough to just say, "I want my own record label." Your vision for that label has to be very specific for it to be successful. You have to have a vision for what the label will be called, what your logo is going to be, what sort of distribution deal you want, what sort of artists you're going to sign, what your office is going to look like, even the color of your stationery. From the root to the fruit, you have to have a clear vision for every part of your idea. Because when you have your own label (and you will) and it's time to pick a distribution deal, or it's time to sign an artist, you won't have to wonder what to do. You'll just look back to the vision you froze and know exactly what move to make! See every single last detail of what you want to accomplish. That detailed vision, frozen in your mind, will be your road map to success.

I'll admit that MBAs can usually do one thing very well, and that's help you formulate the details of your ideas. I might have a lofty vision, but I'll bring in an MBA to help articulate the details. I'll have them list the details as an exercise, to make sure that the vision is sound. That's the point of creating a business plan. However, the idea doesn't begin or end with a business plan for me (any good business plan will always change and evolve). The business plan is just my way of making sure that the details are right and everyone on my team is literally *starting* on the same page.

But using MBAs is a luxury I can afford at this stage in my career. You might not be so fortunate right away. That's why, when you're first getting started, you have to be the dreamer *and* the MBA guy. You have to dream up the lofty idea and work out the small, mundane details.

Lofty ideas can be more fun to kick around in your head, but the details are what will help attract support and attention for your vision. Details allow a vision to materialize into a fundable plan. Details give people confidence in you. Let's say I'm meeting with two people, both of whom are trying to pitch me on investing in a new venture. Both people might have great ideas. But the person who can provide me with a detailed vision is more likely to get the check. Make sure you're that person.

Be Clear in Your Vision

After you've frozen the vision you feel passionate about and have articulated its details, your next step is to make sure that your vision is clear. By that, I mean that the idea isn't so lofty that the average person can't see it. Or that it's not filled with so many details that they're overshadowing your original idea. A clear, unobstructed vision of what you want gives you an advantage in dealing with other people. Remember how I said Baby's vision was so clear that it became contagious? That's what you want for your idea. Clarity and confidence.

When you do have a clear, strong vision, you will see results. People love to be around someone who is crystal clear on their future. *Your* confidence is going to give *them* direction. People will follow someone who's clear with his vision, probably because they're not clear on their own. It's true in my company, Rush Communications. I don't care if it's your first day on the job or if you've been with me for ten years: If you have a clear vision for something, I'm going to listen to you.

Share Your Vision

The final step in realizing your dreams is always to share them with the world. This should be the easiest step. But for some people, it's actually the hardest. They might spend months up in their room dreaming up a new idea, freezing it in their mind, and working out the details. It might be all they think about. But when you see them on the street and ask them what they're working on, they'll just say, "Oh, not much." Not because they haven't been working hard on sculpting their vision, but because they're afraid to share it.

Why? It really comes down to a lack of faith. Even though that idea was given to them by God, they still don't trust it. They're afraid that their idea is going to be rejected. And that fear is what you have to get over if you want to realize your dreams.

One of the easiest ways to get over that fear is by focusing on the process. Don't look at sharing your idea as a chance for people to judge it. Just look at it as another baby step in the process you've already committed to. It would have been great if the Phat Farm store had immediately sold a ton of shirts. That would have made things very easy. But good things don't come easily. They take time to develop.

The reality was that not many clothes were bought after we first opened the store. Financially, the store was a mess. But I didn't trip over the bottom line. I was too focused on my greater vision, which was building a classic clothing company. When you're only focused on the bottom line, a win is when you make $5 million in your first year. But when you're focused on the process, a win is when someone walks into your store and buys a shirt because he loves it. A win is when that person tells you that maybe the shirt should have been a different color, or the collar should have been a little wider. Because that person is helping you learn from your mistakes. You might be losing money but you're gaining the knowledge you need to reach your ultimate goal. You're taking more baby steps in the process. Always put your vision out there. Never be afraid to share it.

Another great reason to share your vision is that once you share it, you're stuck with it. Once you share your idea, people are expecting something from you. Some of them will encourage you. Some of them will criticize you. But all that attention will just make it harder for you to give up on your vision. That attention will force you to continue the process.

I saw this approach work for my brother Danny when he was having a hard time with drugs. Nothing was working, so eventually I just said to him, "Tell everyone that you've quit. Because that way you'll have to live up to it." And it worked. So many people told him, "Oh, it's so great that you got your life together," that he became inspired and felt he couldn't let them down. Plus, hearing them say he was sober so many times actually gave him the confidence to *stay* sober. Before, he questioned his vision for a sober, healthy life. But by sharing his vision, he was ultimately able to live up to it.

If you've ever met me, you know that the importance of sharing isn't something I just preach, but something I really live. Because if I have an idea I feel passionate about, I'm never going to shut up. That might annoy some, but at least I know that people are never unclear about my vision. You might not buy into it, but I'm going to make sure that you're aware of it. A lot of people have good ideas, but they keep them inside, wanting you to draw them out. Don't take that risk. Most people are too busy or too self-centered to even consider that the quiet guy in the corner might have a good idea. Be proud of your idea and always promote your vision. Because if *you* don't, who else will?

Focus on One Vision at a Time

I believe it's also very important to focus on one vision at a time. You want to try to live with what the yogis call "single-pointed focus." By that they mean, never lose sight of your original vision and give it all your attention until you realize it, even if it takes a lifetime.

I know many talented people—most of them more talented than I am—who I always have to remind about "single-pointed focus." These people have been successful at so many different things, but at times it seems their ability to have multiple visions has been both a gift and a curse. It's hard for imaginative people not to share their visions, since they're filled with such incredible ideas. These people can pitch an idea and everyone wants to sign on. Their vision is so clear, you'd be ready to sink your time and money into it after five minutes.

The problem is, *you'll* go to work on their vision and *they'll* quit it. They're already focused on their next vision and have forgotten whatever they pitched yesterday. These creative types don't feel like they have to prove anything—they just want to share their vision and then jump into the next thing they feel passionate about. These people are very successful, in a variety of fields, so it's hard for me to fault their style. But I still wish they would follow their visions all the way through. Because as much success as you can achieve jumping from one idea to another, you can always achieve so much more with that single-pointed focus.

A perfect example of this truth is my old friend Andre Harrell, who is the greatest visionary I know. Andre is legendary in the music industry as the founder of Uptown Records, where he birthed the careers of such artists as Mary J. Blige, Jodeci, Heavy D, and Guy, not to mention the career of a young intern named Sean Combs. He's also had tremendous success creating TV shows, magazines, and advertising agencies. So when I started working on the concept of *Run's House* (a reality show starring my brother Reverend Run that I'll speak on in more detail later), Andre was one of the first people I went to for help in shaping the vision. And true to form, he gave me numerous ideas that would later be the cornerstone of that show's success. But before we even started filming the show, he became so passionate about another vision that he left *Run's House* in order to work on it instead. I'm not faulting him—instead I'm grateful for his contribution. Certainly myself and Puffy (the show's executive producers), and many others are all indebted to him for the ideas that he's birthed but we ended up raising. The fact is, every one of his ideas makes money, even if he doesn't stick around to see all of that money himself. Still, sometimes I encourage Andre to be more focused on his visions, so that he'll not only get a bigger cut of the profits he's helped create but will also get recognition for being the incredible visionary that he is.

I admittedly struggle with the same issue (not that that would stop me from giving advice). There are so many things I'm passionate about and interested in, but they can't all get my full attention. To stay with the Phat Farm example, if I focus on selling shirts and lose track of our jeans, then the jeans will probably be stagnant. But when I put all my focus on jeans, then that's going to start selling. I find that where my attention is, that's where my success is too. I know it drives my staff crazy and I have to keep working to balance my attention. But like I said, this is a process for all of us.

This struggle with focusing on one vision at a time is especially true in hip-hop, where there is a trend where everyone wants to be a rapper *and* an entrepreneur. Sure, Jay-Z and Puffy have done it, but they're geniuses. For the rest of us, it's important to focus on what we do best and master one craft at a time. It's hard for any artist to be a successful businessman. You can always find someone to run your clothing company who's better at it than you. But you can't find someone else to articulate your artistic vision better than you do. Focus on one vision until you realize it and *then* move on to the next challenge. When you are involved in fifteen businesses, or fifteen visions, at one time, it makes it much harder to be great in any one of them. It's much easier to promote clarity one endeavor at a time.

When Can You Let a Vision Go?

One question I get asked a lot is "When is the right time to let go of a vision?" It's a hard question to answer, especially because a lot of times I think some people are really asking, "When is it all right to quit?" To that question, the answer is "never." But to the first question, I tell people that sometimes you have to let a vision go, but you should only do that as a last resort. Because as we know, some visions, especially the important ones, take years and years to realize. So I would never discourage people from following their dreams, even if it seems like those dreams are never going to be realized.

But if you are wondering if it's time to move on, I would encourage you to look deep inside and ask where is that feeling coming from. Is the world telling you you're never going to realize your dream? Or is that message coming from your inner voice?

As long as you're passionate about your vision, you should keep moving forward. I like to say that as long as I'm doing God's work, "I ain't going to stop until they put me in the box." But if your passion is really missing from the process, then it's probably time to focus on something else.

Just make sure that's how you really feel and is not a reaction to what you perceive as failure. Some people change their dreams every day like they're changing their drawers. That's a mistake, because you must be patient with your vision and understand that, while some aspects of the vision might change, your greater vision shouldn't. No matter what you put on paper, no matter what you freeze in your mind, along the way you will have to compromise things. There will be sacrifices you have to make. Some plans will have to be abandoned. Others will have to be changed. Just make sure you compromise on the details. Not the big picture.

In the end, the overriding factor in whether or not you realize your dreams is going to be *you*. Not the world. *You*. If your faith is strong enough, that vision will come to pass. And when I say faith, I'm not talking about blind confidence or ego, or the kind of faith that comes after you have a couple of drinks at the bar. That's not real faith. Real faith is a constant connection to what's inside you and inside all of us. Connection to real faith is what will motivate you to write fifteen business plans. Even if you get rejected by every record label you pitch, connection to the real faith inside you will motivate you to press up your record and sell it out of your trunk. Connection to the real faith inside you will motivate you to keep taking the law boards, even after you don't pass the first few times. If you really want those things, imagine yourself as a winner. Then your faith will make that image a reality.

Value Your Vision

Finally, never doubt your vision because of your background. Just because you've faced struggles, or don't have the best education, never think your vision isn't as important as anyone else's. Nothing could be further from the truth.

I've actually found that people coming from struggle are the *most* creative people I encounter. People in the struggle have to be creative, because they haven't had anything handed to them in life. That's one of the great things about hip-hop: It provides a forum for people in struggle to realize their visions. Look at

Biggie, Tupac, Jay-Z, or Eminem. They had to work harder than people who were privileged or had things handed to them. It might be difficult to accept now, but the struggle you face coming up will become the most important aspect of your character. Remember, pressure can crack pipes. But it can also create diamonds. You can turn your struggle into a jewel. That's why, when people ask me what they can do to be successful, I always tell them, "Anything you want." Because when you follow your dream with persistence and resilience, that dream will always become reality.

Too many times people in the struggle don't have the confidence they should have. Again, that was the problem that we faced with Phat Farm. It wasn't about the clothes, it was about people's perceptions of themselves. But hip-hop has shown that anything is possible. Whatever you dream will become a reality.

RECOGNIZE THE REAL:

Your vision makes your world. If you see the world as a happy, loving place, then that's where you're going to live. But if you see the world as a messed up, negative, and dangerous place, then that will be your reality.

Never change for the mainstream—stay in your lane, and if you're talented and resilient enough the mainstream will come to you.

LAW NUMBER TWO:

ALWAYS DO YOU

It takes courage to grow up and turn out to be who you really are.

—E.E. CUMMINGS

I'VE BEEN CREDITED, deservedly or not, with several innovations in my career. But none have earned me as much respect (and created as many new opportunities) as my perceived ability to identify and build brands. For over twenty years, I've been blessed with a reputation as a tastemaker, someone with a finger on the pulse of what's cool in music, film, clothes, technology, and even politics. So how has an old bald guy like myself been able to maintain such a precarious perch in the hot-today-cold-tomorrow world of hip-hop? It's simple. I always try to follow the Law of Do You, which stresses staying true to who *you* are and what *you* like instead of following trends.

That's something I learned growing up in the hip-hop nation, which has always put a priority on integrity and respecting what's real. Over the years, I've tried to apply this law to all my endeavors, making sure I only promote products that I believe in, rather than those that seem to have the most profit potential. Adhering to this law is what has allowed the Def Jam and Phat Farm brands not only to survive in the ficklest of markets but actually to thrive every year too.

Out of all the laws in this book, this is the one I feel the most confident about, because I've seen it work *so* many times, not only for myself but for the people around me as well. I've seen Kimora Lee find tremendous success with Baby Phat and her other endeavors by Doing Her. If you choose something with Kimora's name on it, whether it's a pair of jeans or a TV show or a perfume, you know you're going to get her fabulous attitude. Even if the fashion gods announced tomorrow that fabulous was "out" and shabby was "in," Kimora would still be fabulous. She's going to personify that attitude no matter what's trendy at the moment. So if that fabulous attitude is what you're looking for, you'll always know that Baby Phat or Simmons Jewelry is where you can find it. By always Doing You, Kimora has been able to build a strong, lasting brand.

But while there will be considerable discussion about business in this chapter, never forget that, like every law I promote, Do You really is a spiritual law. When I talk about Doing You, I'm really just asking you to listen to that voice of God inside of you again. Because without that voice, you'll never be able to tap into the resources God has blessed you with. Instead, you'll end up following the world, which will never be as rewarding as Doing You and following the path God has laid out for you.

So if it seems at times during this chapter I'm using material success to prove this law, keep in mind that the toys are just one of the many rewards you'll receive from staying true to yourself. Most importantly, you'll get the happiness that comes from having a positive impact on the world while doing God's work. From Gandhi to Bob Marley to Tupac, so many people throughout history have been able to change the world by Doing You. Not even because they're confident in their own ability, but because they have such a strong faith in the ability that God has put inside them. They take the time to listen to that voice and have faith in it. When you find that kind of faith, you can use the Law of Do You to take yourself to tremendous heights as well.

THE TRUTH RINGS BELLS

The concept behind Do You is fairly straightforward: Always try to be yourself. Even though that sounds very simple, it's actually one of the most difficult laws to follow. The first step is knowing yourself—who you are and what you stand for. And the only way to do that is to be in touch with that higher voice inside of you. To be present and at one with who you are. Because even with that presence, the temptation to act or dress or talk the way the world tells us to (to conform) is very strong. I'm the first to admit that it's often easier to blend in with the crowd than stand out on your own; but at the end of the day, changing your true colors in order to blend in won't make you successful (or more importantly, happy). That's because when you play a role, you're really just playing yourself.

Any kind of lasting success is rooted in *honesty*. We understand that truth on a personal level—certainly no one seeks out a long-term relationship with someone who's dishonest. And it's no different in business. As a consumer, you're not going to keep supporting a business or an individual who doesn't feel authentic. Trust me, authenticity sells, no matter what you're selling. If people think you're being authentic, they're going to support you. But if they think you're fraudulent, then your success, or the success of your business, is going to be very fleeting.

Take Vanilla Ice, who could have experienced much more longevity, and much less ridicule, if he had just been more honest about his experiences. In my opinion, in addition to having a great track in "Ice Ice Baby," he also had a good voice and fairly witty poetry. The tools were there. Vanilla Ice didn't become the butt of a national joke because he was white. He became a joke because he wasn't honest. His mistake was saying he was from the hood when he really wasn't. What he should have said was "I'm a kid who loves rap music. I'm a white kid from the suburbs. I honestly love rap. I'm a good rapper and I made the best record I could." If he had had the courage to Do Him, instead of trying to be someone else, his career would still be going strong today. But he was dishonest about his history, and as a result, now he's history too.

I share Vanilla Ice's story as a cautionary tale, but I want to be very honest here—you *can* break the Law of Do You and still have a very big hit. You just won't have many more. That's why the history of music is littered with artists who had one hit record (Vanilla Ice is the most obvious example) but were then rejected after people realized they weren't authentic. Frauds can always sell singles. But only truthful artists sell albums time and time again. Frauds are one-hit wonders. Authentic artists have careers. Look, Milli Vanilli sold fifteen million records. But when you fake it, you can only make money (or, in the case of Milli Vanilli, infamy). When you Do You, you can make history.

In many ways, this book itself is an example of Doing You. I understand there are a lot of people who have picked this up because they want advice on how to get ahead and make some money. They're looking for a traditional business guide and probably aren't interested in hearing a "hip-hop mogul" talk about God's laws. But they're the ones I'm going to keep speaking on, because they are the only laws I believe really work. Besides, I don't believe there is any one "business law" that applies to every situation. You can pick up *The Wall Street Journal* on a Monday and read a compelling article about some CEO who saved his company by firing all his overpaid executives and focusing on the bottom line. Then you can pick it up on a Wednesday and read about a CEO who saved his company by giving his executives lots of freedom and ignoring the bottom line. And both CEOs did the right thing in their particular situation. Sorry to disappoint you, but there isn't one strategy that's automatically going to make you a lot of money. Instead, I really believe that every business venture requires a unique approach.

Getting back to Doing You, I feel that an emphasis on honesty has not only kept hip-hop alive but actually helped it thrive over the years. The driving force in hip-hop isn't a powerful bass or drums, but honesty and integrity. That honesty creates a connection that people can feel with a 50 Cent or an Eminem, whether they live in the projects, the suburbs, in Amsterdam, in England, in Israel, in Africa, or any place on the globe. Sure, the music is great and the videos are a lot of fun. But the honesty is what brings it all home. On the surface, a kid growing up in Tel Aviv might not have much in common with 50 Cent, but he's still going to connect with 50's *honesty.* He might not even want to lead 50's life, but he will respect that honesty with which 50 expresses his condition. Never forget that the truth rings a bell that the whole world can hear. A truth that will bring you more fans, more customers, and more love than you ever imagined possible.

I've noticed that no matter how many times rappers perform overseas, they're always shocked by the impact their music has had globally. They can't believe that they can stand on a stage in Denmark, or Brazil or Japan, and hear the people recite their rhymes word for word with them in English. Even someone as seasoned as Jay-Z, who's been around the world many times, told me that it blew his mind when he recently performed in the Czech Republic and the crowd knew the words to every one of his songs. Not just the big hits, but the album cuts too. He was amazed that people who had been living behind the Iron Curtain a decade ago had so much knowledge of and love for his career. But I told him he shouldn't have been surprised, because when his poetry rang that bell, the world responded. Because the truth is something that doesn't know race or class or languages or borders. It's something that connects *all* humanity. No matter who you are or where you live, you can always *feel* the truth.

My experiences with both the Beastie Boys and Run DMC taught me the importance of Doing You very early in my career. We might not have even realized it at the time, but in retrospect, following the Law of Do You was extremely critical to the initial success of both the groups. I'll talk about the Beasties first.

When I first met the Beastie Boys, I loved their music, but I didn't love how they dressed. I noticed right away that they were rocking Kangol hats, sweatsuits, chains—all the stuff that was hot in hip-hop at the time. It was very trendy in the streets, but it didn't feel authentic on them. I felt like they were dressing up as "rappers" instead of allowing their clothes to express who they really were. Then a few weeks later, I saw them perform as part of a quasi-punk group called Young and Useless. This time instead of wearing their "costumes," they were running around in ripped jeans, T-shirts, and baseball hats. Evidently that was their natural look, because they seemed so much more alive, much more comfortable in their own skin. And because they were being truthful (or Doing You), I gained a much greater appreciation for them that night, even though I didn't enjoy punk as much as hip-hop.

You see, from the beginning, they were making music that was honest and pure. Their music truly made them laugh and be happy. But that authenticity was lost behind their outfits. It wasn't anything intentional on their part, they were just so focused on their music that they hadn't put the same effort into making their image authentic too. So after the Young and Useless show, I told them, "Look, it's OK to be yourself. You don't need the costumes." Artists will often get very defensive when you ask them to change their image, but the Beasties were completely cool with it. In fact, after that one conversation, we never even discussed it again, because I suspect losing the costumes was actually a relief to them. I think they felt much more free when they stopped trying to play a role and started Doing Them.

Without giving myself too much credit, I believe that honesty was the key to the Beasties' early success. After they started wearing their own clothes, two important things happened to them. The first is they were instantly able to connect with the millions of white kids who dressed in holey jeans just like them. Meanwhile, the streets responded to the "holey jean" look too. To kids on the street who grew up obsessed with keeping their jeans immaculately pressed and their sneakers spotless, the concept of actually running around onstage with holes in your jeans was something new. Performing in holey jeans and old T-shirts became theatrical and garnered them more attention than they would have received if they had worn their old "rappers" costume. And that's what we all have to strive for in life if we want to be successful. We have to find the thing inside us that stands out as an individual, but at the same time is very honest.

Furthermore, if the Beasties had kept dressing like "rappers," then we never could have released "Fight for Your Right to Party" as their first single. "Fight for Your Right" sounded so rock 'n' roll that people would have had a hard time accepting it was coming from "rappers." If they had insisted on keeping their "rappers" look, we would have had to release "Hold It Now, Hit It," since that fit the hip-hop image much better. "Hold It Now" was a great song in its own right, but it would have never made the impact that "Fight for Your Right" did. That song earned them so many white fans right off the bat and quickly became one of the biggest-selling singles in history. But they would have lost all of that if they didn't Do You. Only by being completely honest were they able to embrace what was already theirs, namely both hip-hop *and* rock.

The irony is that at the time, I caught a lot of flack from black folks for putting out the Beastie Boys. Far from finding them honest, they thought the whole concept was exploitative. There was an assumption that white kids rapping had to be a novelty and that I was attempting to sell out hip-hop. Now, if the Beasties had come out of the gate wearing chains and pretending they were from the hood, then maybe those critics would have had a point. But they didn't. They dressed and acted like what they were, which was middle-class Jewish kids from New York with an honest love for the hip-hop culture that was all around them growing up. In retrospect, it would have only been dishonest if kids like the Beasties had acted like they *weren't* influenced by hip-hop. But at the time, not everyone appreciated hip-hop's impact. Not everyone could see that we weren't exploiting black culture, we were just developing it further. And I think history has proven that the Beastie Boys didn't open the floodgates and kill all the black rappers. Instead, the Beasties helped open up a whole new audience for hip-hop. But we could have never collectively done that if we hadn't recognized the value of Doing You.

Run DMC might have come from a different background than the Beastie Boys, but they faced a similar obstacle at the beginning of their career. The difference is while the Beasties had to learn to Do You when it came to their image, Run DMC's challenge was to Do You musically.

Don't Be a Sucker MC

When Run DMC came onto the scene in the early eighties, most hip-hop at that time was based on an R&B model. By that, I mean all the popular songs featured a rhythm guitar, bouncy bass line, and a melody. The most conspicuous example was the Sugar Hill Gang's "Rapper's Delight," which was a huge, huge hit. Since "Rapper's Delight" had sold so many records, most people, especially at the record labels, felt like they had to copy that sound in order to be successful themselves. But Run DMC didn't want to make a hip-hop record that sounded like R&B. We were from the streets and we knew that the streets needed something else. We knew that R&B was for the slick cats with silk shirts and Jeri curls, not the kids on the streets rocking sneakers and sweatsuits. We understood that even though "Rapper's Delight" had been a hit, its sound didn't really reflect what was happening on the streets. The streets where we lived were powerful and raw. Not smooth and melodic.

In fact, if you look back at the early days of hip-hop, rappers were as interested in rock 'n' roll records, or alternative records, as they were in the disco tracks that dominated radio at the time. They considered the sound of a rock track like Billy Squier's "The Big Beat" or even light jazz like Bob James's "Take Me to the Mardi Gras" much more "ghetto" than Chic's "Good Times" (which provided the bass line for "Rapper's Delight"). Black radio wasn't playing James Brown anymore by the late seventies, but rappers loved the sound of his old songs like "Funky Drummer" or "The Payback." Those songs had the beat rappers needed, which was more important than a melody or even a bass line.

That "big beat" was what we were trying to articulate when we went into the studio to record "It's Like That" and "Sucker MCs," our debut twelve-inch. And to this day, I consider producing the beat for "Sucker MCs" the single most creative thing I ever did in my life. I consider it such an accomplishment because at the time, no one thought you could make a hit record only using drums, which was the formula for "Sucker MCs." It seemed like a great idea to us, but most people couldn't wrap their heads around it. Even Larry Smith, our producer, who was a very talented musician, went crazy when he heard our idea. Larry had come up with all these chord structures and melodies for the song, but instead we told him, "Nope, we're not using a bass. We're not using that guitar. We're not using any instrumentation that sounds like R&B. There ain't going to be nothing but drums on here!" Larry couldn't understand what we were up to, but he stopped complaining once he heard the beat.

And of course, the reaction was even worse when we played "Sucker MCs" for the record executives. They absolutely hated it! To them, if a rap song didn't sound like "Rapper's Delight," then it was worthless. But those executives were too busy *listening* instead of *feeling*. You see, we understood that while "Sucker MCs" might not have *sounded* like a hit record, it *felt* like a hit record. We knew the streets would go crazy for it. It might not have had production that people were used to, but it had the elements people *wanted*. We just weren't giving it to them in the traditional packaging. Just like there are a lot of ways to skin a cat, there a lot of ways to make a beat that's going to rock the streets. That's why you should never think that the best thing to do is copy what someone else has been successful with. History proved us right, but at the time it was a very difficult concept to sell. Thankfully, Run DMC was blessed with the instinct to always Do You. We felt the pressure from the record labels but would just laugh at the idea of copying something that wasn't us. Even as a young group, we were totally committed to being heartfelt with our music.

The irony with Run DMC was that "Walk This Way," the one instance in our career when we weren't heartfelt, turned out to be our biggest hit. It was Rick Rubin's idea to collaborate with Aerosmith and we just went along with it, mainly because Rick was so passionate about it at the time. We wanted to help him follow that vision, but looking back at it, I think it was our least interesting song. Because it didn't represent us.

Now you might be asking, "How can you preach about Doing You when Run DMC's biggest hit came from the one time you *didn't* Do You?" It's a perfectly legitimate question, so here's the answer: If Run DMC hadn't been committed to Doing You throughout their entire career up to that point, "Walk This Way" would have absolutely ruined us instead of taking us to the next level. Because our core fans knew "Walk This Way" wasn't authentic. But they accepted it because we had always been so honest with them in the past. But if "Walk This Way" had been the rule, instead of the exception, then that would have been the end for Run DMC. Then the real hip-hop fans would have written us off as fakes.

When Doing You Gets Distorted

I also want to point out that Doing You comes with risks. While the odds are in your favor that people will support you when you're honest with your message, it's not always the case.

I can say that with complete confidence, since I've been guilty of judging people unfairly for Doing Them. One example that still bothers me to this day was my negative reaction the first time I heard OutKast's debut *Southernplayalisticadillacmuzik*. At the time, I didn't understand their music—it sounded so different from what I was used to that I foolishly made some negative comments about it, claiming that they "weren't hip-hop." The same way people didn't understand "Sucker MCs" a decade earlier, I didn't understand that instead of operating outside of hip-hop, OutKast was actually expanding hip-hop. They were offering one of the most honest expressions, an expression so honest that it went completely over my head at first.

Luckily, no one listened to me and Andre and Big Boi went on to become one of the best-selling and most critically acclaimed acts in not only hip-hop, but all of pop music. And of course today I respect the hell out of them, not that they need, or ever needed, my endorsement. Still, I offer up that example because you have to realize that when you Do You, there is always the chance that people are not going to understand you at first.

Another example took place recently when Reverend Run released his debut solo album *Distortion*. Almost twenty years after making "Sucker MCs," *Distortion* was slated to be the first release from Russell Simmons Music Group, a label I launched with my old friends at Def Jam. And since we knew people would be watching us in these new roles, we really wanted to do well with the album.

A lot of people in Run's position would have felt that pressure and as a result have played it safe and tried to copy what's hot in hip-hop right now. They would have tried to make the most commercial record possible. But just as he had twenty years before (and more than twenty pounds ago too), Run refused to do that. Run is going to Do You until the day he dies. Instead of copying what he was hearing on the radio today, Run recorded an album that sounded like it was made in the eighties. Instead of the big bass lines, soft melodies, and strings that are used on so many tracks today, Run stayed with rock guitars and hardcore rap that has always defined his sound. Not because that's what he thought would sell more, but because that sound is what spoke to him, what was in his heart. And I certainly didn't discourage him, because what made Run great in the first place was that he never sounded like everyone else. Besides, I still love that eighties hip-hop sound, and I banked on that appealing to other people out there with similar tastes. Whenever I get excited about something, it's because I know that there are people out there who feel the same way as I do. And since Run's album was so honest, I was sure that my passion would be contagious.

But it wasn't. The kids simply did not respond to Run's sound, and the album was a disappointment commercially. But Run and I were OK with that, because we hadn't compromised a thing in making that album. I'm not trying to downplay the fact that we wanted the album to do better. I spent many hours on the phone pushing the label to do more and trying to convince radio stations to give it a chance. We worked very hard to find an audience for that album. But at the end of the day, we would rather have a disappointment Doing You, than a success copying someone else. Run could have sold a few more albums by changing his image, but in doing so, he would have lost whatever sort of credibility he had built up over the previous twenty-five years. It was important that while people might have said, "I didn't like that album," they couldn't say, "I don't like Run anymore." Because they knew *Distortion* came from the heart.

And the value of that honesty was proven just a few months later, when his reality show *Run's House* debuted on MTV. That show was able to become a huge success, but only because Run hadn't compromised his integrity with *Distortion*. Imagine if every song on that album had been about Run riding around on rims, wearing grillz, and acting like he was twenty-five years old. People would have remembered that and never given *Run's House* a chance. But since Run was so honest with *Distortion*, people were willing to accept him in another space.

In fact, that commitment to Doing You not only made *Run's House* possible but became the cornerstone of its success. The honest portrayal of Run and his family is what people really love about that show. Which is ironic, because there was tremendous pressure on us *not* to be so honest with it. (I'll describe in greater detail the battles we had to fight to get the show made in "There Are No Failures, Only Quitters.") The TV people were open to *Run's House,* but only if Run appeared to be more dysfunctional than he really is. Not because he's a particularly dysfunctional person, but simply because dysfunction is the common denominator among most hit reality shows. The philosophy was essentially that people liked to watch reality TV in order to see bad moments. They wanted to see older pop stars do stupid things so they could say to themselves, "Look how stupid Bobby Brown is. I'm glad I ain't that stupid." Or "Look at that girl pretending to be in love with Flavor Flav. Please, you know you're faking. . . ." And by saying those things, by putting down the people they saw on TV, maybe they would feel better about themselves. But even though that had worked for a lot of shows, we wanted to break that mold. We knew we could never find success on TV by chasing a trend. We had to let the world see Run and his family for who they are and then decide for themselves whether or not they were interested. And we suspected they would be, since there was such an obvious void in the market. We knew people would respond to a reality show about a reverend with children who are straight-A students, instead of a father who's in out and out of rehab and whose kids are dropouts and promiscuous. We knew that even though dysfunction had worked in the past, Run's honesty could work just as well, if not better. We knew that if we filled that void with an honest light, people would respond because so much of what's on reality TV caters to the darkness.

And ultimately we were proven right when the show became a huge success. (And it really has been an impactful show—whenever I walk down the street now, I'm constantly stopped by young people who say, "Hey, aren't you Reverend Run's brother?") However, I can't stress enough how that show only became a hit because of its honesty. If we had catered to television people's vision, the show would have had a very short life span. If people had seen Reverend Run pretending to be a gangster, or pretending to be a playboy, or pretending to be out of control, then we would have lost our connection with the fans. People would have *felt* that the show was fake, turned off their TVs, and *Run's House* would have been dropped after a few episodes. But by staying in our lane and being honest, we were able to make the mainstream come to us. It might not come the first time you ask (as was the case *Distortion*), but it will come eventually.

Your Truth Can Never Be for Sale

I also want to address another issue, which is that in order to truly Do You, especially in the business world, you're going to have to turn down some very attractive opportunities. Every day, it seems like I get pitched a new business venture. But if I don't feel comfortable attaching my name to a product, then I'll leave that money on the table. I won't compromise my name, because I know once I do, I'll never be able to get it back.

I won't lie, walking away from opportunity can be difficult. There's a part of me that still thinks about all that money my partners and I could have made if we had let Phat Farm produce hockey jerseys. But I try to ignore that voice, because I know that while those jerseys would have made us a lot of money in the short term, the long-term effect would have been disastrous. The jerseys would have compromised our foundation, which is Classic American Flava. And once you ruin your foundation, you can never build any higher.

And sometimes Doing You isn't just about protecting your brand. It can be about protecting your beliefs too. For instance, a few years back I was looking for a distributor for my energy drink Def Con 3. I had been working on Def Con for several years but couldn't get it over the hump. Just when it seemed like we'd exhausted all our possibilities, Pepsi stepped up and said they wanted to distribute it. It seemed like the answers to our prayers. With Pepsi handling the distribution, I was sure people would have an opportunity to see how great a brand we were building. But then Pepsi learned that I was also working with PETA (People for the Ethical Treatment of Animals) in calling attention to the abusive practices of Kentucky Fried Chicken. And that caused some issues, because KFC is currently owned by Yum! Brands, which is a spinoff of Pepsi. So even though Pepsi doesn't technically own KFC anymore, the two companies have a close working relationship. It didn't sit too well with Pepsi that I was talking about how KFC abuses over 850 million chickens a year by painfully debeaking them, crippling them, and eventually scalding them alive. Because of my outspokenness about KFC, they were forced to take their deal off the table. And I didn't have a problem with their decision—I understood protecting their brand's image was more important than any distribution deal with me. And to their credit, since that time they've continued to be very supportive of my social programs, particularly a partnership between Pepsi, the Hip-Hop Summit, and the Ludacris Foundation that has put back more than $3 million toward inner-city arts and music programs.

But at the time, their decision hurt, because it seemed like a crushing blow for the Def Con brand. Not surprisingly, a lot of my business associates were upset with me because they felt that I had let my personal opinions come before my business. For years, people have been telling me, "Russell, who cares about chickens? Please keep your mouth shut. All you're going to do is piss off some powerful companies!" And they were right. My views have cost me plenty of checks. But even though I would have loved to work with Pepsi, I could never do it at the expense of staying quiet about the millions of chickens being killed inhumanely. Sorry, but that's not me. I'd rather speak out about something I believe in and be broke than stay silent and get paid.

BUILDING A DEF BRAND

We've just seen examples of how Doing You might affect your bottom line. But I also want to stress that Doing You can just as easily create tremendous growth for you in the business world. That's because Doing You is an essential part of building what every company needs to be successful in today's marketplace: a trusted brand.

Throughout my career, building brands seems to be the skill I've received the most recognition for. The first one I was successful with was the Def Jam brand, which really captured the attitude and spirit of hip-hop. People had so much trust in that brand, they used to buy albums on the strength of the "Def Jam" logo alone. Even if they had never heard of the artist, people would still snatch it up. Why? Because fans trusted us not to put out anything that was wack. They believed that if we were comfortable putting the Def Jam name on it, then they could be comfortable buying it. And that trust is what allowed me later to branch out into the *Def Comedy Jam* and *Def Poetry Jam* with HBO, as well as video games through Def Interactive. Even though comedy or poetry might not have been on our core fans' radar, because those shows had the Def Jam brand on them, they were willing to take a chance. The "Def" was maybe the reason why you turned the show on, but once they were tuned in, both of the shows spoke for themselves. And that's what's kept them coming back.

Another example is Baby Phat. Because consumers trusted the Phat Farm brand, when it was time to launch Baby Phat, people were willing to give it a chance, even though there had never been a women's hip-hop clothing line before. Now Baby Phat is even more profitable than Phat Farm, and we were able to use that visibility to build ventures like Goddess perfume and Simmons Jewelry. But all those companies were only possible because we had never compromised Phat Farm's original vision.

Those successes took years to develop, but my strategy for building a brand is actually pretty simple. The first step is always identifying a cultural space where I want to operate. By that, I mean identifying a feeling. You can do that by walking down the street, being around people and just sucking in the way they live. Walk the streets and suck in the way the jeans are being worn. And if that energy inspires you, then try to capture it with your own product. Do you want to start a record label? Then you need to walk the streets and suck in the way the music sounds and inspires people. Do you want to start a comedy show? Then you need to check out as many comedians as possible and suck in the way the jokes fall. Or if poetry is your thing, then go to a poetry slam and suck in the way the words move people.

And once you've sucked it all into your heart, then you can express those attitudes in a way that hasn't been explored yet. Your translation of what you've internalized will be what makes you unique. For example, Phat Farms jeans weren't that different from the other jeans people were wearing in hip-hop—they were just a little bit less baggy, because that was something I was more comfortable with. But just that little touch of individuality helped them seem more authentic to our core audience.

Branding with the Youth

Another question I often get asked by aspiring entrepreneurs is "How can I build a lifestyle brand that's connected with youth culture?" They're curious because it seems like young people's tastes change so quickly. Entrepreneurs might be able to react to what's *already* hot, but they have a very hard time predicting what's going *to be* hot. When they see my success with a Phat Farm, or a Def Poetry Jam, they assume I have some sort of crystal ball into youth culture. I hate to disappoint them, but all I try to do is remember to remember that youth culture is centered around Doing You. And when you never forget that basic truth, you'll be able to ride that tiger, instead of always chasing its tail.

Throughout history, youth culture has emphasized having a free spirit and challenging what's perceived to be the adults' mistakes. It's a collective way of Doing You. It's necessary because no matter the culture or country, people have a tendency to become more rigid as they get older. They tend to want things a certain way, and then they try to make the world conform to those ideas. So young people's emphasis on individuality is a reaction to that rigid mentality. Young people are always going to want freedom of choice, not someone else making choices for them. And that desire is going to be reflected in what they wear, what they drive, what they listen to, how they dance—you name it. Even if they all are driving the same car, wearing the same shirt, and listening to the same song, it's fine as long as they believe they made those choices themselves. Young people will accept anything as cool as long as they don't feel it was forced on them.

Let me be clear. When we talk about youth culture in America today, we're talking about hip-hop. That's not an overstatement. Hip-hop *is* youth culture today, not only in America, but all over the world. That's true on so many levels—artistically, politically, socially—but right here I want to talk about its impact economically. Because hip-hop has truly become the voice that makes the choices and sets the trends globally. Hip-hop isn't the first culture to do that, but it is the first to make an impact on such a massive scale. Jazz and rock 'n' roll in particular promoted a lot of cool ideas, but not in the same way as hip-hop. And certainly none of them were able to build brands the way hip-hop has.

That's because hip-hop is much more specific and sophisticated in its tastes than the youth cultures that came before it. Much of that is due to hip-hop's visual power, being the first cultural phenomenon born in the video age. For example, we loved James Brown back in the seventies, but our visual access to him was very limited. If you wanted to dress like James, you had to study the picture of him on an album cover or go see him in concert. But today, if you want to wear the same watch as Kanye

West, or drive the same car, all you have to do is turn on the TV and watch one of his videos. Rappers are incredibly accessible. Young people aren't studying an album cover anymore. Instead, they're watching Kanye's style develop every time they turn on the TV. One day Kanye is wearing a Rolex watch. The next day it's a Cartier. Then it's a Franck Muller. And in the process, all of those watches become cool. You can actually watch as the brands are being built. You can see it happening. It's such a dramatic difference.

I know this all sounds very materialistic, but we can't ignore the fact that materialism has always been part of hip-hop. From almost the very first time an MC picked up the mike, hip-hop has been rhyming about Cadillacs, gold chains, and designer jeans. This wasn't something that was forced on hip-hop by corporate culture— it was completely organic. And I believe that's due to the fact that hip-hop has always been an aspirational culture. It's always been the voice of poor people, a form of expression for people who perceive themselves as being locked out. And for better or worse, people who've grown up poor usually express their initial success through toys. That's why rappers are such incredible taste makers. If they say a Bentley is better than a Rolls-Royce, it's because they've tested both of them just to make sure they're getting the flyest shit. To them, buying a car or a watch isn't really about the car as much as it is about articulating their success. And they don't want anyone to be unclear about just how far they've made it.

And while I love it when people celebrate overcoming the struggle, my hope is that eventually we realize that the toys can't really make you happy, only giving can do that. But at the same time, I'm not going to tell people not to buy those toys. Just like I'm not going to stop selling toys either. The fact is, this emphasis on fashion and style is in hip-hop's DNA. We just need to make sure it doesn't become our only focus.

For entrepreneurs, the challenge is how to tap into that energy. Because despite all the sneaker, car, liquor, clothing, and even computer companies that have already embraced hip-hop, there's still so much energy that hasn't been captured. If you're a hungry entrepreneur with an ear to the street, there's still so much room for you to build a brand in. You just have to be listening to those subtle details that go with the hip-hop attitude. If you watch and listen to what is happening on the streets, what is happening in the videos, in the chat rooms, in the blogs, you'll know where those voids are. And once you identify those voids, it all comes back again to Doing You. When you have a brand that people on the street can trust, they will always support it.

Wear Your Truth

Another advantage of Doing You is that it keeps you closely connected with your brand. That's why every time you see me, I'm wearing something by Phat Farm. I know some people say, "Why is Russell always rocking Phat Farm? He needs to give it a rest." Well, the answer should be obvious: I make shit that I like! Hopefully you'll like it, too, but I'm never going to make clothes that I don't personally think are fly. My clothes reflect me. I respect my brand, so why wouldn't I wear my truth on my back?

Now, don't get me wrong. Occasionally I'll wear a shirt by Sean Jean or a Rocawear jacket or something by Marc Ecko. But that's about it, because if I'm not representing my own brand, at least I'm going to represent hip-hop on a larger scale. To me, that's still Doing You. *Because I am hip-hop.* And by supporting those other companies, I'm supporting myself too.

That's a message I feel is getting lost these days. If you're part of the hip-hop nation, then you have billions of dollars in economic power. When you said the Polo man is hot, that's what everyone scrambled to buy. When you said the Timberland tree is what's in, then that's what everyone wanted. So why can't you say the Phat Farm crest, or the Sean Jean logo, is what's cool instead? After all, Timberland has never embraced hip-hop culture. In fact, when Timberland first became a major brand in hip-hop, they actually tried to distance themselves from that energy. Or consider what happened when rappers started drinking Cristal Champagne. Cristal's CEO admitted he'd rather rappers *not* mention his champagne in their songs and videos. In fact, his exact quote was "What can we do? We can't forbid people from buying it. I'm sure Dom Pérignon or Krug would be delighted to have their business." Wow. Is this the man you want to support with your money?

To me, that's the same kind of attitude that created a need for hip-hop in the first place. It's similar to how, back in the late seventies, the R&B clubs basically said, "We don't want no street niggas in here." By making us feel unwanted, they forced us to hang out in the parks, throw our own parties, and create a new reality. We took that negativity and built something lasting out of it. And that's what we need to do today in the business world too.

I realize that when I ask you to patronize hip-hop brands, it sounds very self-serving. But I promise I'm not using this book to push my own products. Instead, I'm asking you to not only understand, but to utilize your power. Despite all our success, we still need to improve when it comes to supporting brands that *are* hip-hop, instead of brands that *target* hip-hop. For some reason, we still have an aversion to it. We've made ourselves to be the new face of America. Now let's use that leverage to uplift ourselves, to educate ourselves, and to *pay* ourselves. I know that sounds kind of rugged, and you could correctly argue it's a very unyogilike attitude, but that's how I feel.

Again, I'm not trying to dis the other clothing companies out there. And when they come out and start really uplifting the streets where hip-hop comes from, I'll stand up and salute them one by one. In fact, I'll salute Tommy Hilfiger right now. He's helping build the Martin Luther King memorial in Washington and he's always there when hip-hop needs him. So I'd rather you wear Tommy than some of these other brands.

I'm not dissing Phil Knight and his Nikes either. But if you're part of hip-hop, why wouldn't you want to buy a pair of sneakers made by 50 Cent or Dame Dash first? Trust me, no one in corporate America knows you better than Dame does. So wouldn't you rather put that money back into your community? When you automatically assume that Phil Knight's Nikes are better than Damon Dash's Pro-Keds, you're revealing a real lack of faith in your community and ultimately in yourself. Have confidence in yourself and in your community. Be conscious about the choices you make with your money and always try to support the people who support you. I like to call it Doing You by Doing Us.

Speak Your Truth

Finally, I'd like to end this chapter by reminding the politicians out there about the importance of always Doing You. From my perspective, it seems most politicians tend to listen to the polls instead of listening to their hearts, which is in direct opposition to this law.

I believe that if you have love and compassion in your heart (and if you don't, you shouldn't be in office anyway), then you must have the courage to reflect that in your policies. If you're against the death penalty, or for gun control, or against war, then you can't stay quiet just because conventional wisdom says that those issues don't play well in the polls. You must have the courage to speak up for them publicly.

I'm disappointed that so many public servants, especially on the left, seem afraid to live up to their ideals. They're afraid that love and compassion won't translate into votes, the same way that MTV was afraid a reverend in prime time wouldn't translate into ratings. They're afraid to promote peaceful solutions the same way that the record labels were afraid to promote records that didn't sound like "Rapper's Delight." But just like the TV and record executives learned the power of Do You the hard way, eventually these politicians will realize that being honest is the only way to be successful in their industry as well. In fact, I believe the next great leader in this country will be someone who unflinchingly speaks what he or she perceives to be the truth. It's not going to be someone who's afraid to make waves, or is constantly checking the polls. It's going to be someone who's in touch with his or her higher self and isn't afraid to go against the grain and Do Them.

RECOGNIZE THE REAL:

From the beginning of my career, I've always tried to stay true to who I am. I figured it was about time there was a black man who doesn't have to give up his blackness in order to play with the white guys.

I don't belong to any particular religion or sect. But I owe much of my success to finding time for prayer and meditation in my life.

LAW NUMBER THREE:

GET YOUR MIND RIGHT

All the things that truly matter—beauty, love, creativity, joy, inner peace—arise from beyond the mind.
—EKHART TOLLE

IT SEEMS THAT WHENEVER we turn on the TV, listen to the radio, or pick up a magazine, we're bombarded by the message that our *life* will improve once we get our *body* in shape. It's a potent message, witnessed by the millions of people who get up every day and trudge off to the gym, hoping to find happiness through getting their abs flat, their chest bigger, or their butt tighter. And while it's fine to get your body in shape, I would suggest that it's more helpful to get your *mind* toned first. Remember, your mind is your most powerful muscle. A six-pack on your stomach won't really make you happy unless you're also keeping your mind in shape through prayer, reflection, and self-study. How you look on the outside doesn't really matter if you don't have your spiritual self in shape first.

One of the best ways to get your mind in shape is through the practice of meditation. While physical exercise makes you stronger by building things up—like muscle or stamina—the mental workout that you get through meditation makes you stronger by clearing things away. It clears away the distractions of the world and gives you the clarity to see and the focus to pursue the God-given visions that will be the foundation to your success. Building up your body or your bank account will bring you short-time happiness, but you can't take those things with you on your journey through life. No matter how many weights you lift, eventually your body will sag. No matter how much money you make, eventually it will lose its value and its appeal. But a clear and focused mind will last a lifetime. Getting your mind in shape is nothing less than the key to sustainable success in the world.

This may seem like a daunting task, since we're much more conditioned to working out our bodies than our minds. But while you might feel mentally flabby, always remember that getting your mind right isn't as hard as it might seem. Your challenge isn't to take your mind to a place it hasn't been before. Instead, you only need to return it to where it's already been.

That's because every single one of us is born perfect. I really believe this. Our physical forms might not have developed yet, but our minds are perfect the moment we enter the world. We are blank sheets created by God. All we can hear are the high notes of love, which nourish us with all the spiritual guidance we'll ever need. When we're born, everything is in place to lead a beautiful and rewarding life. The problem is we just don't stay that way.

Even though we are born with this pureness *inside* of us, we also have to struggle with the world *outside* of us. And in that struggle, our pureness gets dirty pretty quickly. The first way is through physical impurities, as the world teaches our body to accept things that aren't actually good for it. Everywhere you look you see little kids, toddlers even, drinking cow's milk (which is bad for them, no matter what any doctor tells you), eating French fries, and gulping down sodas filled with sugar and high-fructose corn syrup. That's not what their bodies really want—in fact, most children spit out cow's milk the first time they taste it! Kids are supposed to eat fruits and vegetables and natural juices. Nevertheless, they eventually learn to accept what they instinctively rejected as harmful. They start drinking the milk, eating the French fries, and chugging the soda, not because it's what they want, but because it's what society tells them is desirable. And it keeps happening over the course of our lives.

When we're teenagers, we take a puff of a cigarette and cough. But instead of acknowledging that smoke doesn't belong in our lungs, we keep smoking, because that's what the world says is cool. Just like when we drink too much alcohol and get sick, we get up the next day and do it all over again. Not because it's good for us, but because it's what we see the world is doing around us.

Just like we pollute our bodies, similarly, we pollute the purity of our minds. Emotionally, we're taught to act in ways that are harmful to ourselves. We're taught to have egos, to be envious, to be selfish, to be insecure. Soon that beautiful blank sheet that we're born with is filled up with the physical and emotional vices that the world pushes on us. It's an inevitable part of being. And the end result is usually an adult who's totally lost touch with his inner self, who feels lost in the world and keeps making the wrong choices. We're born, and then we're separated from God. The beauty of meditation is that it brings us back.

Meditation can help bring you back to a place that you probably forgot even existed. A place where you will know the right choice to make in every situation. A place where you can be in control of your emotions and ignore the distractions that keep you from focusing on what's really important to you.

I've been able to make meditation a larger part of my own life through the practice of yoga. Yoga has not only helped me get healthier and happier but, most importantly, has brought me closer to God. While yoga was the route that led me toward meditation, it is only one of the sciences that can help you form that elusive union with your higher self. If you're more comfortable meditating in a mosque, or in a synagogue, or even in a Quaker meeting, then God bless you. My only hope is that after reading this chapter, you'll have a better appreciation for the power of meditation and be able to use it as the key to unlock the incredible potential that's inside your mind and your heart.

HEARING THE GOD INSIDE OF YOU

Before I embraced meditation, I used to have a hard time falling asleep because there was so much noise in my head. And by noise, I'm not talking about car alarms, police sirens, or the dog next door barking too loud. No physical noise was keeping me awake. Instead, it was my emotions that wouldn't let me sleep. It was the noise bouncing around in my own mind that kept me from being at peace.

You might have experienced it yourself. Even though all you want to do is fall asleep, you can't seem to turn off the conversations taking place inside your head. And to make it worse, it's usually trivial stuff that's keeping you awake. You'll replay something someone said to you at work. You'll worry about whether you locked your car door. You'll worry about whether you're gaining weight. I spent many nights lying awake like that, worrying and stressing over a million different things coming in and out of my mind. Was my new record going to sell? Did I get the right deal for one of my artists? Was that girl I'd been sweating ever going to call me? It was like there was a soundtrack playing in my brain that I couldn't turn off. Those are common examples, but there are also bigger terms that we can use to describe noise. Doubt is noise. Criticism is noise. Insecurity is noise. The past is noise, just like the future is noise too. These are the sounds that slow us down.

Indeed, I eventually realized that all the noise in my head was doing more than just keeping me awake at night. More importantly, it was drowning out the most important voice any of us has, which is the voice of God inside us. The truth is, when you can't hear God inside of you, you're always going to struggle in life. There might be stretches when things are going good and you feel like you're happy. But without that connection to your higher self, that happiness can't last. Sooner or later that noise will creep back into your mind and you'll be listening to the world, instead of the God in you.

The only way you're ever going to find that happiness is by focusing on your higher self and letting go of your lower self. I understand that's easier said than done, since there are constantly going to be hurdles to overcome, obstacles to get around. But that's fine because reality isn't here to trip you up. Reality is here to make you better. Listening to your higher self helps reality do its job.

Admittedly, the terms *higher self* and *lower self* might seem a little vague, but I think they're concepts that we're already familiar with subconsciously. All of us know what the right choice is to make in any situation. So when I say "higher self," I'm referring to that positive choice, to the choice that will contribute something to the world. Conversely, your "lower self" is reflected in the greedy choice, the choice that doesn't benefit anyone (and that includes you). For example, I don't believe in eating animals. I'll explain my reasons in greater detail later in the book, but essentially I think eating meat creates negativity in the world. Yet sometimes I also find myself desiring a piece of fish. When I'm focused on my higher self, I'm able to ignore that desire. But when I'm distracted by the world and my lower self has my attention, I end up taking a bite of fish. My higher self knows that I shouldn't even pick it up, but because I'm not focused, my lower self wins out.

Maybe the best way to define what I mean by "higher" and "lower" self is through people's actions. When I'm at work, I can tell which of my employees is listening to her higher self. When I see a person who is happy and focused, who's inspiring the people around her through their dedication and hard work, I know that person is listening to her higher self. Then I see employees who are subservient to their lower selves. They are selfish, takers rather than givers. They sulk around the office and don't put in the hard work, but still try to take the credit when something goes right. Those kinds of people might think they're "getting over," but their success is always temporary. Time and time again I watch as the people who listen to their higher selves move on to bigger and better things, while the people who listen to the low notes either end up stuck in one place or fade away altogether. They never realize that by ignoring their higher selves, they're blocking their ability to be blessed.

I can hear many of you asking now, "That's fine. But how to do we hear that higher voice?" Well, the first step is to understand where that voice is coming from. And that's from *inside you*. A lot of the time it seems like people are more comfortable listening to the God that is outside them. But I believe that God is already inside of you. When they take "you" out of God, that's when I start to lose the connection. I can't imagine God as a guy sitting on some golden throne. That doesn't seem real to me. The only God that seems real to me is the God in my heart. The God that's in *all* of our hearts.

I guess that's why if there's a space where I feel slightly disconnected from the Judeo/Christian/Muslim way of seeing the world, it's probably in prayer and meditation. In fact, I've felt that way for a long time. When my parents used to take me and my brothers to church and the preacher would tell us to pray, I didn't like it. I was closing my eyes and saying the words, but there was a disconnect. At the time, I chalked it up to being too young. I figured I wasn't smart enough, or worthy enough, to have the same conversation with God that everyone else in the church was having. But now I realize that's just not the way I personally connect with God. I still go to church on occasion, but I've learned that I'm much more comfortable when I'm trying to connect to God through my own heart, rather than through someone else's vision of what God is.

That's why I want to make a distinction between prayer and meditation in our culture. When most people pray, I feel like they're asking God to help them. They're asking the God outside of them to help them with a job, help them find love, or help them keep their families in good health. But I believe that meditation lets you help yourself. Meditation gives you the power to go get that job, or find that lover, or support your family with your own God-given talents. I'm not suggesting that prayers don't get answered. They do, as long as the person praying has very, very strong faith. The kind of faith that many of us can't find.

The difference is that when you get in touch with your higher self through meditation, you're *guaranteeing* that your prayers will be answered (for lack of a better term), because you're holding yourself responsible. The voice of God *inside* of you is always going to tell you how to find that good job. The voice *inside* you will always help you find a beautiful person to share your life with. The voice *inside* you will steer you toward the right choices in life. Even if your faith is weak, that voice will always be strong. Never forget that *you* are the Holy Spirit. You have the power to see goodness or sorrow in the world. *You* have the power to be happy or not happy.

I don't think it's blasphemous to make these statements. In fact, this is really the message that's at the heart of the Bible, or the Holy Koran, the Buddhist scriptures, and so many other great spiritual books. I'll say it again—Jesus and Muhammad didn't reveal themselves to prove what they could do. They revealed themselves so you could see what *you* can do. And with some very simple steps, you can begin to realize that potential.

BEING PRESENT

The most powerful step in realizing your potential is simply to be present in the world. That might seem so obvious that it barely bears repeating, but operating outside of the present is actually what separates all of us from the happiness we desire. We talk about living for the here and now, but in reality we're much more comfortable avoiding it. Too often, we spend our lives drifting between the past and the future, instead of rooting ourself in the moment. And living like that, you become your worst enemy. You wait for things to happen instead of making them happen. You imagine what happiness is like instead of appreciating the happiness that is already present in your life. You dream about making money, or about the money that you've lost, instead of appreciating that you're rich this very second! You must embrace the present. Never, ever forget that. You can't make money in the future and you can't make money in the past. The present is the only place you're going to get paid. Just as the present is also the only place you'll ever be truly happy, or ever be able to experience true love.

The world is so loud that we almost forget that we're capable of being present. We forget that we can experience seconds when we feel truly alive. That's why it's so important to remember to remember that we are capable of being present. Like when we see a beautiful woman, or a beautiful sunset, or even a beautiful piece of art, and just say, "Wow." Those are moments of pure presence. Moments when you stop thinking about everything else that's happening in the world and totally focus on *being present*. You don't hear the traffic, or see the other people on the street. You forget where you are, or where you were heading, and become transfixed by how powerful the orange sun looks as it begins to drift behind the clouds. Those are moments of presence.

If you've ever been in a car accident, then you've experienced pure presence. One second you're moving fast, distracted by the world. The next second, everything is happening slowly. You can hear the rubber screeching on the pavement. You can hear the metal crunching. But you don't feel anything. You're not scared. It's almost like a movie. Because you're completely present.

I bungee jumped once, and that was definitely a moment of pure presence. You're standing on top of the platform and suddenly you're totally awake. And at the moment you jump, you're not thinking anymore. You're flying through the air, but there's no fear, no noise, no world. Just you and the moment. You become totally present.

A book that really helped me understand this concept is Eckhart Tolle's *The Power of Now*. It's very powerful, especially when Tolle explains that being consciously present in the now is the best way to realize the immense potential of the future. After I read *The Power of Now*, it had such an impact on me that I started giving copies to everyone I met. One day I took Puffy to yoga with me and after the class I tried to explain the concept of presence to him. I started talking about car crashes and bungee jumping when Puffy cut me off. "Oh, yeah, I get what you're talking about," he said. "I feel that way every time I get shot at." And we both couldn't help but laugh. Not long afterward, my yoga instructor, Steve Ross (more about him later), called to say that Eckhart was staying as a guest with him in Los Angeles and asked if I would like to meet him. Of course I said yes and quickly flew out so I could meet this man who had inspired me so much. When I arrived at Steve's home, he led me into the little guesthouse where Eckhart was staying. I sat down and for about ten minutes, neither of us said a word. Instead, we just stared at each other. At first I was a little freaked out, but after a while I realized we were having a meditative conversation. Finally, after almost ten minutes of us staring at each other, I decided to break the silence and told him how I tried to describe the concept of presence to Puffy. After I shared the story, the only words he had for me was laughter. He kept laughing and laughing, to the point that I finally got up and left him in the guesthouse. I said good-bye to Steve and as I got in my car to leave, I could still hear him laughing in the guesthouse. At first, it seemed a little crazy that this guy found my story *so* funny, but the more I thought about it, I realized that Eckhart's reaction made perfect sense. It wasn't that he found anything funny about Puffy getting shot at, but that he was so pleased to hear such a great example of pure presence. His whole book was about trying to explain presence, and in one sentence, Puffy has summed it up perfectly!

Of course car crashes and getting shot at might seem like extreme examples, but these moments of presence aren't that rare. They're really all around us, every day. If you watch basketball, you'll see people who are completely present. When a player like

Michael Jordan or LeBron James gets "in the zone" and is able to score ten straight points at the end of a playoff game, that's just another way of saying that he was completely present. When they're in that zone, they're able to shut out the fans, the defenders from the other team, the refs, and just be. Every shot goes in because they're not thinking about the distractions, they're just being. They're stuck on stupid, which might sound funny, but is exactly how you have to be to find sustainable success.

I've shared all these examples because I want people to under-stand that pure presence isn't elusive—it's something that we're all capable of, something that we actually encounter in life. Once you accept that, then you can set your sights on the ultimate goal of meditation, which is to be able to string these moments of presence together.

The goal is to be able to live your life the way Michael Jordan played basketball, or Marvin Gaye sang a song. To be able to feel the way you feel when you laugh at a joke, but feel that way *all of the time*. To be able to feel the way you feel when you're having great sex, but *all of the time*. It really is possible. If you feel a certain way even if only for a second, that means that you're capable of it. It's just that we're taught that we can only laugh when we hear something funny, or experience the joy of a climax when we're hav-ing sex.

Again, we're talking about car crashes, basketball, and sex, but at the end of the day all these things are rooted in a spiritual state, a state that every religion has a name for. The yogis call it "Samahdi," or "walking meditation," while Christians call it "Christ Consciousness," Buddhists call it "Nirvana," and Muslims call it "Taqwa." My brother Reverend Run, who's what I like to call a "Christian yogi," has his own term for it. He calls it a "State of Grace," that space where you can walk around and practice love in everything you do. To walk around all day with a smile and, instead of seeing the world as bad, simply seeing opportunities to make the world better. That's Run's practice, and I think it's a very valuable one. But the truth is, *every* religion has a name for that special moment when you're able to extend the experience of presence.

Of course, only very special people like a Jesus or a Lord Buddha or a Muhammad are able to be totally present, all of the time. The rest of us mere mortals are just trying to be a little more present than we already are. We're just striving to be present enough to appreciate the godliness around us. Whether it's a mountaintop or a project rooftop, a sunset or a dark alley, a newborn baby or a corpse, the signs of God are posted all around us. We just have to try to be present enough to see them.

Remember, there's never any fear or anxiety in the present. There's only consciousness. That's where every good idea comes from. It's the space where scientists discover the atom. The space where artists paint beautiful pictures, or make beautiful songs. It's where businessmen make fortunes, and teenagers fall in love. It's the space from which you do every good thing and experience every bit of happiness. When we talk about being present, we're talking about real success. When you accept this truth, you understand that what you've always been chasing, you already have. Or as the great Buddhist monk Thich Nhat Hanh put it, "The miracle is not to walk on water. The miracle is to walk on the green earth, dwelling deeply in the present moment and feeling truly alive."

THE PRACTICE OF YOGA

There are many spiritual paths that you can follow that will lead you to that state of presence. But the one practice that has had the greatest influence on *me* is the science of yoga. When I started working on this book, one of my goals was to never sound preachy. But when it comes to yoga, I'm going to get high up in the pulpit and speak my piece without any apologies. Because I really think that yoga is a practice that can show every one of us how to lead a more rewarding life. It's certainly done that for me. I'm going to talk more about yoga later, but for now I want you to know how I got into the practice.

Back in the early nineties, I was living in Los Angeles, learning my way around the movie business. On the surface it looked like I had *everything* going on. I had a fancy house, plenty of friends, and was surrounded by beautiful women. But inside I felt empty. I was financially successful but wasn't at peace. The truth is, I was fearful of real success, fearful of what was around the corner. I wasn't content because I was searching for something real. Thankfully, I didn't have to search for long.

That's because one day my great friend Bobby Shriver dragged me into a yoga class with him. Any doubts I had about doing yoga (my perception had been that only gay men did yoga) evaporated pretty quickly once I took a look around. I couldn't believe how many beautiful women were there, bending and stretching and contorting right in front of me. It seemed like every one of them had a better body than the next! But it was more than the beautiful scenery that excited me. Even though I was struggling with the physical poses, I realized that I had stumbled onto something incredible. Just through sweating and focusing on my breath, I began to find more peace than I had ever found in the bottom of a bottle or a line of coke or a StairMaster. When I came out of that class an hour and a half later, I was high as hell. But it was a beautiful, natural high, without any of the negative baggage that comes with drugs or alcohol. It was only one class, but I was hooked. I knew I had found something special. I had entered a space where there was no fear, no future, no nothing. And I wanted to go back. In fact, I've been chasing that high ever since, just like a crack addict chases his first high. But the difference is, I'm not chasing something *de-structive*. I'm chasing the high you get from finally getting your body and mind on the same page. And that's actually one of the most *con-structive* things you can do.

I believe one of the reasons I also had such an instant connection to yoga was my teacher that day, an incredible man named Steve Ross, who I just mentioned. Steve was, and continues to be, the ideal teacher for me. Firstly, Steve shares my weakness for beautiful women, which probably explains why his classes are always filled with some of the most stunning models and actresses in Los Angeles. But much more importantly, Steve is very open-minded and believes strongly in having fun during his classes. He'll play loud hip-hop music, make jokes, and goof around in his class. He's very committed to yoga, but he doesn't push it like a religion. He's completely nonjudgmental. If he had pushed it hard, I probably would have been turned off. The same way I rebelled against organized religion when I was younger.

Soon I was going to yoga every chance I got. But even though yoga was making me so much healthier and happier, very few of the people around me understood my passion, let alone shared it. They were like, "Man, what are you talking about? What the hell is yoga?" They thought it was something for old white ladies or gay men. And I could understand why. When I went to that first class, there were probably fifty-six women in it (Steve knew what he was doing), two gay men, plus me and Bobby. There was nobody there who looked like me or seemed to come from a similar background. Not because those people were being shut out, but because it simply wasn't on our radar.

Or the few people who did have a vague sense of yoga felt weird about yoga because they were raised a Baptist or a Muslim. They didn't understand that yoga really shares the same space as all those other practices. That the messages you find in the yoga scriptures are the same you'll find in the Bible, the Koran, or the Torah. The only difference is that the yogis aren't trying to tell you to separate yourself from other religions. They're letting you know that the sameness is there. That as long as you're getting in touch with God, it's all good.

And it was definitely all good for me. After a few years in L.A., I decided to move back to New York. But instead of leaving yoga behind, I got into the practice even more heavily. I started going to classes at Jivamukti Yoga, a highly technical center that explores the spiritual science of yoga. The center was founded by Sharon Gannon and David Life, who were some of the first American instructors to study in India and emphasize the spiritual aspect of yoga. Through promoting books like the *Yoga Sutras,* the *Bhagavad Gita,* and *The Hatha Yoga Pradipika,* David and Sharon have taught thousands of students how to bring their bodies and minds into union and free themselves from the entanglements of the world. In fact, the term *Jivamukti* means "liberation." I know that their classes really opened up a new dimension of yoga to me. Which is not to discount what I learned from Steve, who always taught that the technical science of yoga is valuable but not necessary. His philosophy could probably be summed up as "Without love and humor, yoga is just a lot of hard work." And I can't argue with that.

Though there are subtle differences among all teachers, Steve, Sharon, and David have all been incredible blessings to me. If you live in Los Angeles or New York, I encourage you to go and meet them for yourself. No matter where you live, try to find a yoga teacher that you like. Because they will be able to share so many beautiful insights into the world with you. They will be able to share simple ideas that can promote a happier existence. Just the other day, I was talking to a friend who was going through a difficult divorce. She was telling me about how she was depressed and was going to start seeing a psychiatrist. I told her that therapy can be great, but I knew of a more rewarding way. I suggested she go see a yoga instructor I knew well. And I reminded her that not only is yoga a lot cheaper than therapy, but it can be much more inspiring too. She told me that she was interested but was afraid her legs "weren't flexible enough for yoga." I had to laugh, because to get something out of yoga, you don't have to be able to touch your toes. Physical flexibility is only a small part of it. The flexibility in your mind and in your heart is all that matters.

MEDITATION OVER MEDICATION

Gaining clarity through yoga is an especially important message for people who struggle with drugs and alcohol. So many black and brown people in this country, whether through addiction or incarceration, have been tragically disenfranchised because of their addiction. I say tragically because most people aren't involved with drugs because they're bad people. I believe they got hooked on drugs, or on alcohol, because they had trouble getting the noise out of their heads. Because they can't afford a doctor and a prescription, they self-medicate. And when you're on the street, self-medication eventually leads either to jail time or death. That's why I want to promote a better way to kill that noise. It won't cost a cent, any of your brain cells, your relationships, or even your freedom.

Please understand that I'm not judging anyone who uses drugs. That would be very hypocritical of me, since I've been there myself. When I was much younger, I used to get up at dawn and get high because the noise in my head was so loud. I want to make it clear that I'm not preaching from the mountaintop. I've been down in the valleys too. I'm just suggesting that when you're faced with fear and anxiety, don't medicate. Meditate instead.

If you live in a housing project, instead of going up on the roof and smoking a blunt every time you get stressed, try practicing yoga instead. Sure, people might not understand you at first, but if you stick with it, I promise you'll find a more lasting peace than you'll ever get from weed. If you live in a trailer park, instead of trying to escape your condition through speed or crystal meth, try practicing yoga instead. See if you can change your condition that way. Don't worry if that's not what your friends do, because what they're doing isn't really working. Have the courage to try something different.

Or maybe you're living in a beautiful house with a backyard and a pool, but you still feel empty inside. Instead of reaching for those antidepressants in your medicine cabinet, or the bottle of Scotch in your glove compartment, try joining a yoga class instead. See if a different path takes you to a better place. Because all the pills or pints of Scotch in the world won't ever fill your void. Only your higher self can do that. Only a union with God can do that.

I'm preaching so hard because I've seen all the ways in which yoga has empowered me. I married because of yoga. I learned how to drive because of yoga. I became more philanthropic because of yoga. I bought my first house because of yoga. I became more focused because of yoga. On so many different levels, my life has more value now because of yoga. And it's not just me. I think if everyone in the hood consciously started practicing yoga tomorrow, in a year that hood would really be a much better place to live. People would be lifting each other up instead of pulling each other down. The streets would be filled with compassion instead of conflict. That's how powerful this thing is. In fact, I believe that if people who practiced yoga were the only voters in this country, then we *really* would be the greatest nation on earth.

HOW TO MEDITATE

Practicing yoga led me to another powerful way of being present—and that's meditation. Every morning when I wake up, before I turn on the radio, pick up the newspaper, or have a cup of fresh juice, I try to spend a few minutes in meditation. Sometimes it's for fifteen minutes, sometimes for less. But it's always an essential part of my daily routine, because I know without it, I'm not going to have a productive day. I'm not as likely to have the focus I need to run my business and the clarity I need to be happy with my life.

And I'm very blessed. I have a space in my home with high ceilings and soft lighting where I can easily get into peaceful, reflective state. But the truth is you don't need all of that to make meditation part of your own routine. You can meditate in the projects or meditate in a penthouse. It's all up to you. Because no matter who you are, or where you live, you just need to love yourself enough to believe that inside you is an answer. I don't care what you have or haven't done with your life up until today. You must believe that inside of you is an answer. Otherwise, all the hard work that you put into meditation won't be worth it. You have to believe that answer is already there, waiting for you to find it.

The next step is to accept that meditation is a process. You're not going to hear God the first time you close your eyes and count to ten. It doesn't work like that. You also have to accept that the work you put in will be very hard. When you first start, five minutes will seem like an eternity. So don't be discouraged if you only do two minutes your first time. Even if you just sit still for a minute and watch your breath go in and out, at least you're starting the process. Before you know it, two minutes will turn into five. Five minutes will turn into ten. Ten minutes will turn into fifteen. Soon you'll be meditating for a half hour (which is what I aim for) and you'll start to see real results. And here's how you can start.

Be Still

If you're trying meditation for the first time, first find a quiet room where no one is going to bother you. If the bathroom is the only place in your home that fits that description, then let everyone else use it first and then go in there and set up shop. Whatever space you're working with, try to find a comfortable spot where you can sit in a cross-legged position. And no matter what, commit to a position you can sit in without moving. No matter what happens, don't move. If you feel like you have to scratch your nose, don't move. If your ass itches, don't move. It will all go away. Just sit still. And as the stillness begins to settle, things that are happening on the outside become less important. Some thoughts come in your mind, but you'll begin to realize how insignificant they are. You'll find the distractions will eventually disappear.

Breathe

The way you'll make the distractions disappear is by focusing on your breath. The relationship you have with your breath is the most intimate relationship you have. Because breathing is something we do all day, every day. But are you really aware of that relationship? Do you spend time working on it and focusing on it? Probably not, because most people still don't know how to get the most out of their breath. But your breath is actually the most stable thing in your life. Whether you're rich or poor, happy or sad, you'll still breathe in and out, all day, every day. When you stop doing that, it's time to get in the box.

That's why your breath is your most important tool in meditation. Focusing on your breath coming in and coming out is how you can clear your mind of all the distractions. Whenever that noise comes into your mind, just breathe it out. Let it go. You can't fight thoughts from going into your mind, but you can always breathe them out. That's the process.

In fact, put down this book and try it for yourself. Take a deep breath. Count in one-two-three-four. Breathe out at the same rate. Count out one, two, three, four. Do that a few times and you'll start to feel the world slow down. When the world is slowed down, you can start to be a bit indifferent to all that goes on around you. Not that you're not working hard, but so that you're not attached to it. Attach yourself to your breath instead. If your breath could be your soundtrack all day long, you'd be very happy.

If you can just be more conscious of your breath, your life will be more rewarding. Because no matter how bad things get, when you remember to slow down and breathe, things always get better. If you feel like someone is trying to get over on you, before you react, take a second and breathe. You'll find a better way to handle the situation. If your girl breaks up with you and you feel like the world is closing in, just breathe. If you're about to take a test in school and you get nervous, just slow down and breathe. As long as you remember to breathe no matter what kind of obstacles life throws at you, you'll always be on the right path.

When people ask me for advice on situations, I often tell them, "Just smile and breathe." Some might feel I'm not taking their problem seriously when I say that, but that advice is very real. It's the same advice I would give to my own daughters. Because breathing allows you to strip yourself of anxiety and stress. And people make bad choices a lot of times, not because they're bad people, but because they're stressed and anxious. Especially in the hood. But if you just remember to breathe and smile before you act, you'll always make the right decision.

Silence

The final piece of the meditation puzzle is silence. There's a reason you have two ears and one mouth. Once you stop talking, you'll be able to start listening to your higher self.

Of course, appreciating silence is easier said than done (pun intended). If you're like me, running your mouth comes much more naturally than shutting it. Sometimes I still talk too much and can't hear everything God is trying to tell me. I'm trying to do better every day, but it's still a journey for all of us. So stay with it, because eventually you'll understand that God has instructions for you and they will be heard if you're silent.

In fact, before you try meditating, first just try sitting in silence. You can start off by embracing silence for just a half hour a day. That means no talking, TV, music, computer, or reading. Just you and your thoughts. After you get that down, try being silent for forty-five minutes a day. It will be hard, but if you stick with it, you'll start seeing results. Once you stop talking, you'll be able to start listening to yourself. And then you'll be able to hear the helpful hints God's been telling you all along.

The Watcher

Once you have an appreciation of breathing, stillness, and silence, the fruits of meditation will be within your grasp. When you spend those fifteen minutes breathing slowly in silence, you'll start to see all your issues and dramas for what they are: distractions. And soon it won't feel like they're holding you down anymore. You might *think* about your job, or your relationships, but you won't get tangled up over analyzing them. Instead, you'll understand how to let it all go. When your mind is quiet, you can be what yogis call "the Watcher." You're in a state when you can just watch what's happening in your head instead of being controlled by it.

One practice that can help you become the Watcher is to focus on a mantra while you meditate. In English, we usually think of a mantra as a phrase that describes someone's philosophy. For instance, Jesse Jackson's mantra is "Keep hope alive," while 50 Cent's might be "Get rich or die trying." But in meditation, its meaning is a bit different. The word *mantra* comes from two Sanskrit words *man,* ("to think") and *tra* ("tool"). So the literal translation is "a tool of thought." And that's how mantras are used in the Hindu and Buddhist practices, as tools that clear your mind of distractions. Because when you focus on repeating that mantra over and over again, soon the noise will die down and all you will hear is your inner voice.

And a mantra doesn't have to be a phrase, or even a word. It could just be a sound. In fact, the most basic mantra in yoga is "Ohm," which yogis believe is the original sound of God. If you don't believe it, try repeating "Ohm" over and over again for five minutes. You'll see that it connects you with your heartbeat, which is a very powerful experience. Start with "Ohm" and eventually move on to longer mantras. Really, though, any mantra will work. Just so long as it helps you become the Watcher while you're meditating.

Remember, when you can watch your thoughts, you have better control of them. When you become the Watcher, it's literally like you're watching a movie of your life. You can rewind the good parts, fast-forward through the bad ones, and always be in control. You'll be able to watch the world and invest your emotions and actions in the things that you really care about, instead of being overwhelmed by what the world is throwing at you.

EVERYTHING IS PRAYER

I know we've been talking about meditation, specifically through the science of yoga, but I want to end this chapter by getting back to the concept of prayer. Specifically, I want to touch on the idea that everything you say and think is a prayer. *Everything.* I feel this is an important point to stress, because a lot of people think that prayer is only something you do in a church or a mosque. But we have to realize that prayer is really what you're saying and what you're thinking every day, twenty-four/seven.

It's great if you practice yoga and meditate for an hour on ways to make the world a better place. Just like it's wonderful if you go to synagogue and spend an hour focused on an inspiring sermon. But if you keep your thoughts positive only during those times, then you're never going to really change your condition. You have to understand you're talking to God all day, every day.

And that conversation, whether it's conscious or unconscious, will transform itself into actions. So if you think about negative things, those thoughts will turn into negative actions. But if you're able to focus on the positive, you're going to create positive actions. And the more positivity you create in the world, the more positivity the world will give back to you.

You've got to tell God thank you every day. When I call up Reverend Run's house, he answers the phone by saying, "Praise the Lord." Because he understands that you've got to praise God every chance you get. It's a small gesture, but it helps him keep his mind on God. Not just when he's in church, or when he thinks he needs God, but all of the time.

RECOGNIZE THE REAL:

God has already put a lot of time into you. When you put a little time back into God through prayer and meditation, that investment will always pay off. That's why when I start my day by reflecting on all the things I have to be thankful for, I'll have a much more rewarding day.

So many people are wondering what to do with their lives. Well, my advice to them is to *stop* wondering and to *start* looking inside for one of the many talents that they have. Put that on your drawing board and go to work.

LAW NUMBER FOUR:

STOP FRONTIN' AND START TODAY

I've heard of Monday, Tuesday, Wednesday, Thursday, and Friday. But I've never heard of Someday.
—REVEREND IKE

THE PRECEDING QUOTE (courtesy of Harlem's legendary Reverend Ike) really sums up the Law of Stop Frontin' and Start Today. So many people spend their lives waiting for "Someday" to arrive instead of having the courage to start following their dreams "*to*day." If you wait for "Someday," you're going to be waiting for a very long time. But once you Start Today, you'll find that success is much closer than you ever imagined. In fact, the day you start, you're already a step closer.

One of the main reasons people break this law is because stalling is much easier than starting. But in this chapter, I'll try to explain that though stalling might seem easier, it actually makes your life *harder*. When you allow yourself to be swept up by your ideas and follow them wherever they lead, your life will immediately become richer and more rewarding.

I've struggled with stalling and a lack of initiative at times, so I know how tempting it can be to put things off. But in this chapter, I want to share the practices that have sometimes allowed me to get past that fear (because we only stall when we're afraid) and focus on the jobs in front of me. The most important of those practices is getting in touch with your Dharma, the Sanskrit term for "purpose in life." God has blessed all of us with a purpose in life, and when you use prayer and mediation to realize that purpose, you'll have the energy and confidence to start working on it immediately.

When you're in touch with your Dharma, you'll stop waiting for someone to hand you something and be able to take it yourself instead. When you're in touch with your Dharma, you won't spend years wondering what to do with your life but will begin fulfilling your purpose right away. You'll realize you're never too old to start something new. You'll understand that the only time is now. So stop frontin', because there is tremendous power inside you. All you need is the courage to reach for it today.

FOLLOW YOUR DHARMA

Stalling is only one of the conditions that keep people from Starting Today. Another is that many people are unsure of what path to start *on*. They might be ready and willing to put in the work, but they can't *see* the jobs that are waiting for them out there. However, once you embrace your Dharma (it's a noun, not a verb), you'll understand that there are actually many jobs for you and all you need to do is choose one and start.

Dharma has taken on many meanings over the centuries, including "work," "religion," and "duty." But for this chapter, I want to focus on a meaning it has taken on in yogic practice, which is "purpose in life." Essentially, Dharma reveals that without exception God has blessed each of us with a variety of resources and ideas. That means you and I and everyone we know has numerous talents waiting to be realized. Not everyone's Dharma is the same, but it does exist in all of us. Maybe your Dharma is to run a television network. Or maybe it's to be an architect. Or perhaps it's to be a poet. Any one of them is possible. You just won't know until you start doing the work.

That's because God's not going to tell you, "You're here to be an architect. Now go design some buildings." Sorry, but it won't be that easy. However, he (or she!) will show you the signs. You might start to notice that you are interested by the way buildings look, and then one day start to make sketches of ones you really like. And by starting that process, you're already getting closer to your Dharma, because those sketches will lead you to art classes in high school. And the ability you show in art classes might result in a college scholarship. And after you excel in college, you'll get into architecture school. And before long, you'll be creating buildings that make other people happy too. But it only happened because you started acting on that initial Dharma.

To me, that's what a good life is all about: taking one of the skills God's blessed you with and actually acting it out. Conversely, when you don't pursue your Dharma, it's very easy to become stagnant and unhappy. That's why you must understand that you do have a purpose, and if you're ready to do the work, it'll only be a matter of time before you realize it. You don't even have to make the right decision about which job to start. Any decision is the right decision as long as you start working toward it today.

Now, some of you might say, "Suppose I'm ready to start today but still can't find my Dharma?" My reply is, stop *looking* for your Dharma and start *listening* to it. Just listen to that inner voice we described earlier and pay attention to what it tells you. All you have to do is lie in bed, letting the ideas come into and go out of your mind. As soon as one starts to seem a little bit more important than the others, really listen to it. Because that one is your Dharma! Don't dismiss it and go back to bed. Instead start to do something about it right away. If you hear that idea and never act on it, you'll become one of those stagnant, sick people. Remember, your purpose is to act on the resources God gives you. If God gives you a bucket of fish, you have to distribute those fish. If you don't, they're going to rot, attract a bunch of flies, and starting stinking up your soul.

After you listen to your Dharma, don't hesitate acting on it. A person who doesn't understand Dharma might stall by saying, "Man, there's no way I could do all of that," or "That looks way too hard." Not because the job is so hard, but because he's afraid of doing the work. Yet the truth is that *no job* is so difficult that you can't start working on it today. Chances are what's stopping you from getting started is the fear *inside you*. Not the task *in front of you*.

A person who understands Dharma will have the opposite response to starting a "hard" job. That person will be eager to get started, no matter what kind of work is in front of her, because she understands that she's doing God's work. And when you're working for God, nothing is too hard. Even if you decide that your Dharma is to cure cancer, or to help starving people in Africa, you won't feel that task is insurmountable. No one is going to cure cancer overnight, but by making the decision to *try* to do it, you'll light a fire inside yourself that will keep you motivated no matter how many obstacles are in your way. You'll be motivated to put your head down and get down to work today. When you start to follow your Dharma, all that fear that's been holding you back will just fall away.

What Am I Going to Do with My Life?

I want to take a moment here and speak directly to all of the recent college graduates, or those about to graduate, who are reading this book. Now that you're out of school and in the "real" world, you're probably asking, "What am I going to do with my life?" That's a perfectly legitimate question to ask, but don't spend the next ten or fifteen years pondering it. Instead, dig deep inside of yourself and try to find an answer *now*. I know of so many talented, educated people who are just floating around, still waiting for something to happen many years after they've graduated. Don't fall into that trap. Instead, *stop* wondering and *start* listening to your Dharma. Devote yourself to identifying your true passion now and start pursuing it with all your energy. Instead of asking, "What am I going to do with my life?" you should be asking yourself, "What *aren't* I going to do with my life?" because there are so many different things you can succeed at.

I also want to remind all of you who are still in school that it's not too early to Start Today either. Sometimes there's a perception that you can't start following your dreams until you graduate from high school, or before you get your college degree. But the truth is, you don't have to wait. You *can* Start Today. Generally, I would recommend that you get a high school diploma and do everything you can to graduate from college too. But if you're one of those people who know their Dharma from an early age, then please don't wait for a date that society has set to start pursuing it.

Back in the late seventies, I made a decision to drop out of college and dedicate myself to hip-hop. That decision did not go over very well with my parents, who had always put a strong emphasis on education. My father in particular thought that hip-hop was just a fad but that the benefits of college education would last a lifetime. As much as I hated to disappoint him, I still decided to put all my energy into my passion for the culture. I had the confidence to do that because I instinctively sensed my Dharma, even if I didn't know what Dharma was yet. It was very difficult at the time, but that decision to Start Today was one of the best I ever made. That's why one of my hopes for this book is that it will give a young person out there the confidence to make a similar decision. If this message connects with you, then try to spend a few minutes in prayer and meditation every day. Then use that clarity to really focus on what you think your Dharma is. And if you get a clear answer, start working on that job right away! You don't even have to drop out of school like I did. You can start doing the work in high school, or in college, so that when you do graduate, you'll hit the ground running. While the rest of your classmates are wasting time trying to figure out their next step, you'll already be in full stride toward your dreams!

Age Ain't Nothing but a Number

While it's important for young people to have the confidence to Start Today, the same is ultimately true no matter how old you are. It's very unfortunate, but there's a mentality in this country that at a certain age, you become "too old" to start on a new path in life. That might be true in fields like sport or dance, where you need to be in your physical prime to perform. But otherwise, you are never too old to start pursuing a new dream. Never.

I know in hip-hop, there's a perception that once you're past your mid twenties, you're too old to be a "new" artist. But the truth is, there are plenty of great artists who got their start at that age. For instance, I happen to know of a popular "new" rapper who was actually forty years old when he released his first album! I'm not going to name names, because he decided not to publicize that fact. Personally, I think it's beautiful and he has nothing to be embarrassed about. It's great that he had the courage to keep following his Dharma at an age where most people are completely settled in their lives.

Everywhere you look, there are stories of people who didn't start working toward their Dharma till relatively late in life. I'm no fan of KFC, but I appreciate that the actual Colonel Sanders didn't begin building his franchises until he was in his sixties. Or take Taikichiro Mori, the Japanese builder who was once considered the richest man in the world. He didn't start his construction company until he was in his mid fifties. Anthony Burgess, who wrote *A Clockwork Orange,* didn't publish his first novel until he was thirty-nine. Rodney Dangerfield didn't start doing comedy until he was forty-two. None of those people accepted that their path in life was set at twenty-five, or even thirty-five. They all had the courage to start on a new path one day, no matter what decade of their life that day fell in.

But maybe the best example is someone like Lord Buddha himself. If you're not familiar with his story, let me share it briefly, because it's a very inspiring illustration of what can happen when you Start Today. Thousands of years ago, in an area that is now part of northern India, a prince was born named Siddhartha Gautama. The prince spent his first twenty-nine years living the good life in his family's royal palace. He was literally treated like a prince and enjoyed a life sheltered from any of the unpleasant realities of the world. He was very set in that lifestyle, until he one day decided to venture outside of the palace walls. Once outside, he was startled by the sight of an old man, then a sick man, and finally a rotting corpse. It was an incredible revelation to the prince, who had never had to confront the realities of life and death before. The experience was so shocking to him that at once he decided to abandon the luxuries of the royal court and dedicate himself to becoming a wandering monk. He spent the rest of his life as a monk wandering through India, helping people understand the reasons for suffering and pain and teaching his followers about the path to enlightenment. Today, we know that monk as Lord Buddha.

Try to remember that Buddha made that radical change from a rich prince to a penniless monk when he was almost thirty years old, at a time when thirty was well into middle age. That's why one inspiration, out of many, that we can take from Lord Buddha's life is that you are never too old, too rich, or too poor to set out on a new path in life.

That's also a message found at the heart of Islam. Muhammad was almost forty when he received his first vision from God. Before that, he had led a normal life as a merchant in Mecca. Yet when Muhammad started to receive his visions, he didn't shy away from the new path God had laid out in front of him. Instead, he embraced it and went on to build one of the most important spiritual practices in the world. Admittedly the stories of Lord Buddha and Muhammad are extreme examples, but I think they serve to underline that Starting Today is a message that can be found in all faiths. Very few of us will be able to embrace our Dharma with the faith and passion of those men, but their stories should inspire us to take whatever steps we can in our own lives.

YOU MUST START IN ORDER TO SUCCEED

You have to *start* before you can *succeed* at anything. I know that sounds very elementary, but it's a concept that's still elusive for many of us. Almost every day, I'm approached by people who want me to help them jump-start a project. While I definitely want to share my resources with as many people as possible, I also want those people to understand that they don't need my help. Just like they don't need Puffy's help or Bob Johnson's help or even Bill Gates' help to get their idea off the ground. If you have a marketable idea that you feel passionate about, don't wait for *me* to say it's a great idea and hopefully throw a couple of dollars your way. An investor will always be much more attracted to your idea after you've gotten it up and running than when it's just a concept in your mind.

Just getting started is also critical on a personal level. I know a young guy who keeps telling me he's going to be a lawyer every time I see him. It's always "Yo, Russell, I'm a good arguer, they won't be able to fuck with me in the courtroom. I'm going to be a big-time lawyer!" But when I ask him what he's doing about it, all I hear is, "Well, once I get my degree, I'm going to think about law school." But I don't want to hear about waiting on a degree! That's why I tell him, "If you want to be a lawyer so bad, then where are your law books? The libraries are wide the fuck open. Get in there and study the law!" Because you should never wait for a school to accept you before you start studying the practice of law. Head down to a library and start studying the law today. So when you do hear back from those schools, you'll be ahead of the game because you'll already be *practicing* the law. And you'll have a better chance of getting into law school because your passion and knowledge will be obvious. A lot of cats have even taught themselves to be lawyers while they're in *jail*. They didn't apply to any law school. They studied the books until they were lawyers, without the benefit of spending a day in school. So why can't you start studying the law when you're free on the streets? Don't wait for someone to give you the green light to follow your dreams. Live your life as if you are already where you want to be!

People are always trying to put off until tomorrow what they could be doing today. If you want to lose some weight and get in shape, go and hit the gym today (or better yet, take a yoga class). Don't say, "Things are kind of hectic right now, so let me wait until I have some more free time." Make the time and start getting in shape right now. If you want to stop smoking, don't say, "I'm just going to finish this pack and then I'll quit." Walk to the trash and throw those cigarettes out today. Don't even have a "last one." Your last one was *already* your last one.

Try not to be like that wanna-be lawyer, someone who's always talking about what he's *going* to do. Don't be one of those people saying, "Man, as soon as I get that settlement from my accident, I'm going to open this barbershop." Or, "Once I get a new computer, I'm going to write this screenplay I've been thinking about." You see, it's very easy to spend your whole life waiting to make a move without ever actually making one. "I'm going to wait till I have some more free time" will turn into "I'm going to wait until my kids get older," which will turn into "I'm going to wait until I retire," and the next thing you know, it's time to get in the box and you still haven't opened that barbershop. Don't just talk about what you're going to do. Instead, be present in this moment and decide what you want to be doing. And once you decide, then go ahead and do it.

The key is really to just start moving. Start the process and keep pushing forward no matter what sort of obstacles you face. If you want to open a barbershop, start cutting hair in your basement and try to build up some loyal clients. If you get enough clientele, a barber might notice and offer you a chair in his shop. And when you continue to bring in new customers, instead of risking the chance you might leave with those customers one day, he might offer to make you partners with him. Then you won't need that settlement money, because you'll already be in business. Or if you want to write that screenplay, start working on it today. Don't wait for a new computer. Write it on a notepad if you have to. Or if you really can't find time to write, carry a little tape recorder around with you and record your thoughts while you're sitting on the bus, or riding in your car. Those moments will create a momentum that will force you to make the free time that you thought you had to wait for. Cutting hair in your basement or recording chapters during your commute might seem very far from your plan of opening a barbershop or being a screenwriter. But they are really very important steps in moving you closer to your dreams.

Let me also say this to you: We're talking a lot about starting today in your professional life, but the exact same principle applies to your personal happiness too. People are always waiting for something to happen in their personal lives before they can be happy, instead of having their eyes open and appreciating everything great that is already happening for them *right now*. To say that you have to wait until something happens for you to be happy is actually making it more likely that you never will be happy. That whole "just wait until" rap in itself is a denial of personal happiness.

Don't Wait for Someone to Put You On

Another mindset that keeps many people from Starting Today is the belief that someone else is going to "put them on," or create opportunities for them. This is really one of the most dangerous attitudes you can have, because no one is going to put you on. Please understand that. Your hard work is going to put you on. Not another person.

As I mentioned earlier in the chapter, I witness this mindset all the time, because people are constantly looking for me to put them on. They believe that because I've enjoyed success in the music industry, I'll automatically be able to "hook them up" with the position or deal that they're looking for. Sorry, but it doesn't work that way. If you want to launch a record label, then don't wait for someone like me to "bless you" with a deal. Start blessing yourself. Don't wait for me to write you a check. Instead, put your name on a record and start selling it online or out of the trunk of your car. Call your company John's Records if that's your name. Start selling those records *today*. Even if you're operating out of the trunk of your car, you'll already be doing better than a lot of the major labels out there, because at least you won't be *losing* millions of dollars a year. After you sell some of those records and you create a good buzz, eventually a major record label will come looking for you. And *then* someone like me will write that check you were looking for. But they'll pay you because they were impressed by the work you already started. They'll never pay for work you haven't done.

Trust me, no one in hip-hop was just put on. Even someone like Jay-Z, who is so talented and charismatic, wasn't put on. Jay-Z put *himself* on. It took many years for him to get a deal, and when he did eventually get one, it was only after he had founded his own label and started releasing his own records. Jay didn't sit around waiting for someone to hand him something. He went out and jump-started his own success.

It was the same way with Kanye West. He's become one of the biggest stars in the world, but no one put him on either. In fact, Kanye had to struggle for years before he got signed. If you're not familiar with his story, you should listen to "Last Call," which is the last song on his debut *College Dropout*. It's a very inspirational song that details, step by step, his struggle to break into the record business. It's over twelve minutes long, so you know there was a lot of struggle. It begins with Kanye's efforts to make a name for himself while living in Chicago. When he realized he couldn't create a buzz for himself there, he didn't stall. Instead, he packed up all his equipment into a U-Haul truck and drove to New York. Once he got there, he spent months locked in a room, making songs day and night. Eventually, he was able to get some of his songs into the hands of people at Rocafella Records and gained some recognition making beats for Jay-Z. Even then, he was still struggling to realize his ultimate dream, which was to release his own album. The record labels thought he was a talented producer but didn't believe he could rap on his own. Label after label turned him down, even after he played them "Jesus Walks," which later became a huge hit. Finally, Rocafella realized the talent that was right under their noses, gave him a deal, and the rest is history. But when you listen to "Last Call," you realize that Kanye was only able to make that history because he was willing to start following his dream instead of waiting for someone to pull him out of obscurity.

Don't Wait for a Check

One of the keys to Kanye's story is that he didn't wait for someone to cut him a check before he moved to New York. He was working on his art whether someone was paying him or not. A lot of people in his situation wouldn't have moved until someone was willing to pay for them to come to New York. Kanye was smart enough to know that you can never wait on a check. When you're just starting out, you have to share your services with the world and not worry about the payment. That's true no matter what field you're in. The successful people are the ones who start working on their jobs whether there seems to be any money in it for them or not. There are many talented people out there who never start their journey because they're waiting for someone else to pay for their ticket. That's an attitude that will keep you standing in place for a very long time.

And it will also stop you from realizing your true potential. A true artist like Kanye or Alicia Keys makes music out of his or her heart, not out of any desire to win Grammys or sell a million records. The world might end up labeling you "Grammy Winner," or "Platinum Artist," but those tags should never be your motivation. Because if you're working just for those titles, even if you're talented and end up getting them, then you're not really doing your best. Anyone focused solely on the payoff is just going to play himself. Your best only comes out when you're creating for love, not for accolades.

I'll give you another example of the danger of waiting on a check. Someone was recently telling me about a friend of his who calls himself a journalist but doesn't want to write any stories unless there's a check in it for him. He's very bright and could be contributing to the world in many ways, but instead he's unemployed, living with his mother, waiting for someone to put him on. He thinks that because he's so talented, someone should hook him up with a job at a newspaper like *The New York Times* or *The Wall Street Journal*. But of course, no one has yet. Because just as record executives only want to sign rappers who are already hot in the streets, newspapers only want to hire writers who are already writing hot stories. They don't want to hire someone on the potential of what he *might* write. They want to hire someone on the strength of what he's *already* written.

That's why my advice to him is if you want to be a writer, then write. Go write about what's happening in your community and then try to pitch those stories to newspapers or magazines. And if you can't generate any interest in those stories, then start your own blog and post your stories online. Or if you can get a little money together, buy a ticket to China or South Africa or even Iraq and start to write about the fascinating things that are happening in those countries. Maybe writing stories about those parts of the world will help you stand out from the pack a bit. As long as you keep grinding, people will notice you. And after you start to collect some clips, and thousands of people are visiting your blog every day, then maybe the *Times* or the *Journal* will be willing to cut you a check and put you on staff. Just don't sit around waiting for someone to pay you for your talent. Start writing today, whether there's a check in it or not. If you want to rap, start rapping today. Whether you think anyone is listening or not. If you want be a doctor, don't wait until you get into a medical school. Go to the library and start diving into those medical texts on your own. Whatever your dream is, the joy and excitement you'll get from starting to follow it is all the payment you need.

Another reason some people have trouble getting started is because they have a sense of entitlement. They think that because they're smart, or they come from a wealthy family, someone else should do the heavy lifting for them. But rich or poor, black or white, none of us are entitled to *anything*. My former partner at Def Jam, Lyor Cohen, is a great example of someone who understood this truth. As a young man, much to the chagrin of his family, Lyor had a strong desire get into the record business. His parents were very well off and thought their son should be a lawyer or a doctor instead of wasting his time with rap music. They even told Lyor they would cut him off if he didn't give up hip-hop. Most people in Lyor's position would have either given up on their vision, or maybe waited for their parents to soften up and then used their connections to get a job at a label. But Lyor wasn't interested in either of those options. He knew he wanted to be in hip-hop, so he got on a plane and came to New York to work with Run DMC, even though no one had promised him a thing. Once he got to New York, he spent a month living on the floor of a hotel room, working for free, just to get his foot in the door. Eventually he turned that small foothold into becoming the head of Warner Music and one of the most powerful people in the music industry. But it would have never happened if he had waited for someone to hand him something. Instead, he secured his own success by starting out after his dreams as soon as he had them.

THE HIP-HOP SUMMIT

A great example from my own life of the power of Starting Today is the Hip-Hop Summit Action Network. Today, the HSAN is a high-profile organization that has held dozens of voter drives, financial summits, and town hall meetings across the country. With the support of artists like 50 Cent, Jay-Z, Beyoncé, Will Smith, P. Diddy, Eminem, and countless others, the HSAN has made great strides in politically and economically empowering the hip-hop nation. But just over five years ago, it was nothing but a vague idea in my mind. How I was able to turn that idea into something tangible and useful is a testament to why you should always Start Today.

It all began back in 2001, when I read a news story about a rapper (I can't recall exactly which one) getting arrested. The story really upset me, because at the time I was growing increasingly frustrated by how the media seemed to emphasize hip-hop's low notes. I wasn't trying to ignore those notes, but I also knew the culture contained many high notes, notes that don't seem to receive the same attention. I felt very strongly that as a community, we needed to not only shine a light on our high notes, but also create an environment where there would be even more high notes to share.

It would have been easy to feel frustrated and then move on, but that day I decided to act on what I was feeling. So I picked up my Motorola pager and sent an e-mail to AllHipHop.com (a very influential hip-hop Web site), announcing that I had organized a meeting between Minister Louis Farrakhan and several prominent rappers to address the negativity in our community and its coverage in the press. Now, I admit Minister Farrakhan and the rappers hadn't agreed to any meeting when I sent that e-mail. However, I had already discussed the idea of a meeting with the Minister and I knew he was open to it and I figured once the Minister was on board, the rappers would follow suit. So I was confident in my ability to organize the meeting. Yet if I had waited to confirm everyone's participation, then coordinate everyone's schedules before I announced the meeting, the moment would have passed. So I sent out the e-mail, even if it was a little premature. And that single e-mail, which maybe took me five minutes to write, set a very powerful chain of events into motion.

By composing the e-mail, I had made sure the meeting was no longer just an idea floating around between the Minister and myself. Now that I had put it in the air, I was compelled to actually make it happen. Sure enough, as soon as I put the word out there, the idea started to take on a life of its own. Within a couple of days, Will Smith, Jay-Z, Puffy, LL Cool J, Reverend Run, Queen Latifah, Jermaine Dupri, and Damon Dash all agreed to participate, as well as Dr. Benjamin Chavis (my great friend and former head of the NAACP), who was instrumental in organizing the event. And on a hot summer day, all those rappers, plus many more, came out for what we decided to call the Hip-Hop Summit. Additionally, the Democratic candidates running for mayor of New York that year showed up, as did Kwame Mfume, then the head of the NAACP, and Hugh Price, the head of the Urban League. It was a very impressive collection of minds. And of course, the event was highlighted by the Minister's speech, just as I had said it would be several months earlier.

If our movement had never extended past that day in New York City, I still would have still been proud of what we accomplished. But once you put an idea in motion, it usually goes even farther than you originally dreamed. Indeed, throughout the day people kept asking me, "When's the next summit, Russell? We need to build on this." At first, I said I wasn't planning to promote another event. Still, more and more people kept volunteering their services and encouraging me to organize something. By the end of the day I had not only announced that we were holding another summit, but that we going to start an organization dedicated to pursuing the summit's goals. Again, I didn't wait until I had organized a board of directors, or secured the funding we needed to make the announcement. I felt so motivated by the energy of that day that I spoke the organization into existence on the spot. The following morning, my announcement was all over the media and suddenly my initial idea had even more momentum and had developed even more possibilities. Within a few months we had organized a board of directors that included people like Puffy, Lyor Cohen and Cornel West, Michael Eric Dyson and

Dr. Manning Marable. So even though my announcements might have been premature at the time, by putting them into the air, I gave them the power to mature into actual facts.

You must understand that words take on their own life in the universe. My words, expressed in an e-mail, first become equity and then became reality. That's why you must speak your idea as soon as you have it and then put it on paper (or in this case, in an e-mail). Words alone can start you down the path toward your dreams. It started with an e-mail, but that e-mail turned into the Hip-Hop Summit, which in turn became the Hip-Hop Summit Action Network. In just five years, under the incredible leadership of Dr. Ben, we've held summits in New York, Los Angeles, Philadelphia, Houston, Detroit, Miami, St. Louis, and Atlanta, registering thousands of new voters and teaching even more the basics of financial literacy. It's been an incredible blessing and I hope to do even more good work through HSAN in the future. The HSAN was always a good idea, but my words are what took that idea to the next level. Of course, none of it would have happened if I hadn't immediately acted on my initial inspiration.

Don't Stall

When people say they're waiting for things to happen before they make a move, all they're really doing is stalling. Just like I would have been stalling if I had waited for commitments from a bunch of rappers before I sent out that e-mail. You must fight through that urge, because stalling is one of the most harmful things you can do to your dream. When you put things off, it creates incredible anxiety. It'll make you very sick to sit at home watching TV, talking about "someday," when you have dreams that you're not living up to today. Or if you already have a job, but are sitting back and letting your work pile up on you, you're going to become very miserable as well. The pain that's created by avoiding hard work is actually much worse than any pain created from the actual work itself. Because if you don't begin to work on those ideas that God has blessed you with, they will become stagnant inside of you and eventually begin to eat away at you. You might seem OK on the outside, but inside you will be ill from not getting those ideas out of your heart and into the world. Stalling leads to sickness. But taking steps, even baby steps, always leads to success.

If you find yourself stalling, there are several ways to break out of that condition. The easiest is to simply put your head down and start working. Yet sometimes we've been stagnant for so long that we forget what it means to truly work hard. So if you can't seem to find the energy or the focus to put in that hard work, allow yourself to be swept up by the world instead. You see, stalling keeps you chained to one place and prevents you from moving forward. It prevents the world's natural momentum from carrying you closer to your dreams. That's why when you stall, in addition to *not* moving forward, you're actually holding yourself back.

When you allow yourself to be swept up by the world, you'll bump into so many great ideas that would have never hit you if you had just been standing in that same place day after day. It's worked for me that way so many times. When I surrender to the natural movement and unpredictability of the world, I'll look up and find that I'm not just talking about my dreams, but I'm actually doing something to make them a reality. Again, that was the case with HSAN. One day it was sending an e-mail about holding a meeting. The next day I was hosting that meeting. By the end of that day, I had started an organization. All because I had allowed myself to get swept up. That was also how it happened for me with Phat Farm. One day I'm talking about a clothing company, a month later I look up and it's like "Wow, I'm really investing in a clothing company." And a month after that, it's "Wow, I'm really starting to manufacture clothes." But those steps were only possible because instead of stalling, I allowed myself to move with the momentum. I didn't say, "I think this clothing company is a good idea, but let me wait till I have a few more investors." Instead, I dipped into my personal account and rode the little ripple (it wasn't even a wave) that action created. And when we actually had the ability to make clothes, I didn't stall and say, "Well, let's not start manufacturing until we're guaranteed placement in the department stores." Instead, I said, "If we can't get in the department stores, then we'll just make the shirts anyway and sell them in our own store until somebody notices." And then I allowed myself to ride that little wave, and the wave after it, until eventually the company was moving closer to where I wanted it to be.

Whether you take that baby step yourself, or just allow yourself be swept up, you'll get a real sense of satisfaction and freedom the first day you start pursuing your dream. If all you do that day is go to the library and do some research on your idea, or sketch out some rough plans, you'll immediately notice a real difference. During even that very first day, you'll get an "I can't believe I'm doing this" feeling. There will be an excitement that had been missing from your life. And when you lie in the bed that first night, that excitement will be replaced by a sense of relief. You will feel incredibly relieved in having used the energy that God gave you.

Try it for yourself. Put down this book and ask yourself, "What's the one thing I've always wanted to do, but keep putting off?" Be honest with yourself, and then at some point today, take a baby step toward actually doing it. Maybe it'll be spending a few minutes online checking out classes at a community college. Maybe it's just doing a couple of push-ups. Or maybe it'll just be turning off the TV and picking up a book. Whatever path you decide to start off on, I promise you'll feel real excitement the moment you take your first steps. And when those baby steps eventually turn into major strides, you'll realize how much better you feel about yourself. You'll see that you enjoy life so much more when you handle your business immediately instead of putting it off.

Go Where the Action Is

The final step in Starting Today is the physical component. As was the case with Kanye, often you have to make a physical move to Start Today. That's especially true in the entertainment industry, where so much of the action is centered in cities like New York, Los Angeles, and, increasingly, Atlanta. You must go where the action is today, because you ain't going to become a rapper or an actor living in Idaho. Nothing against Idaho, but the opportunity just isn't there. You can't sit around on your tractor hoping some A & R guy is going to drive up to your farm and offer you a deal. Instead, start saving up some money today, and when you have enough, then pack up your bags and move to New York or Los Angeles. And after you spend some time hustlin' in the Big City and start to work on your album, you can share what life was like on that farm through your art. You just can't stay on that farm and hope that one day someone will pay attention. You can't wait for the action to come to you. You must go to the action.

Or, if you live in Ohio and want to be a fashion model, then you have to move to New York and walk up and down Seventh Avenue until some agent notices you. If that doesn't work, then you have to stay out in the clubs, not to party, but to meet other models and then find out who their agents are. It's the same thing if you want to be a fashion designer. You have to go to that same stretch of Seventh Avenue, because that's where most of the designers work as well. You have to make it your business to find out who those designers are, where they go for lunch, or what parties they go to at night. And then you have to start working toward becoming part of their world. Because being around similar people who are dedicated and interested in what you're interested in will increase your opportunities exponentially. I'm not saying you have to be one-dimensional to succeed in a particular industry. I think it's actually healthier to have other interests and hobbies. But you do need to be around that common energy to create momentum for yourself.

This might seem like very basic advice, but so many people are afraid to take even these simple steps. Why? Because they're afraid that after they move to New York or L.A., they still won't ever "make it." But in reality, that's impossible. There can be no wrong decision when you're following your dream. Any decision that gets that process started is the right decision.

Let's say you want to be an actor and you find the courage to move to L.A. Like thousands of other aspiring actors in that town, you might spend years going to auditions during the day and waiting tables at night. If you're determined enough, and resilient enough, eventually you might become the next Denzel Washington, or the next Halle Berry. But even if you don't, you will still be in an environment where your dream can take on a new shape. As I said, your Dharma isn't just limited to just one skill or job. You might have come to Los Angeles to be the next Denzel, but you might wind up the next Steven Spielberg instead. Or maybe you'll become a great TV producer like Stan Lathan. Or even a talented gaffer, which might not bring you public recognition but will earn you tremendous respect (and very good money) within the industry. Any of these jobs are possible, but only if you Start Today and make that move to L.A. I can't promise you exactly which job will become your Dharma, but I can promise you that you won't become Halle, Stan Lathan, or a great gaffer sitting on your couch in Ohio. Again, you have to live your life as if you are already where you want be.

Detach Yourself

Going where the action is might seem like a very obvious concept, but it's one that can be very difficult to put into practice. It's human nature to become attached to our homes and our communities, where we're surrounded by family and friends. But while it's always good to respect and love something, it's usually not good to be *attached* to it.

Attachment is just another snare that can keep you from being swept up by the world. You gain a certain freedom when you let go of the past and submit yourself to the unknown. I spoke about that in the last chapter, when I said, "The world is filled with uncertainty, but it's also filled with opportunity." Free yourself from the attachments of a single place or a lifestyle and give yourself the ability to pursue your dreams unfettered. Detachment is a very powerful strategy, and I'll talk about it more later on in the book. I also encourage you to read about it more in Deepak Chopra's *The Seven Spiritual Laws of Success.* I believe so strongly in that concept and several other ones found in that book that I make all my employees read it before they come to work for me. I certainly don't want people working for me who are rooted in a rigid space, whether it's physical or spiritual. I want to work with people who have the freedom to pursue any opportunity *the day* it presents itself.

RECOGNIZE THE REAL:

Right now is the only time that there is. Yesterday is gone and tomorrow never comes. Whatever you need to do in life, start it today. Put down this book and go follow your dream.

Happiness isn't going to come knocking on your door. You have to go find it. And the only way to do so is by working your hardest.

LAW NUMBER FIVE:

NEVER LESS THAN YOUR BEST

The dictionary is the only place where success comes before work
—VINCE LOMBARDI

You PROBABLY DIDN'T GO OUT and get this book just to read "Hard work leads to success." I know that seems painfully obvious, but there's simply no way around it. Without a dedication to hard work, you're never going to find any lasting success in life.

We've just finished stressing the importance of Starting Today, but, frankly, unless you work your hardest once you do start, you'll just be making a series of *false* starts. That's why the key ingredient to any kind of happiness or success is to never give less than your best.

The phrase *Never Less than Your Best* might conjure up images of double shifts, long nights in the office, or putting your body through extreme tests, but to me, it's not just about testing yourself in the world. It's really more about your inner condition. That's because I view Hard Work as a spiritual practice, as a tool with which you can cut through the distractions of the world and give yourself the space to start doing God's Work.

People who embrace that spiritual component often give their best at every job, even when that job seems painfully far from their dreams. That's why I promise that when you dedicate yourself to working your hardest at EVERY job, whether you're working for minimum wage at the mall or for millions of dollars on Wall Street, you'll lead a much happier and more fulfilling life.

Hard Work is something I certainly try to practice every day. You might wonder how true that statement really is, considering I spend my day getting driven around in a luxury car, meeting with interesting people, and sleeping in a beautiful home. To most people, there's nothing hard about the type of work I do, or the lifestyle I lead. That's why I hope to demonstrate in this chapter that Hard Work has very little to do with what sort of job you have, or how much you get paid to do it. Those are the worldly components of Never Less Than Your Best. Instead, it's important to focus on this law's spiritual component.

It's also important to understand that there's no such thing as a dead-end job. No matter what sort of work you do, your effort will make that job worthwhile, especially here in America. That's because for all its faults and frustrations, today America is filled with so much incredible opportunity. Perhaps more so than any other place in the world, America is a country where the only thing between your current condition and your dreams is effort. The majority of the immigrants who come to this country are able to see this truth—which is why they're willing to make such tremendous sacrifices to come here. I encourage you to see a similar reality, whether your ancestors came here on the *Mayflower* or in the bottom of a slave ship. When you clean off your lenses, you will see that the doors to unlimited success are right in front of you. And your hard work is what will allow you to stride right through them.

STAY FOCUSED ON THE PROCESS

Not long ago, a woman working as a nurse approached me for advice on how to improve what she *perceived* to be her position in life. I can't recall her exact situation, but essentially she didn't want to be "stuck" working as a nurse her entire life because she was afraid she would never make enough money in that profession to be happy. She was hoping I could show her a way to make it in the business world instead. I get that question a lot, and it's always a tough one to answer. Everyone's life is nuanced, so it's very hard to give someone advice on his or her particular situation. I tried to be very honest with her and explained that while I couldn't give her a specific route that would take her from a nurse to a successful entrepreneur, I could share a basic strategy that would help her find that route on her own.

The strategy I shared with her is the same one I'd like to share with you now: Always focus on your effort, instead of the results of that effort. That means don't get hung up on the size of your paycheck, or the title next to your name. Instead, focus on the actual work itself, which is the process. So in the case of the nurse, I encouraged her to simply concentrate all her energy on helping the sick people in her care. I encouraged her to do everything she could to bring comfort to those people and their families. Not to suggest she hadn't been doing that before, just to do it now without *any* concern over the payment or perception. I told her that if she put all her effort into helping her patients, the results she was looking for would take care of themselves. They might not come in the form she was expecting, but they would come. I promised her instead of feeling like she was toiling in obscurity, she would start to feel noticed. That instead of feeling stuck, it wouldn't be long before she could feel the momentum of hard work taking her closer to where she wanted to be in life.

Whatever profession you are in, when you get attached to the results of your hard work, you'll be in for a rude awakening when those "results" finally do come. It's happened to me several times, even when I received multimillion-dollar checks for selling Def Jam and Phat Farm. Now, a lot of those checks went to my partners, but you'd still think I'd be jumping up and down for joy over my piece of those pies, right? Wrong. In both cases actually getting the money was a major letdown. Cashing those checks was anticlimactic. Because as soon as the money was in my hands, I realized the actual hard work that I put into those companies brought me much more happiness than the money ever could.

I know many of you are probably saying, "Please, give me half of that $130 million check and I'll be the happiest person on the planet!" Well, I hope you do get it, but in my experience it usually doesn't work that way.

I've been working with rappers for over twenty years, and they always have the same reaction when they get their first big check. The first thing most of them do is run out and buy a $400K Mercedes Maybach, or whatever car is hot at the moment. They'll go crazy with excitement the first time they drive it around the block, but once they park it, there's a feeling of "Now what?" Because it's hit them that all they have is a piece of steel with some rubber wheels. Suddenly that sense of having finally "made it" is actually empty. They had counted on the payoff being more rewarding than the process, and it comes as a shock when they realize that's not the case. The cars and the houses can look great, but they realize nothing they buy can match the happiness they found from working on the album that made them rich. They might have been living with their moms instead of in a gated community, but nothing was better than those long hours in their rooms, working on their rhyme skills. They might have had to take a bus to the studio and then spent weeks eating on cheap takeout and sleeping on the floors, but nothing can top those days they spent surrounded by their friends, crafting their art. They realize no toy can bring them as much satisfaction as the feeling they got the first time they heard a song they spent so long working on actually played on the radio. That's where the joy is. Not under the hood of a $400K car. It took me a few cars to realize that myself, but now I know it to be true.

It really comes back to the singled-minded focus and clarity that you can find in being present. The key is taking that focus and applying it to the *process* of working hard, instead of the result of that hard work. I know some people say "Keep your eyes on the prize," but I disagree. When your eyes are stuck on the prize, you're going to keep stumbling and crashing into things. If you really want to get ahead, you've got to keep your eyes focused on the path. Instead of staring at the prize, stare at the process. If you wake up thinking about what you're going to get, instead of what you're going to do, it will destroy your inspiration. Don't think that there's going to be gold at the end of the road. Instead, value the process and you'll see that the road has been paved with gold all along.

Use Positive Energy to Break Down Negative Energy

I think most people accept that a commitment to hard work is central to any kind of worldly success. From rappers to star athletes to famous actors to media moguls to presidents, most successful people credit hard work as what's taken them to where they are in life. What isn't as well known is hard work is also a stepping-stone to spiritual fulfillment. (Are you noticing a trend here?) I believe that a commitment to hard work won't only get you paid but will also purify your spirit. When you get off your couch and start working hard, you'll find that work itself is making you happy and whole. Not just the results of your labor, but your labor itself. The work itself becomes the process by which you obtain happiness. The work becomes your savior.

Do you believe that hard work can be incredibly rewarding for your spirit? You should, because you probably already accept that it's rewarding for your body. You know that if you go to the gym and have a great workout, you'll not only look better but feel better too. You know that when you have a good workout, or smile through a grueling yoga class, it not only makes your muscles stronger, but it also burns away the extra physical energy you're carrying around with you. Well, hard work does the same thing for your spirit. If you put in a long day in the office, or spend an extra hour working on your homework, it will actually make you feel better about yourself. That's because we all carry around a lot of junk in our hearts and minds. And by junk, I'm referring to worthless emotions like desire, resentment, apathy, pride, and envy (in yoga, these are known as "the five Kleshas"). These are the emotions that the world sticks in our way to slow us down. But that extra hour in the library or in the office will burn through that junk and clear a path toward that Higher Self I keep talking about. And a connection with your higher self is the foundation that all true happiness and success is built on.

Remember, when you get disconnected from your higher self, it often leads to depression. You can spend all day coasting and avoiding hard work, but when it's time to go to bed, you'll find that going to sleep is what's *hard*. That emotional junk will keep you tossing and turning all night long. However, when you put in a hard day's work, you're going to sleep like a baby. Not because you're physically worn down, but because you're spiritually lifted up. A person who's too lazy to burn through that baggage during the day will regret it at night. A person who keeps her head down and focused on her job during the day will be rewarded with rest.

In the yogic tradition, this principle of using intense effort to burn through life's distractions is called Tapas. It's another Sanskrit word, roughly defined as "heat" or "essential energy." The concept is that through a disciplined approached to work and self-sacrifice, Tapas will burn away the negativity that separates us from God. By working our hardest and happily enduring the hardships of life, we are able to create a sense of peace and clarity in ourselves.

That might sound complicated, but when the yogis speak of using Tapas it really just means using positive energy to break down negative energy. To me, that's the true value of hard work. Not buying toys or building muscles, but using your positive energy to overcome the negativity around you. Because no matter what your job is, in order to be truly successful at it, you have to have faith that concentrating on that work will bring you closer to God.

Again, when you're using your work to burn away the junk and clearing a path to God, then that work no longer is your own. It becomes God's work, because you're working to get closer to that higher voice inside of you, instead of getting closer to the toys, the money, and the material things that the world is constantly promoting. That's why what sort of response I get to my hard work isn't important to me. Why should I care whether people approve or disapprove of what I do? Why should I care whether they think a spiritual reality show, or a spiritual fragrance, is a bad idea? Because as long as I'm doing God's work, I can never be wasting my time.

I really want to stress here that when I speak of God, I'm only speaking of that higher self. And I'm going to keep stressing that, so no one gets confused. I'm not talking about a third-party God up in the sky who's keeping score of everything you do down here on Earth. If you want advice on how to work for that God, then you need to pick up another book. When I say "God," I'm referring to that little piece of God, the little piece of consciousness that represents the best in you. Maybe when you find that piece, you'll flip it over and it'll say "Jew" or "Christian" or "Buddhist" or "Mormon" or "Muslim." That's your personal choice. They're all beautiful, but truthfully the labels don't matter to me. What matters is that your commitment to Never Doing Less Than Your Best is so strong that it burns through the rubble and allows you pick up that piece. What you want to call it is up to you. I'm just promoting a process that helps you find it.

Many people never find the focus that's needed to burn through that rubble, and end up getting weighed down by the world their entire lives. I don't want to use examples of those I've seen this happen to, since this book isn't about judging people. But I will share an example from my own life when I've felt myself getting stuck in the rubble. I'm stuck in the rubble every time I hold a grudge. I'm stuck in the rubble every time someone says "fuck you" to me and I say "fuck you" back, rather than looking for the good in that person and addressing that instead. I'm stuck in the rubble every time I hurt someone but don't take responsibility for what I've done. I'm stuck in the rubble every time I find myself getting satisfied with my toys, instead of focusing on how I can use my blessings to bless others. I'm stuck in the rubble any and every time I ignore my higher self. And trust me, I find myself stuck every day. Thankfully, through mental focus and hard work I have the tools to dig myself back out again.

NEVER LESS THAN *MY* BEST

As I said earlier in this chapter, I'm not just preaching for *you* to work hard while *I'm* chillin' in a penthouse, getting a massage, and living the good life. Despite having "made it," I still put in the work every day, sometimes even more than when I was first getting started. Believe me, Biggie wasn't joking when he said, "Mo' money, mo' problems." I'm carrying a lot of baggage these days—my family depends on my success, my investors depend on my success, my employees depend on my success, and people who are inspired by my career expect it, if they don't depend on it. I'm not complaining about those responsibilities—in fact, I consider them an incredible blessing—but I'm conscious of their weight. So it's especially important for me to always work my hardest, because without focusing my Tapas, I could never carry those loads. It would start pulling me down overnight and I would lose what little connection I enjoy with my higher self. If my dedication to hard work ever started to waver, I know my spirit would suffer a lot worse than my checking account. So no matter what task is in front of me, I'm never going to give it Less Than *My* Best.

Almost every day, I try to get up with the sun, get right to work, and don't come home again until it's dark out. I know you might see pictures of me in the papers that make it look like I'm out on the scene, but don't get it twisted. It's true that I do like to *go* out, I just don't *stay* out. No matter how hot a party it is, I'm usually still back in bed by midnight. No matter how great a *night* I'm having, I've come to understand that I'll have an even better time the next day if I'm up bright and early putting in the hard work.

Since it's hard to keep your mind focused all of the time, I try to create a set of rituals to follow every day. By dedicating myself to those rituals, I manage to keep working hard even when I don't always feel the motivation or the inspiration. My first ritual is meditating as soon as I wake up. As I said earlier, I find those few minutes of peace really set a positive tone for the rest of the day. During the summer, when I spend a lot of time at my country house in the Hamptons, I like to drive to the ocean and meditate on the beach. I'll spend a few minutes meditating on the empty sandy, take a quick dip in the water, and then head straight to a yoga class. I've found having that salt water on your body makes you sweat even harder during class. Between the difficult poses and the salt making me sweat, I can almost feel the junk burning away. After class, I like to come home and make a fresh fruit and ProEndorphin shake. (Endorphins are the natural opiates that your body manufactures to create a sense of peace; I cheat a little bit and buy ready-made endorphins that you can put into a shake. The energy boost you get is much more rewarding than caffeine.) Then I get right to work on whatever is on my agenda that day. I'll take meetings and make phone calls until around five, at which point I'll head to another yoga class if I have time. After yoga, I try to do more work, then grab a vegetarian dinner and head home. If there's a fund-raiser or party going on that night, I might try to stop by, but I'll never stay late enough that it might jeopardize my ability to get up and do it all over again the next morning.

Admittedly, the day I've just described wouldn't be possible for most people out there. I've been very blessed to be able to have a house by the ocean, or to have the freedom to leave my office in the middle of the day for a yoga class. I realize most people can't afford those luxuries. That's why I'm not trying to promote these *particular* rituals (though *everyone* has the ability to spend a few minutes in meditation), as much as I am promoting the *power* of those rituals. Those rituals keep me focused on the process of Hard Work even when the distractions of the world are very loud. When the world tells me it would be more fun to stay out all night, the rituals remind me that I need to be up early so I can meditate. When the world tells me that a nice steak dinner would hit the spot, the ritual reminds me that I don't eat meat. The process is what's hard for me, but adhering to the rituals makes it easier.

If I look up from what I'm doing and get distracted by the prize, the rituals keep me in line and bring me right back to the process. If I'm working on a hip-hop clothing line and the buzz is growing louder that I'm crazy, that I'm wasting my money, then I stay focused on my hard work to burn through those distractions. If everyone tells me I'm crazy for trying to get a show with a bunch of niggas telling jokes on HBO, I just put my head down and keep working until I can't hear that noise anymore.

If you don't already have some, create a set of rituals that will help you "remember to remember" to stay focused on the process of hard work. They don't have to be extreme. You don't need to be like the yogis who spend hours standing on their head every day just to remind themselves. You don't need to do two thousand sit-ups everyday, or spend an hour in confession, or even get up early in the morning. You can create a very small set of rituals that will keep you focused on your hard work. And no matter what sort of rituals you create, you are going to miss some days. I certainly do. I call myself a vegan, but like I said, I'll grab a bite of fish when I think no one's looking. Sometimes I'll skip a yoga class because I'm tired, even though I know that getting on the mat would actually be the best way to get my energy back. I'm going to slide, so I try not to beat myself up over it. I've learned that it's OK to forgive yourself. I'm not saying it's OK to forgive yourself and then spend the next month being sloppy, but it is OK to forgive the occasional lapse from your rituals. So long as the next day you get right back to work.

I'll say it one more time. The actual work is the process by which you obtain happiness. Not the results. Please understand that. Most of us can't fully digest this idea, but you must embrace it on some level if you want to be happy.

Work Your Hardest at Every Job

When you understand that your happiness comes from the process, instead of the results, it becomes much easier to embrace the importance of working your hardest at *every* job. I know that's tough if you're that nurse struggling to get by on ten dollars an hour. Or if you're stuck working at one of the big retail stores, putting in a full week without any benefits. Or if you're stuck working for a boss who's more interested in exploiting you than rewarding you. But no matter what you're doing, try to work at that task like it's your dream job. Because your happiness ultimately comes from the *way* you work, not *where* you work.

No matter what sort of job you have, take responsibility and pride in it. If you accept a dishwashing job, don't say to yourself, "Oh, this ain't really me, I'm just doing this to get paid," and then leave spots on the dishes. Because a lot of people keep saying, "This ain't me," until one day they look up and it's time to get in the box. The fact is, whatever you're doing at this moment *is* you and you have to give it your all.

When you start to take shortcuts, you'll not only disappoint your customers and your boss, but most importantly, you'll disappoint yourself. You can fool some people with an "I don't care" attitude, but inside, you'll know that you're doing less than your best.

You have to learn that your dedication to hard work will pay off. I can promise you that. Because the world loves people who work hard at everything they do. The world notices those people and rewards them for that dedication. It might not be an immediate financial reward, but you will get something. Let's go back to the dishwasher analogy. If you come in early to wash the dishes, and smile and breathe throughout the process, several things will happen. First, your day will go a lot quicker washing dishes with pride than it would if you were bitching and moaning the whole time. Secondly, your boss will notice your hard work, which will lead to a better job in the restaurant. And maybe one of the waitresses you work with will notice your attractive attitude (because hard work is attractive) and you'll start messin' around with her after work! Which is definitely better than washing dishes! So in a short time, you will be able to see the value of your hard work. You will see that it has helped you rise up. It might not necessarily make the numbers in your bank account rise right away, but it will make your spirit rise right away. And it's part of a process that will let you rise up out of the distraction and entanglements of the world and into your dreams.

I think that when some of you hear me or other "successful" people talk about the importance of working hard, you take it with a grain of salt. You might think, "Of course I'd be working hard if I was running my own TV show, or directing my own movie. But there's no point in busting my ass when I'm only washing dishes." I can certainly understand the frustration, but understand that you're not wasting your time when you're washing those dishes. You only waste your time by washing dishes while you think there's a better job you could be doing. You can never forget that every person running his own labels, or directing his own movies, or running his own corporations did not start out with that job. He started out as an intern, or as a gofer on the set, or in a mailroom, and then worked his hardest at every job along the way. And that commitment to all those shitty jobs, and only that commitment, is what eventually led him to the job that seems so fabulous from a distance.

When you think that only certain jobs are worth your energy, that means your ego is making too much noise in your head. I like to say that *ego* stands for "Edging God Out." Because you *will* edge God out of your life when you think you're too good for a certain job. Instead, humble yourself and realize that every job is worth your while. Certainly any job is better than sitting at home eating Twinkies and watching TV. Any job is better than depending on the government for a handout. Any job is better than sitting on your stoop smoking a blunt and talking about what you're *going* to do. Remember, in Proverbs it says, "All hard work brings a profit, but mere talk leads only to poverty."

SWEEP THE DAMN STREET!

If you're willing to work hard but don't know where to start, just look around you. Go out on the block and find a store with a dirty sidewalk and start sweeping it. Don't worry about whether the owner is going to pay you or not. Just start sweeping. Don't worry if your friends come down the block and start calling you a sucker. Just keep sweeping. Don't worry if a girl you like walks by and sees you with a broom in your hand. Just keep sweeping and working your hardest at making sure the sidewalk always looks good. Because if you come out every morning and sweep the front of that store every day with a smile, it won't be long before the owner notices you and finds you a job inside the store. Maybe he'll put you in charge of stocking one of the aisles. And if you stock those aisles with the same dedication to hard work and the same smile, before long the boss might make you the weekend manager. And after you apply your hard work to that job, before long you'll be the regular manager of the store. After you're successful at that, and build up business contacts and a real understanding of how the store works, you'll save your money up and open your own store. And because you'll run your store with that same dedication to hard work, in a few years you'll own a chain of stores. But it was only possible because you were willing to humble yourself initially and start sweeping that sidewalk for free. Now, some of you might hear that example and say, "But I can't eat if I'm sweeping a sidewalk for free!" Well, if that's your attitude, then you're a greedy son of bitch. Sorry, but I don't feel for people who want more than they're giving. If you're broke and don't have an outlet for your Hard Work, then you have to take what's available. If all that's available is a dirty sidewalk in front of a store, then take that sidewalk and make the most of it. Keep working your hardest until you own the store.

Where's That Dude Kevin?

That "sidewalk" scenario might sound very farfetched to you, but trust me, I've seen it happen. I've seen people create a toehold for themselves in a business by starting for free and then keep giving that ultimate effort until they're actually *running* that business. A perfect example is Kevin Liles, who's now one of the biggest executives in the music business at Warner Music. Kevin is at the top of the food chain, but he got his start in the game as an intern at Def Jam, working for free. When Kevin came to Def Jam, he wasn't making a penny more than that street sweeper I was talking about. He wasn't getting paid, but if someone told Kevin to be in at nine A.M., he would come in at eight A.M. with a big smile on his face. And no matter how early Kevin came in, he would make sure to be the very last person to leave at night, even later than his bosses. Certainly later than me! Now, most unpaid interns would balk at working those hours, let alone create that schedule themselves. Their attitude would be "Hell, no, I'm not working later than my bosses! They're getting paid and I'm not making anything. Let them stay late." Or if they did stay late, they'd grumble and complain about their situation to anyone who'd listen. Kevin didn't fall into those traps. He worked harder than anyone in the company, always had a smile on his face, and never once mentioned money. Not once. In fact, Kevin used to say, "You can't pay me to work harder. You can't pay me to be nicer. Because I love what I'm doing."

When his internship finally ended, suddenly Kevin was very much in demand. Everyone was looking for him, saying, "Where's that dude Kevin? I can't operate without him." Because his hard work was not only noticed, it began to be counted on. Where just a few weeks earlier he wasn't earning a dime, now departments were fighting each other to pay him. The promotions team had to outbid the marketing team just to keep him in their department! So Kevin turned that internship into a position as promotions associate but very quickly became a promotions manager. From the promotions manager, he became the head of the promotions department. From the head of the promotions department, he became the head of the company. And now he parlayed his success at Def Jam into becoming the head of all black music at Warner Records. How did he do it? By working his hardest at every step of the process and never asking for a thing. All Kevin did was put his head down and work. Because he knew as long as he worked his hardest, the rest would take care of itself.

Kevin Liles is one of my favorite examples of where hard work can take you, but it happens all over the world, every day. No matter what sort of job you start out with, as long as your hard work serves the people you're working for, you're going to be very successful. Even if your boss isn't paying you at first, he (or she) will start to depend on whatever sort of work you're doing. So if one day you decide you want to take your hard work somewhere else, your bosses will immediately start crying that they can't live without you. Then they'll have to cut a check just to keep you around. You'll end up with a much bigger check than if you had just walked into the store and said, "Hey, let me get a job stocking shelves," or walked into a label and said, "Hey, why don't you pay me to be a promotions guy?" No one's going to pay you if you come at them like that. But when you have the patience to share your hard work without worrying about a check, when you finally do get paid, that check will reflect all your effort and dedication.

Believe me, every day someone comes up to me and says, "Yo, Russell, lemme get a job." I smile at those people, but I also keep it moving. Because the way to get a check from me isn't to come with your hands out. The way is to start working hard for me without asking for a dime. Start putting in that hard work and make me depend on you. I'm not trying to exploit anyone, I'm just being real. Employers are human, we love free labor. So coming in as an intern, or clerking for a judge, or sweeping the floor, is often the easiest way in the door. Take advantage of our greed and work as hard as you can and as long as you can without worrying about money, and it will eventually pay off.

This approach certainly worked for my "son," Brett Ratner. Today, Brett Ratner is one of the most successful directors in Hollywood, with blockbusters like *Rush Hour* and *X-Men* on his résumé. But when I first met Brett, he was a hungry kid just looking to get his foot in the door in the entertainment business. In fact, he brought me a bunch of the hooded sweatshirts he'd seen me wearing on a cover of *Right On!* magazine. He didn't know enough about the record business yet to serve me professionally, so he figured he could help me personally with the sweatshirts. He was willing to do anything to be of use. After he hung around a bit and figured out that I liked models, then he made it his business to take me to every model's apartment he could find. Bringing me sweatshirts and hooking me up with models probably wasn't Brett's idea of a dream job, but he knew I had Hollywood contacts through producing movies like *Krush Groove* and *Tougher Than Leather* and figured that making himself useful might lead to some filmmaking opportunities for him. We finally did notice Brett, not because he had a loud mouth, but because he was relentless in working hard for me and my company. We let him direct a PSA for Public Enemy, and when he did a good job with that, it led to several rap videos. Brett spent a few years working hard on videos, which led to an opportunity to direct *Money Talks* with Chris Tucker. His hard work on that film led to an opportunity to direct *Rush Hour*, and the rest, as they say, is history. But Brett didn't get that initial break because he came to me and said, "Hey, let me direct a video for you," even though he was probably thinking that. He got that initial break because he was willing to work his hardest for free until people began to notice his effort and dedication. I still call Brett my "son," but the fact is he's been an incredible inspiration to me over the years as well.

To tell you the truth, I got my start in the music business the same way. My man Rudy Toppin used to throw these parties that big-name players in the music business always used to go to. Well, I wanted to be in the party business, so I approached him and offered to hand out flyers for free as a way to get my foot in the door. I was selling weed at the time and actually had some decent money in my pocket, but I didn't view spending hours handing out flyers as a demotion. I was happy to humble myself by working hard at promoting Rudy's parties because I didn't want to be a drug dealer. I wanted to be a party promoter. I was inspired by the music and wanted to be around it any way I could. I was happy to focus on the process of handing out flyers instead of worrying about what sort of payment I would get for it.

The Kevin Liles and Brett Ratner examples are very important, because I suspect that a lot of the people who bought this book did so because they're looking to duplicate my success in the communications industry. So if you're looking for a surefire way to get into the game, there's your answer. You have to come at the game like Kevin and Brett did. Whether it's film, records, television, digital media, or fashion, you have to find someone who's doing what you want to do and bring her her lunch. You leave your ego at home and bring that person the tools she needs to do her job. And after you catch her attention by bringing her those tools every day with a smile, one day she'll let you use those tools too. And when that day comes, it's just a matter of putting your head down and working your hardest to make the most out of that opportunity.

Hustle Like You're the Immigrant

I believe one of the reasons successful people are able to make such a strong commitment to hard work is because they appreciate just how much opportunity there is in America. Kevin Liles might have come from the streets of Baltimore, but he never for a second thought that his hard work wouldn't take him where he wanted to go. I was the same way. Even when I was handing out flyers, I was absolutely convinced my focused effort was going to help me break into the music business. I could sense so many openings around me that I figured it would only be a matter of time. That's not to suggest that we still don't face tremendous obstacles in America—I'll be the first to admit that racism, sexism, classism, homophobia, and prejudice are still much closer to the surface than many would like to admit. But never let those obstacles obscure the fact that we do live in a country where hard work can elevate us to the greatest heights. I can't say that to most people in this world. For millions and millions of people overseas, no matter how hard they work, the opportunities just aren't going to be there. They're going to work harder than most Americans and they're still going to have to live on less than a dollar a day for the rest of their lives. At home, there's no opportunity. Despite the continuing classism and racism, they want to come here.

That's why it saddens me that as a community we still don't take advantage of all the opportunity that's available to us in this country. It seems that our struggles have made many of us blind to that opportunity. People can't see that the obstacles that blocked us a hundred or even fifty years ago are largely gone now. Our people are still walking the streets frustrated, when there's a library on the corner they could be walking into instead and using what they find there to improve themselves. Trust me, the doors to those libraries have not always been open. Just like the doors to the radio stations and TV networks and record labels and gated communities and universities have not always been open either. Even though pioneers had to pry those doors open for us, we still won't walk through them. That's very frustrating to the previous generations who fought such a terrible fight for us.

Conversely, I feel like when most immigrants look at America, *all* they can see is opportunity. Do you know what many Chinese call America? They call it "Mei Guo" or "the Beautiful Country." While there are certainly many "middle class" Chinese who immigrate, we're talking largely about very poor people who aren't going to have many beautiful things when they get here. We're talking about people who are probably going to spend a generation here working in sweatshops or delivering food for dollar tips. That's a very tough existence, probably tougher than most of our own, but they're willing to do it.

They're willing because beyond the struggle, they see opportunity. And to them, even if they can only catch a glimpse of it, that opportunity is beautiful. Just like it's beautiful to the immigrants coming here from Mexico, from Africa, from the Caribbean, or from dozens of other places. These immigrants aren't just willing to work their hardest once they get here. They're willing to walk through deserts, swim across rivers, crawl under fences, cross the ocean on rubber rafts, stow away in shipping containers, and hide in the wheel wells of airplanes just *to* get here. In contrast, a lot of the people born here can't find the motivation to get off the couch and walk over to a free library to start bettering themselves. Not because they're lazy or because they don't care. But because their lenses are dirty.

You have to be able to see that America in the twenty-first century is *still* the greatest place you could ever live. Despite the fact that much of our success was achieved through exploitation, and despite the oppression that remains in our country today, in the history of the world there has never been a society that enjoyed as much freedom and opportunity as we do right now. When you look back at all the great civilizations of the past, none of them afforded the same freedom and opportunity that can be found in America today. Whether it was ancient Egypt, ancient Rome, the Ming Dynasty in China, the British Empire—whatever society achieved great heights, none offered as much opportunity as America in 2006. Understand that by living in America, you've hit history's lottery! You are living in a time of incredible advancement and possibility. Despite everything messed up that's happening in the world, we're still living in an incredible period!

So be honest with yourself. When you see America, do you see a beautiful place where your Hard Work will ultimately lead to success? Or do you see a country where your Hard Work will never pull you out of the struggle? Do you see the lack, or do you see the abundance? If all you can see is that struggle, then wipe off your lenses. Make sure they're clean enough to see the opportunity that's right in front of you. Don't let the struggles of the past cloud your vision. I really believe the last generation removed the physical barriers of the struggle. Now it's up to you to overcome the *mental* barriers. The final struggle is the spiritual barriers in your *mind*. And you can overcome that struggle by working your hardest to take advantage of all the opportunity we have in this country.

I want it to be very clear that I'm not just talking about black folks here, or in the book in general. When I talk about the struggle, I'm talking about the struggle that is faced by all people who are locked out. That's why poor white people, poor Asian people, poor Latinos—really poor people of any background—need to wipe off their lenses, as well, and see all the opportunity. People from all backgrounds let self-esteem issues fog up their lenses. And I take some responsibility for that. I realize if you're living in the projects or in a trailer park, when you turn on *Cribs* and see me walking around a forty-thousand-square-foot mansion, subconsciously it probably makes you feel bad about your home. Or maybe when you see pictures in the papers of me getting out of a new car, subconsciously it might make you feel like your old car doesn't have much value. Of course, that's the exact opposite of my actual intention. Instead, I hope that when you see my house on TV, it'll inspire you to believe that with hard work, one day you can have a mansion of your own if that's what you want.

One of the main reasons I've written this book is to remind you that you *can* do it. To remind you if you're riding the bus every day, with hard work, dedication, and faith, you can get the car you've been dreaming of. To remind you that your sneakers might be dirty right now, but with hard work, dedication, and faith, you will get a fresh pair soon. Of course, I would also encourage you not to worry about the toys so much and instead use your efforts to get your spirit right *first*. But no matter what motivates you to get out of "poverty," you must understand that so-called poverty is only in your mind. Just like often prosperity is only in our minds too. The world is going to be what your hard work makes it. It's just a matter of what we see when we open our eyes.

I know this message can sound very judgmental, and I've bristled, at times, when people have laid it on me. That's why I want to stress that I'm not *criticizing* anyone out there. I understand everyone is already doing the best they can in life. I'm just encouraging you to use your hard work constructively, so that you can do even better than you are doing right now.

This isn't the old, right-wing "American Dream" rap I'm giving you. This is a "Nu American Dream" rap. The old American Dream was bullshit, because not everybody was allowed have it. In fact, for a lot of people it was a nightmare. That's why hip-hop has been so important. It's opened up the American Dream so that it truly includes everyone. So now a Kevin Liles, or a Jay-Z, or an Eminem can invest all of their effort into their dreams, because they know that dreams can come true. All I'm promoting is that everyone recognize this—not just a motivated rapper, or an immigrant desperate for a better life. The opportunity is available to all of us. You've just got to put in the work. Trust me, it's all about the Hard Work, because nothing is going to fall into your lap. Sometimes in this country we get a little soft. Don't get soft. Don't wait for something. Hit the streets today and hustle like *you're* an immigrant.

Underpromise and Overdeliver

Hopefully by now I've been able to convince you of the value of Never Doing Less Than Your Best to both your bank account and your spirit. If so, now I want to specifically address the importance of focusing that hard work on a business level. It's great to give your best, but unless that effort is focused, you'll end up wasting a tremendous amount of energy. You can't just put your head down and keep it there. That's why one of the business mantras I'm always preaching to my staff is "Underpromise and overdeliver."

That means don't say you can do something just because you think that's what the person you're working for wants to hear. Or don't say yes just to prove to your boss how hard you're willing work. When most people do that, it usually ends up biting them in the ass. Because when you don't deliver what you promised, your boss isn't going to care that you were just trying to make a good impression. She is just going to care about the fact that she doesn't have what she needs, and she's going to blame it on you.

Instead, be conservative in what you say you can deliver, and then give your best to deliver *more*. That way you've protected yourself if something goes wrong and you've increased the odds that you'll deliver more than what you promised. Which is something every boss likes.

For example, if you're a record producer and a label wants you to turn in a track on Monday, tell them the earliest you can do it is by Tuesday. Then bust your ass to make sure that track is on their desk *first thing* Monday morning. The label will love the fact that instead of making the deadline, you beat it.

Of course, there's no point in underpromising if you don't follow through on the overdeliver part. Don't buy yourself an extra day but then take it easy over the weekend and still hand it in on Tuesday. The *public* deadline might be Tuesday, but your *personal* deadline still has to be Monday. You must put your head down, work your hardest, and live in the studio the whole weekend if that's what it takes to get that track done by Monday.

Let's be clear: I'm not promoting that you lie to people about your abilities. I'm not recommending you purposely put out a number that's radically different from what you're capable of delivering. Instead, I'm recommending you make sure that what you put out there, you can really live up to. It's great to be confident, but you never want to promise the impossible. I've certainly made that mistake in my career, committing to delivering clothes before they were properly designed, releasing albums before they were really ready, or overstating projections for a new business. I didn't do any of those things because I was trying to be deceitful but because I was simply too optimistic. I had such a strong belief in the power of my Hard Work that I assumed I could pull off anything. Now, I know that's it great to have confidence, but it's even better to temper that confidence with a conservative assessment of the job in front of you.

Stress Doesn't Equal Hard Work

I want to end this chapter by emphasizing that stressing about a job does not equal working hard on that job. A lot of people think the time they spend worrying about something is the same as actually working on it. Wrong. The actual work you do is what will change your life for the better. Worrying about that work will just slow your life down. It may seem like I'm talking about removing fear (because that's what worry is) in every chapter, but there's simply no way around it. Fear is one of the biggest obstacles we have to overcome in life.

Stress was an issue I struggled with for a long time, because I definitely used to think that stress (specifically rethinking things over and over again) is what made me work hard. At that time, I believed that worrying about where my next meal was coming from is what helped me *get* my next meal. I figured that without worry, I would lose my motivation to work hard, but in retrospect, it not only made me uncomfortable personally, it caused me to make mistakes professionally that actually set my career back. Worrying about where my next meal was coming from actually kept me from eating right. Now, not only does my hard work produce more fruit, but the fruit also tastes much sweeter. In fact, I've learned that none of the truly good things in my life have ever come from worrying.

I think most people understand this, but they still worry anyway. That's why you must keep reminding yourself of the basic practice we're talking about here: Work your hardest on the job in front of you right now and don't worry about the past or the future. The more you worry about the future, the less engaged you are in the work you're doing today. And when you're not fully engaged in the work you're doing right now, you'll never be able to burn away all that negativity. You can only prepare for the *next* moment in *this* moment.

Even though worrying has caused me to make mistakes in the past, the funny thing is I can't remember what those mistakes were. Whenever I do interviews, the toughest part for me is when they ask the inevitable "What mistakes do you regret?" question. When I hear that, I just sit there with a blank look on my face. I'm not trying to be cocky, I just don't have an answer to that question because I've blocked all the "failures" out. I'm pretty happy where I am this second, and if I were to start messing with the past, then this second might not be as great as it is right now. So I literally can never answer that question. Some people might say I'm in denial, but I prefer to look at it as being committed to working my hardest in this moment, instead of getting stuck in the moments where I didn't work my hardest in the past.

All we can really do in life is try to remember principles like never giving Less Than Your Best. I certainly don't claim to follow it all of the time. What I do try to do all the time is *remember* it. That's really the goal for all of us: Try to remember to remember. I know I say it in every chapter, but I really want to drive that point home. Like all the other laws I promote, this one is a practice. None of us are perfect and we all get distracted by the world from time to time. The happiest people are the ones who remember not only to work their hardest, but to stay focused on what they're working for. And that's to get closer to God than to any sort of earthly reward.

RECOGNIZE THE REAL:

It's very simple: When you're working your hardest, the world opens up to you. When you're not working, your mind becomes cluttered and the world becomes closed.

No one can find success by him- or herself. When you pick the right team you'll always win.

LAW NUMBER SIX:

SURROUND YOURSELF WITH THE RIGHT PEOPLE

Surround yourself only with people who are going to lift you higher.
—OPRAH WINFREY

ONE OF THE NICKNAMES I've acquired over the years is "the Godfather of Hip-Hop." It's pretty flattering, but also pretty far from the truth. That's because to many, the term *Godfather* represents someone who's become powerful through ruthlessly manipulating the people and situations around him. In fact, the logo for the *Godfather* movies was a hand manipulating a puppet's strings.

That's a cool image, but the idea of me climbing the success ladder by stepping on the people around me couldn't be farther from the truth. I didn't become successful because I climbed on the backs of the people around me. I became successful because those people *lifted me up*. I didn't make a name for myself in the music industry, or the fashion industry, or in *any* industry because I was smarter than the people around me. My successes have only been possible because I was surrounded by people who are smarter than *I was*. I can honestly say that without the insight and inspiration of the people around me, I would be closer to the "stepchild" of hip-hop than the "Godfather." From music to fashion to television to movies to my personal life, anything positive I've experienced has largely been made possible by the people around me. If you want to achieve your goals in life, you must Surround Yourself With the Right People. Because whether you're a Godfather or just a rookie, you're going to be defined by the people around you. You can't compromise when it comes to

Surrounding Yourself With the Right People. No one can find success by him- or herself.

Having the Right People around you is such a crucial step toward finding any sort of success in this world. You could break some of the laws in this book and it might take a while before they *break you*. For instance, if you don't Follow Your Vision with persistence, you might not realize you've been missing out on your dreams until it's time to step in the box. If you don't Do You, you still might have a perfectly good career, just not as rewarding as it would have been if you had followed your own path. You can choose not to operate under many of these laws and still lead a decent life. However, *this* law isn't one of them. If you don't have the right people around you, the consequences will be immediate and sometimes severe. That's because having the wrong people around you won't just slow you down on the road to success. Those people will actually lead you down a dead-end path. Don't let that happen. Take control of your life. If you choose to be around spiritual, hardworking, giving people, you'll be a spiritual, hardworking person who's always receiving gifts.

FIND A RABBI

Before we talk about the importance of finding the right *people* in the life, we need to address the importance of finding the right *person* first. Whether it's in business or in life, it's important to not only find, but also to listen to, a person who's had more experience than you. I call these people "rabbis" (the Hebrew word for teacher) because, rather than be selfish with their knowledge, they are willing to share it and teach those who haven't had the same breadth of experience. This is especially important in the business world, which is why I always say no matter what venture you're trying to explore, you need to find a rabbi who can guide the way. A rabbi can teach you, *before* you set out on your journey, where some of the holes may be or where the obstacles might come. They know because they've already experienced those holes and obstacles themselves. And by sharing that knowledge with you, they will save you tremendous time and energy.

That's important, because I think one of the biggest challenges for people is breaking into an industry. When you're on the outside looking in, the obstacles can seem insurmountable. That was certainly the case in my own experiences. Even though I was loaded with enthusiasm and confidence, the major record labels in Manhattan seemed like they were a million miles away when I was just a party promoter living in Queens. And even after I broke into the record industry, the fashion industry seemed impenetrable at first too. Movies, TV, jewelry, sneakers, energy drinks—every market can look very unwelcoming when you're on the outside looking in. The way I've been able to get past that fear in my own career is by focusing on establishing relationships with people who are already behind what we perceive to be the walls. It's very helpful to find that person who will teach you the mechanics of the industry, what the real costs of production are, and what your bottom line needs to be. Who will share what they've gone through, what's tripped them up, and what's brought them success.

Admittedly, I'm contradicting myself a bit (I told you it was going to keep happening!). A few chapters ago, I told you to keep your ears closed and focus on your own vision. Now, I'm telling you to keep your ears open and try to soak up everything the rabbi can tell you. But the truth is, it's a balance. You have to instinctively learn not to trust other people over trusting yourself, while at the same time not being hardheaded and missing out on opportunities to learn. You have to find the experts, the people who've had the experiences, and then listen to them very closely.

You can't take advice from everybody, but when the rabbis talk, you have to pay attention.

My First Rabbi

When I first got into the record business, I loved hip-hop and desperately wanted to be around it as much as I could, so promoting parties or clubs where rappers like Eddie Cheeba or DJ Hollywood or Starski performed was a natural fit for me. And really, I was fine with that. It allowed me to make a little bit of money while I got to hang out with artists I was truly inspired by. One day—I think it was sometime in 1978—my brother Run was putting up flyers for one of my parties when he was approached by a man named Robert Ford, who at the time was a reporter for *Billboard* magazine. Robert was very interested in learning more about this new trend called hip-hop, so he set up a meeting with me through my brother. We hooked up a few weeks later and hit it off right away. I loved the music and was looking for any way possible to become involved in it professionally. I was hoping that through throwing parties, I could start managing some artists. Rob was already involved professionally in the music business, but he wanted to learn more about hip-hop, which he could tell was about to become a very big deal. So right off the bat we had a mutually beneficial relationship. I could show Rob what was happening in hip-hop, and he could be my rabbi and teach me about how to break into the record business. But ultimately, Rob taught me not only how to break into the game, but how to stay in the game by making honesty and integrity the foundation on which you build any sort of marketing or development plan. In other words, Rob taught me the value of selling the truth. That was the first lesson I've learned in the game and it's proved to be the most important one too. And that's why I call Robert Ford my original rabbi.

The first thing Rob helped me with was making contacts.

Relationships, especially in the entertainment business, are so important. If you aren't comfortable networking with people and making new friends, you're going to have a very hard time. For me, networking comes fairly easily, but I had never had a chance to apply that skill in an industry setting before I met Rob. After we'd been hanging out for a while, he invited me to go to the *Billboard* convention with him in New York (I believe this was 1979), so that I could meet some of the players in the game. Of course I said yes and it was a real eye-opening experience for me. Rob seemed to know everybody and wherever he went, I just tried to hang back and observe the way people spoke to each other, what they talked about, what they wore, how they partied, you name it. I wanted to soak it all in like a sponge. That experience not only introduced me to people but also introduced me to the art of networking. A dedication to Hard Work is always the most important quality, but an ability to make and maintain relationships is probably the second most important skill you need to have to make it in this business.

The *Billboard* convention was a very important moment for me. Meeting all these people from labels and radio stations and management companies gave me the confidence that I could really make it in the music business. So it wasn't long before Rob and I decided that instead of just promoting parties and writing about hip-hop, respectively, we would actually take a stab at making some hip-hop on our own. Along with his friends J. B. Moore and Larry Smith, Rob decided to produce a rap record with an artist I had started working with named Kurtis Blow. The record was called "Christmas Rappin' " and even though it might sound a little old-fashioned today, at the time it was a very big deal for us. That record was a hit and it helped Kurtis become one of the first rappers to get a major label deal, but it also opened up all sorts of doors for me within the music industry.

Thankfully, what Rob taught me wasn't about how to get an

artist a record deal, but what to do with that deal once you got it. You see, Rob was a tremendous rabbi because he not only knew industry people, but he understood the philosophy of artist development as well. He was the person who taught me that instead of just getting a deal for a rapper, you could actually build a brand around that person.

That might sound obvious now, but it was a new concept at that time. You have to understand that during the late seventies, record labels believed that artist development was something that only made sense for rock bands and few big R&B acts. Rap, on the, other hand, was seen in the same light as disco (probably because records like "Rapper's Delight" and "Christmas Rappin'" used popular disco bass-lines). And within the industry, there was almost no emphasis on developing disco artists. In fact, most disco "artists" didn't even exist, as the people who performed the songs onstage weren't the same people who actually sang them in the studio. Milli Vanilli would have fit right in back then. So with a few notable exceptions like Donna Summer, the Bee Gees, or ABBA, the disco scene really revolved around the big record producers and the labels. The artists themselves were essentially disposable.

Now, if the industry thought disco artists were disposable, you can imagine what they thought about street kids who only rapped and "couldn't even sing"—to the suits, these kids were completely disposable. Rappers certainly didn't have much talent and no one would ever want to emulate them, so why waste money trying to develop them? That was the conventional wisdom, but Rob was bright enough to see that rappers like Kurtis possessed real potential. He knew that if we could just show the world that rappers were real artists with powerful stories, then they could build lasting careers instead of just cutting a song and disappearing back into the streets. That's why Rob insisted on putting Kurtis's photo on the cover of the twelve-inch for "The Breaks," his classic follow-up to "Christmas Rappin'." The label wasn't even going to bother, but Rob knew that just showing Kurtis's face was part of establishing him as an artist. Rob also suggested that rather than only put Kurtis's name on the cover, we actually give him a nickname, in this case "the King of Rap," which created more of an aura around him. Admittedly, those might seem to be very small steps by today's standards, but they mattered tremendously at the time. Rob knew that by treating Kurtis as something more than a nameless, faceless street kid, we could actually build a lasting and stable career for him. And he was right—now, even twenty-five years later, Kurtis Blow can go to England or Germany and get paid to perform. And I like to think that part of that is because we helped him build his career on something solid—bricks, not bubblegum.

To this day, I use Rob's philosophy when I'm developing any new brand, not just within the music industry: to invest in things that are lasting, honest, and stable, instead of cheap and disposable. Rob taught me to emphasize an artist's honest emotional connection with the people, instead of promoting gimmicks that are here today, gone tomorrow. He taught me that it's so much more fun to sell what's good about an artist and get paid off of that, instead of trying to promote something that's not really there. Again, that might seem like obvious advice, but to a young guy jumping into the game, it was the most important thing I could have heard. Because when you're young, you usually don't care about "lasting" and "stable." You care about cashing checks now and worrying about tomorrow when it comes. You think you already know it all and usually aren't worried about building a career. But Rob slowed me down and showed me how to build something lasting, not only for myself, but for the artists I was working with too, without anyone having to compromise his or her vision. So now, when it's time for me to develop a new brand, I just go back to the model Robert Ford showed me back in the day. Rob's probably never thought of himself as a rabbi, but the success of my businesses attests to what a great teacher he was.

At this point, some of you might be saying, "That's great, but there's no Robert Ford out there for me. I haven't met anyone who's willing to take me under his wing and teach me what to do." Well, my response to that is "*Yes, you have.*" We all meet a Robert Ford *every day.* Here's the key—it's not a matter of *meeting* a Robert Ford, it's about *hearing* a Robert Ford when you do meet him. Every day we meet people who are trying to share their wisdom with us. We just don't always *hear* them. It's not enough to be around a rabbi, or to surround yourself with the Right People; you have to *listen* to those people once you do. Again, there's a reason we have two ears and one mouth. It's so that we can hear all the good advice out there. We should be twice as comfortable listening as we are at talking, but usually it's the other way around. I know I said this earlier in the book, but it bears repeating: Listening is extremely important. You've got to hear the rabbis when they're talking to you. Don't talk over them, or talk through them. Listen to them. Because when you listen to what they're trying to tell you, you'll usually find an easier path in life.

Finally, remember that everybody, and everything, can be your rabbi if you let them. You can learn from everything, even an ant. Think I'm bullshitting? If you really watch an ant, you're going learn about teamwork, you'll learn about hard work, you'll learn about giving. An ant can teach you those things. So imagine what you can learn when you open yourself to the experiences of another person.

Be a Rabbi

I also encourage you to look for ways that you can be a rabbi to someone who needs some advice. Because I think you'll find that teaching someone is one of the most rewarding experiences you can have in life. I'm certainly indebted to Robert Ford for all that he taught me, but I also like to think that our relationship made his life richer too. The success of "Christmas Rappin'" certainly raised Robert's visibility and allowed him to leave *Billboard* and start a new career as a music producer. So while Rob wasn't ever expecting a payout from helping me, the world definitely rewarded him for his hard work.

Personally, my goal is to be rabbi to as many people as possible. If some of what I share is useful, then I'm doing my job. Ninety-five percent of the people reading this book might think it's a waste of time, but if that other five percent reads it and actually feels some of these laws sink in, then I'll consider it a total success. I realize that these messages won't connect with all of you. But I also understand that messages that we've heard a million times before sometimes connect when we hear them from an untraditional source. I saw the reaction at the Hip-Hop Summit when Eminem got onstage and talked about the importance of hard work and faith. It was nothing new—it was the same message you'll hear in this book, or in school or in church. But when the young people heard that message directly from Eminem, it actually sank in for the first time with many of them. I saw kids with tears in their eyes when he was talking about working hard. Not because no one had ever told them that before, but because it was the first time they heard it and then believed it was possible for them. On that day, Eminem, a guy that everyone said was such a negative influence on America's youth, became a rabbi to those young people. And I'm sure if you ask him, he'll say helping those young people that day was one of the most satisfying things he's done. You do the work so that you can teach others.

That's why I always try to work with young people, because through mentoring them, I become inspired to do better as well. I love working with a young person on the come-up who's so inspiring in his own hustle that his mentors end up moving faster too. When that happens, people who've been in the game for years and years end up getting reintroduced to hard work and focus through this young spirit. There's a young lawyer working for me now named Nahshon Craig who really exemplifies this spirit. He came to me looking for a job and guidance a few years ago, and I'm so glad now that I decided to bring him on. That's because every time I get lazy and let something fall out of pocket, Nahshon is right there, picking up the pieces and making sure I put them back where they belong. He reminds me a lot of a Kevin Liles or a Lyor Cohen, though I'm sure he'll make his own name in the industry very soon. (In my office we already call him "the Closer.") Even though I'm forty-nine years old and writing a book from the perspective of experience, I still like to think that I'm just hitting my stride and that there's some more good work. And one of the main reasons I feel so excited about the future is the contagious enthusiasm of young people like Nahshon. I might have started as a mentor to him, but in a short amount of time he's ended up inspiring me.

Certainly the main reason I'm still in the record business is because it gives me the opportunity to be a rabbi for a new generation of artists. Right now, I'm working with a young artist from Brooklyn named Jinx, another guy I call my "son." Yes, I'm trying to teach him the record game, but at the same time, he's inspiring me. That's because even though he's been through so much—when I met him, he was a teenager who'd already been shot, been in trouble with the law, and become a father—I'd never seen someone as dedicated to living his dream as Jinx. I've known him since he was fifteen. He's watched his friends drop like leaves on a tree, but he hasn't let that consume him. It's actually made his heart grow. And I love him for that.

When we talk, it's as much about life as it is about music. In fact, my biggest message to Jinx hasn't been "Get yourself a hit record" but "Get yourself a high school degree." At times I thought maybe he wasn't listening, but in between standing outside radio stations hustling his singles and raising his kids, Jinx made the time to go to school and better himself. Recently, when he came into my office and surprised me with his GED, I swear I almost cried. I didn't cry when my own father died, but the sight of Jinx standing there with that diploma in his hand sure made me watery-eyed. Of course I couldn't sit there and cry in front of a gangster, but there was no denying I was emotional. In fact, I can feel the tears welling up in my eyes as I write this now.

That's why I say that Jinx is my greatest rabbi. His determination in the face of struggle is a constant reminder of what my job is here on earth. It's my job to step in and help someone the same way so many people stepped in and helped me over the years. That's the real beauty of surrounding yourself with the Right People. You can help yourself by helping others. I'm crying not only because of what Jinx has been through, but because it feels so good to actually do your job in life. Believe me, realizing that you've truly helped someone in life will bring you much more pleasure than any of the toys.

PICK THE RIGHT TEAM

As I said, I've received a lot of accolades over the years for my ability to build brands like Def Jam, Phat Farm, *Def Comedy*, and the Hip-Hop Summit Action Network. However, a closer look at my career reveals that every step of the way I've been surrounded by people who not only shared my vision for those brands but actually did the heavy lifting that made those brands a reality. That was certainly the case with Def Jam, where Rick Rubin deserves most of the credit for our initial success and people like Lyor Cohen and Kevin Liles orchestrated our second wave of hits. It was also the case with Phat Farm, where Ruby Azrak helped me build that brand and Kimora Lee helped me focus it and then take the company to another level. I certainly wouldn't have been able to create TV shows like *Def Comedy Jam*, *Def Poetry Jam*, and *Run's House* without the knowledge and steady support of Stan Lathan. Just like how without the knowledge of Brian Grazer, one of the greatest producers of our times, I would have never been able to produce a film like *The Nutty Professor*. The same is true of the organizations I work with. As I've already mentioned, the Hip-Hop Summit Action Network wouldn't have existed without the vision and determination of the great civil rights activist Minister Ben Chavis. Similarly, if it weren't for the hard work of Ellen Haddigan, Rush Philanthropic would be seen as just another vanity celebrity foundation. But under her guidance, it's become an organization that truly impacts the lives of young people. For a final example, the Foundation for Ethnic Understanding only exists because of the passion and enthusiasm of Rabbi Marc Schneier. A lot of names, I know, but that's exactly the point—when you work with the Right People, there's a very wide breadth to what you can accomplish. Without exception, every one of my successes has been spearheaded by someone who's not only interested in what I do but is more dedicated to that vision than I am. I might get the headlines, but the people around me are the heartbeat that moves me forward. Without them, I could never progress.

After twenty-plus years in the game, I know I can't do it by myself. I know the survival of my companies depends not on my talents but on my ability to pick the Right People to support those talents. That's why to this day I still personally interview all my prospective employees, from a vice president to an intern, even though I'm not that good at the process. I don't always ask the appropriate questions and I'm probably not as focused as I should be. Still, I have an instinctual sense of what I'm looking for. The most important quality you can show me is a commitment to giving. The importance of giving will get its own chapter later in the book, but when it comes to employees, I'm looking for people who give by being good teammates. I want to be surrounded by people who uplift each other by focusing on the companies' bottom line, instead of their personal bottom line. In other words, I'm looking for people who aren't worried about the amount of credit *they're* gonna get, but instead are focused on what kind of credit the *company* is gonna get. I'm looking for people who don't have a "tit for tat" attitude about their work. For every effort they make, they don't expect a pat on the back. Instead, they're content with making the other employees around them successful. I'm talking about a receptionist who not only gets coffee for her boss but gets some for your boss, too, so that both of you don't have to make the same trip. I'm talking about someone who sweeps up a dirty floor the moment he see it. Not someone who calls his boss to let her know the floor's dirty so that he'll get credit for sweeping it, but someone who sweeps it without worrying if anyone saw him or not. I'm looking for people who understand that the body of their hard work is what will get them noticed, not the little things they do.

Even though I have the final say on who gets hired at my companies, I really want the person up for the position to make the decision for me. This means I'm looking for people who don't apply for jobs, but *take* their jobs. This is especially true when it comes to promotions. I want to be surrounded by people who make the most of their opportunities. Whether they're an intern, or freelancing, or delivering the mail, these people work so hard that I have no choice but to hire them for more important positions. In fact, they work so hard that they end up hiring themselves.

I want to say one more thing here about the interview process, though I'm going to address it again later. Never go into an interview and blame someone else for your condition. If your last job didn't turn out the way you had hoped, never point the finger at your previous employers or your employees or the market or *any* external force. Always accept the blame for your condition. If I ask you why you left your last job and you tell me, "Well, my boss didn't like me," or "Man, they were stupid over there," then you're finished, in my book. I might keep talking to you for a few minutes out of courtesy, but you're not getting the job. Because I don't want to hear that someone else is responsible for your position. I just don't want to hear it. If you walk into my office and tell me about someone else's faults, or someone else's flaws, then that's probably the last time you're going to walk into my office. I really don't want to be surrounded by people who make excuses. Instead, I want to be surrounded by people who take responsibility and improve their condition through hard work and resilience.

Keep the Office Open Physically and Spiritually

Once you have the right people in place, it's very important to create a working environment where they feel inspired instead of stifled. For me, the best way to create that sort of environment is by giving my employees as much freedom as they need. I like to run a creative shop, where if someone has a new idea for a product, or a new idea for how we can do business, she'll never hesitate to share it. My hope is that this sense of freedom encourages my employees to keep looking forward while also staying focused on their primary responsibilities.

That means that my office can often seem chaotic. On the surface, I'm sure it looks like most other CEOs' offices: an oak desk, city views, leather chairs, flat-screen TV—all the fun toys. But as the day progress, it often transforms into a corporate street corner, a place where employees, clients, and visitors can all feel comfortable hanging out, speaking their minds, and sharing ideas. In fact, I recently had to put a lock on my office door because too much information was being exchanged. I might be taking a meeting about Simmons Jewelry, and someone from Phat Farm would walk in and start talking about our new shirts. I'd get so caught up in looking at the designs that I'd never finish talking about the jewelry. My incredible assistants Simone Reyes and Christina Paljusaj would spend hours planning my schedule down to the last five minutes, but I kept screwing it up. So even though I don't like the symbolism of a locked door, the stream of people wandering into my office has slowed down a bit. Still, my best work tends to get done when there's a natural flow between my staff and me. Locks or not, I know I'm an impossible person to schedule, but you can't argue with the results. As long as you learn how to organize it in an effective way, freedom is often very rewarding.

Of course, not everyone operates well in chaos. Instead of inspiring, many people find it intimidating. They prefer to run an organized, tightly run ship. Instead of delegating responsibility to their staff, they're much more comfortable running every aspect of their business themselves. Personally, I could never operate that way; I believe it's a waste to surround yourself with the Right People, only to keep them on a short leash. If you believe they're the Right People, then you have to trust them to do the job just as well, if not better, than you would yourself. That means a lot of times you might not know exactly what someone is doing, or even where she's doing it, but you have to believe her energy is always focused toward the overall success of the company. My management style depends on trust and probably doesn't work for everyone. As an employee and an employer, you have to learn what style suits you best. But for me, it's about not only surrounding yourself with the Right People, but also giving them the resources and the creative freedom they need to succeed.

Once You Have the Right People in Place, Keep Them There

A final step in this process is keeping the Right People around you once you've found them. One of the best ways to do that is to "incentivize" your employees. Never forget that even when your employees share your passion and your vision, they still have to eat. Their primary motivation is going to be money—that's just human nature. That's why you should never hold back financial incentives for them, even if it cuts into your own profits. When you try to keep all the profits for yourself, those profits will never last. But when your employees are eating well and feel like they're being treated fairly, they'll work harder. And that hard work will in turn lead to more profits for the company. It's an obvious equation, but not every businessperson can see it. If you're one of those bosses who feel that they're entitled to one hundred percent of the profits, then God bless you. In my eyes, though, that's a very shortsighted philosophy. I've always believed that if you want the best from your employees (and who doesn't?), then you have to make them feel excited about the job. The great ones will stay motivated without your ever having to pat them on the back, but you can't expect all your employees to be self-motivated. It's not realistic. That's why I like to share equity with my wallet. Pats on the back are great, but most people want to see that encouragement reflected in their bank accounts. I don't want my employees to just be working for a salary—I want them to always feel like they own a piece of what they're working for. Every day when they get up, I want them to feel that there's a good reason for them to go to work. There's no point in surrounding yourself with the Right People if you just end up chasing them away by being cheap. Don't give those people a reason to want to move on. Make them feel invested, instead of feeling disposable.

I really try to practice what I'm preaching here. For example, after I sold Phat Farm, George Bush decided to give me one of his ridiculous tax breaks. Even though I needed a tax break like I needed a hole in my head, I still found myself getting back millions of dollars from the government. (Tax breaks for the rich is a situation we really have to address in this country. It's so crazy.) I could have easily kept that money for myself and justified it by saying that not only had I worked hard for it, but that I had also paid much more in taxes than my employees. But I didn't look at it that way. Instead, I figured the only reason I was in such a favorable tax bracket was because of my employees' hard work and therefore they deserved that refund as much as I did. So I took that money and handed it out to my employees as bonuses. Every time I sell one of my companies, instead of keeping all of the profits, I give away millions to my employees. In fact, I've probably given away over $10 million in bonuses to my employees over the years. I'm not trying to put myself on the back, I'm just saying that by denying others profits, even if they work hard and never ask for any equity, and by being cheap, you are denying yourself an opportunity to contribute to the cycle of giving and your own happiness.

Joint Ventures

Once you've got the right team in place, it's helpful to start thinking about ways you can help that team improve. If you're fortunate enough to have all the resources you need, then it's just a matter of collectively putting your heads down and getting to work. But if you feel like you need more money, manpower, visibility, infrastructure, or physical space to realistically get the job done, then you might want to consider a joint venture. In theory, a joint venture is a business partnership in which two parties contribute assets and share the risks in pursuit of profits. Traditionally, they've been used by companies looking to get into overseas markets. The foreign company provides the technology and resources, while the local company handles the relationships needed to keep things running smoothly on the ground. But I've found that joint ventures work great anywhere, especially when entering a new field. If you don't have all the resources that you need, then a joint venture might be your answer.

I first learned that lesson in the early nineties with Def Jam, when we were partnering with Sony Records. At the time, we had created several smaller spin-off labels, the idea being that they would create opportunities for some of our newer artists. Unfortunately, once they were up and running, we realized that we just didn't have the infrastructure to support them. The bills started piling up and we eventually fell into some serious debt, to the point where we owed Sony $17 million. It didn't look good and some people were even advising us to cut our losses and close shop. But that didn't make sense to me. It's true that we had made some missteps, but it was also true that Def Jam was still one of the most forward-thinking labels in hip-hop. I knew that someone else would be willing to help us further our vision in exchange for a piece of the action. So instead of quitting, we put out some feelers and eventually were able to create a new joint venture deal with Polygram. It was a tremendous deal for us: With the $32 million Polygram gave us for only half of the company, we not only paid off our debt to Sony but were able to put the remaining $15 million in our pockets. And even better, the deal allowed us to retain control over our catalog, which included Public Enemy, Slick Rick, LL Cool J, the Beastie Boys, and a lot of other classic material. I may never be involved in a better turnaround. There may be bigger numbers one day, but I doubt there will be a better turnaround. And of course Polygram made a tremendous amount of money through the success of new Def Jam artists like Warren G, Jay-Z, Ja Rule, and DMX. It worked out great for everyone and really taught me the value of joint ventures.

Later, I was able to orchestrate a similar move with Phat Farm. The company certainly wasn't in debt, but I understood that in order to reach its full potential, Phat Farm needed more resources. So I spent months trying to find a company whose resources would allow Phat Farm to reach a wider audience, without sacrificing its integrity. After some looking, we were able to find that company in Kellwood Clothing and struck a very good deal that allowed me to retain day-to-day control of the company while totally expanding its possibilities. Thanks to that joint venture, I believe that Phat Farm is now ready to realize its true potential.

In fact, I've been blessed to be part of many successful joint ventures in my career. My name might be on Simmons Jewelry, but it's really a partnership with a great jewler named Scott Rouch. We were partnered with individuals who were owners of Fabrikant and now we've made a new deal to take a larger ownership stake in the Simmons Jewelry Group LLC, which is its own successful producer of private label jewelry. Similarly, my Rush Card is really a joint venture with my great friend David Rosenberg and his Unifund financial group. Again, I might be the CEO of these companies, but they would be nothing without the hard work and insight of people like David and Scott Rouch.

Now, I'm not saying that joint ventures are always the right choice. Sometimes you need to run a business by yourself in order to protect your vision for it. But if you can protect that vision while partnering with someone who has more experience and resources, then you should strongly consider it. You never want to compromise or give away your vision and you always have to make sure you maintain a degree of ownership for your idea. But if someone else shares your vision and has the infrastructure to help make it a reality, then don't be afraid to join forces with him. My philosophy has always been a smaller piece of a big success is better than a big piece of a little success. And so far it's worked pretty well for me.

SAY NO TO YES MEN

It's also very important to realize that the Right People for you *are not* the ones who always agree with you. In fact, those are actually the *wrong* kind of people to have around you. If you're only surrounded by a bunch of yes men who kiss your butt and tell you what they *think* you want to hear, then you're never going to get good advice. Who you really need around you are people who speak from the heart and aren't afraid to question your ideas.

In my company, I never want to be the emperor with no clothes. That's why for me, a good day in the office is when someone tells me the truth. I love it when someone speaks up and tells me that the designs for one of my shirts are bad. Or tells me that my marketing plan for a new business is flawed. Or has the guts to tell me that even though I just spent $250K on it, the video for one of my songs still doesn't look right. When people are honest and openly share their opinions, that's what I want. What I don't want is a lot of people in my office blowing smoke up my ass, telling me how great I am, but then when it's time for the streets to weigh in, instead everyone's talking about how wack I am. That's why I try to reward people for telling the truth. Because I know honesty will take our company much farther than flattery.

I understand that an atmosphere of complete honesty isn't always possible—it's hard to tell the guy who's signing the checks that he made a mistake. Still, I try my best to encourage a free exchange of opinions in my office. One way I do that is by trying to stay surrounded by younger people. I believe young people are naturally more honest because they're not always worrying about the consequences of what they say. I've found that young people are leaders by nature, not followers, and they can lead your business to success if you let them. I can't prove it, but it feels like my businesses run better when I'm working with younger people. But while I do love working with young people, ultimately, as the song says, "Age ain't nothin' but a number." What I really want is to be surrounded by people who are young at heart. And a person who's young at heart is going to tell me what she really thinks, regardless of what she perceives to be the political ramifications.

I need that honesty, because there have been so many times in my career that I would have gone down the wrong path if it weren't for someone close to me telling me the truth. Almost every day I'll be close to making a wrong decision but get talked out of it by someone close to me who knows better. A great example is Run DMC, who I honestly didn't want to sign at first. One of the greatest rap groups of all time was practicing in my basement, but I didn't want to sign them. You see, I wasn't a fan of DMC's voice at first and I also wanted my brother Run to finish school. So I foolishly told them I wasn't interested in working with them. Thankfully, my lifelong friend Spuddy kept telling me I was wrong. He said, "You should mess with your brother, he's got skills. Out of all the people that are around you, he's the most talented. And you should mess with DMC too. He sounds great." After a while, I saw that Spuddy was right and set about working with what would turn out to be one of the most important groups in pop culture history. But if I had let my ego get in the way and hadn't listened to what my friends were telling me, none of that might have happened.

Another great example was my decision to endorse the Republican Michael Steele for Senate in Maryland in 2006. Ultimately my endorsement didn't make much of a difference (Steele still lost), but I'll explain the political rationale behind my decision in the Empowerment chapter, since it caused a lot of controversy at the time. Right now, though, I want to demonstrate why it's important not to have yes men around you when you make a major decision.

After I decided that I wanted to endorse Steele, one of the first people I called was Glen E. Friedman, the great photographer and activist, who's been one of my closet friends for over twenty years. I called Glen because, as a true friend, I knew he wouldn't be shy about sharing his opinion of me endorsing a Republican. True to form, he immediately started yelling at me, accusing me of being a sellout and letting me know that I was making a huge, huge mistake. When I tried to explain that Steele and I actually saw eye to eye on several important issues, Glen accused me of being naive, of only wanting to see the common ground and intentionally turning a blind eye to the many differences we had. In Glen's opinion, I was being careless with whatever degree of political clout I had accumulated over the years. "Don't go out on a limb and support either guy," he scolded me. "Stay independent unless somebody completely blows you away. Don't play these guys' game—instead, use your influence to start a whole separate system. . . ." I started shouting back about Steele's virtues, about the good work he did to uplift poor people, but that just made Glen even more adamant. "You're so stupid," he said. "I might be dumb about selling and marketing things, but you're just as stupid about politics. You have no idea what a terrible mistake you're making and the sad thing is you're so dumb you think you're doing the right thing."

A lot of people get their back up after hearing things like that, especially when they're being delivered at a very high decibel, but I loved that Glen was being so honest with me. Because if I call you up and ask for your opinion, then that's what I really want. If you think I'm being a fool, then call me a fool. If you think I'm being manipulated, then call me gullible. Let me know how I look to the world, because I can't always see how I fit into the big picture. And after hearing Glen's passionate reaction, I realized I couldn't just casually endorse Michael Steele. I needed to really think out and defend my endorsement.

Ultimately, I did decide to endorse Steele. That decision was in no way a reflection of how much I value Glen's advice—I'm going to keep on asking Glen's opinion as long as he has one (which obviously means as long as he's alive!). Because even though his arguments against my endorsement were very strong, in that particular instance I decided to go with my gut instinct. I also consulted my political guru, Dr. Ben Chavis, on the issue, and even though he shared many of Glen's concerns, he also appreciated some of the good things I saw in Steele. And by considering their opinions, as well as those of several other people I spoke with, I was able to have more confidence in my decision. Of course, that didn't stop Glen from standing on a street corner a few days later as we were walking through SoHo and, pointing at me like I was a mass murderer, shouting, "Ladies and gentlemen, here in front of me is a man I promise will be voting Republican in the next presidential election!"

As I said, I'll talk more about the reasons for that decision later on. What I'm trying to convey here is the importance of having people in your life who aren't afraid to tell you when they think you're wrong. You always want to be able to pick up the phone, tell them what you're about to do, and then get their honest opinion. You might not always follow their advice, but you'll always appreciate that honesty.

Thankfully, I've been friends with plenty of people who've kept it real with me over the years, but the person who's probably been the most honest with me has been Kimora Lee. As both a wife and a business partner, she has always told me the truth, whether I've wanted to hear it or not. What she's told me about our private life will stay just that: private. We've got two beautiful young daughters who we both love with all of our hearts and I wouldn't want them to pick up this book one day and read something I said about Mommy, or Mommy said about Daddy. I believe those kinds of conversations should stay within a family. Admittedly, as I'm writing this, there's a lot of speculation in the press about my relationship with Kimora and I know that publishers love confessions and revelations. But I'm afraid you're going to be disappointed if you were planning on flipping through this book for the page where I talk about my marriage with Kimora. Because all I want to say about our marriage is that I don't regret one second of it. Not one single second. I can't say what the future will hold, but I know that Kimora is not only the adult woman that I love the most, but she's been one of the most influential people in my life.

And, getting back to the topic, one of the reasons she's had so much influence on me is because she's been so honest with me. Some people don't like that kind of honesty, but I know that honesty not only comes from love, it's also saved me a lot of time and money. A great example is when I first decided to launch the Baby Phat line. I had put together what I thought was a pretty good collection. Then Kimora walked into the showroom, took one look at it, and said, "This is all a bunch of crap." It stung at the time, but when I thought about it, I realized she was right. I took her suggestions to heart and we ended up redoing the entire line in her vision. And from that day on, Baby Phat has become one of the most successful ventures I've ever been involved in.

But that would have never happened if Kimora had been afraid to say what she really felt. Thankfully she was honest with her vision and wasn't afraid to share it. That's why I say you can never go wrong when you're surrounded by people who love you enough, and feel invested enough in your vision, to always tell you the truth.

Wrong People

Unfortunately, you can go wrong when you are surrounded by the wrong *people*. While being surrounded by "Yes Men" might keep you from getting ahead, being surrounded by the Wrong People will actually move you backward in life. If you hang out with negative people, they'll take you down a negative road. It's that simple. Think of life as a car. Why are you letting those dummies drive? They're only going to crash or get you pulled over. Take the wheel. Take control of your life.

There have been times when I let the wrong people take the wheel, most notably when I was a young man. I grew up surrounded by a lot of drug dealers, and even though my parents tried to push me in a more positive direction, I found myself pulled toward them. It was mainly a lifestyle issue; I wanted to have enough money to keep buying new clothes and keep popping champagne in the clubs, and dealing drugs seemed to be the easiest way to do that. So I started dealing, mainly a little weed and some fake cocaine. But after a while, I could see that it was the wrong route for me. Instead of controlling my own life, I was being controlled by the people around me—the cops, my customers, and other dealers. And none of them gave a shit about me. They were willing to drive me down the wrong road and never think twice about it. They were the absolute wrong kind of people for me to be around.

Luckily I realized that before I got in over my head and made the move from drug dealing to party promoting. I realized that instead of aspiring to be gangsters, the party promoters aspired to be concert promoters, or to find some sort of position in the record business. They wanted to be legitimate. It was a transition that made sense to me: The only reason I sold drugs in the first place is because I wanted to get into the parties. The drug dealers and party promoters were all hanging out in the same parties, so why not cut to the chase and just throw the parties myself? That way I could stay on the scene without having to worry about all the drama. I wouldn't have to worry about getting killed. Shit, I was mainly selling fake drugs anyway. Why risk it all for that?

I was fortunate enough to make that decision to take the wheel before it was too late. But I also know that growing up in the 'hood, sometimes staying away from the dummies is easier said than done. My personal transition was a gradual one—I went from drug dealer to party promoter to manager, while staying high the whole time. I didn't abruptly leave the wrong people—I just slowly moved away from them. Not everyone has that luxury. When you're in the hood, the wrong people are all around you and it's not easy to avoid them. That's why I suggest that when you see the wrong people, smile at them, but keep it moving. Give them a pound, share a joke, chat for a second, but don't hang around. Because if you don't keep it moving, eventually they're going to bring you down with them. So if you're not one of them, then you don't belong around them. I'm not trying to be dramatic, but where I come from, if you hang out with a murderer, eventually you'll catch a body too. It's that deep. Thankfully, the opposite is true as well. If you take the time to find the positive, giving people in your community (and they are there), then you'll lead a positive life that's full of gifts.

Now, I know when I talk about gangs and murderers, it might seem like I'm only addressing people growing up in a certain environment. But avoiding the wrong people is important for everyone. Maybe you're a fifty-five-year-old executive living in Connecticut with a great job and happy family. But you've struggled with drinking in the past. As long as you've stayed around positive people who aren't interested in partying, you've been fine. But one day you start to hang out with a crowd that likes to drink, and suddenly you find yourself getting twisted again. You have to know that those are the Wrong People for you. And you have to distance yourself from them. I always say that Jesus can hang with the wine bibbers, but I can't. I know that I'm in a good place in my life right now, but if I started hanging out with the wine bibbers every night, I'd have problems. Those wine bibbers might not be bad people, but they would be the Wrong People for me.

One of my favorite quotes is "A man's strength is to know his weakness." We all have weakness. Again, no one is perfect. That's why if you sense that certain people might affect your quest to become a better person, then you really have to get away from them. If they're doing things you don't want to do, on a regular basis, then you must move away from them. If you can't weigh their investment in the world as better than the one you already have, then it's time to move in a different direction.

Now, I freely admit that saying "Don't hang out with criminals" if you want to stay out of jail, or "Don't hang out with drinkers" if you have an alcohol problem is very elementary stuff. Still, it has to be said. Because as obvious as this advice is, most people still can't follow it in their own lives. That's why I hope that through my repeating it here, it might finally ring a bell for someone who feels like his life is out of control.

RECOGNIZE THE REAL:

People call me a shot caller, but I'm really a shot sharer. I see myself as more of a collaborator than a boss.

No matter how many times something doesn't go your way never give up. That's because success is a journey, not a destination.

LAW NUMBER SEVEN:

THERE ARE NO FAILURES, ONLY QUITTERS

There is something good in all seeming failures. You are not to see that now. Time will reveal it. Be patient.
—SRI SWAMI SATCHIDANANDA

IN OVER TWENTY-FIVE YEARS of riding out the highs and the lows of the entertainment business, I've learned a lot of important strategies for success. But I can honestly say that few of them are as important as the law that teaches There Are No Failures, Only Quitters. That's because no matter what path you decide to follow in life, you're going to run into obstacles. It's inevitable. So while it's great to Start Today, Do You, Never Give Less Than Your Best, and Surround Yourself With the Right People, following those laws becomes pointless if you're going to quit every time you suffer what you perceive to be a setback.

When it comes to courting success, I consider a "never-say-die attitude" to be more valuable than wealth, connections, or sometimes even talent. In fact, so many of my competitors were smarter than I am and had greater resources, but only got halfway down the road before they quit after the first time they stumbled. Any one of them could have been more successful than me if they had just kept pushing toward the finish line. Some people who are the least talented, but are the harder workers and the more resilient, end up with the most success. I oughta know, because I'm definitely one of them.

The reason most people fail to reach the finish line is because they confuse a setback with a failure. If there's one thing I want to get across in this chapter, it's that a setback isn't a dead end: a setback is just a learning *curve* on your journey to success. In fact, setbacks can actually speed up your journey toward success if you pay attention to them. If something doesn't work for you, you haven't failed—you've just learned what *not to do* the next time.

So many times in my career, I've suffered setbacks that the world would describe as "failures." When Def Jam was $17 million in debt, I'm sure some people wrote me off as a "failure." Just as when Phat Farm lost $9 million over its first five years, plenty of people said I was a failure in the fashion game too. Still, no matter how much money I was down, or no matter how much salt people were trying to throw in my game, I never, ever quit, though at times I was tempted. No matter how bad things seemed to be, I managed to remember to remember that the only way I could actually *fail* was by *quitting*.

It's also important to understand that a lot of times the world doesn't put rocks in our way. Instead, we often put them there ourselves. When we hold on to our mistakes, we're throwing rocks in our own path. When we allow our minds to fill up with fear and worry, that's just more rocks we're going to have to get around. But when we detach ourselves from worry and let go of our mistakes, the road always opens up. That's why if you want to make a commitment to never quitting, one of the first steps is to simply get out of your own way.

I suspect that out of all the chapters in this book, this is the one that will connect most deeply with the hip-hop nation. That's because if you're part of hip-hop, then you were already built not to quit. You're the product of a culture that only exists today because it refused to quit in the face of tremendous adversity twenty-five years ago. The pioneers who created hip-hop never gave up, so there's no reason you should ever give up either. The struggles you'll face might be different than they were twenty-five years ago, but as long as you never quit, you'll overcome them too.

BE RESILIENT

As I said, resilience is one of the most valuable characteristics you can develop in life. Faith, dedication, compassion, and hard work are *good*. But resilience is what makes them *great*. That's because no matter how hard you're working, or no matter how great your faith is, at some point you're going to hit a wall. Whether you lead a successful life or not depends on how you deal with that wall. When you're face-to-face with a wall, do you get intimidated and turn around? Or do you pound away at the wall until it finally falls down? A quitter goes home with his tail between his legs. The successful person is going to go through the wall, over it, around it, under it—whatever it takes to continue on his journey.

I want to make an important distinction here: Hitting a wall doesn't make you a failure. Running into a wall is simply part of the human experience. You only fail when you quit and go home. Similarly, running into a wall is not a mistake either. You can only make a mistake if you keep running into the same wall. That's why, to me, mistakes are really opportunities. If your fashion line is $9 million in the red, you don't look at starting that line as a mistake. You look at it as an opportunity to learn how not to spend the next $9 million. Mistakes only cost you when you don't acknowledge them. But when you pay attention to your missteps, you can *always* learn more from things that people would call a mistake than you do from what people call success.

In the last chapter, we talked about finding a rabbi in a new industry. In this chapter, I also want to encourage you to view your own experiences, both good and bad, as your teachers. See the struggle as your rabbi too. Understand that you learn more from the rocks than you do from the smooth path. What the world calls a "failure" is really your teacher. Every time you "fail," accept what happened. Then, instead of getting emotional about it, or blaming someone else, try to analyze it and understand what you might have done wrong. It might be hard at the time, but learning from your "failures" can be a very effective tool in life. Most people don't analyze their success. Instead, they get so caught up in celebrating it that they never have a clear understanding of what made them successful in the first place. So, ironically, they often have a very difficult time duplicating that success. But when you really take the time to accept your mistakes, the lessons you learn from them will last you a lifetime. That's why someone who builds her career on so called failures will often be more successful in the long run than the "overnight success." Or, as Soichiro Honda, the founder of Honda motors, put it, "Success is ninety-nine percent failure."

Everywhere you look, there are examples of incredibly successful people who've failed at something the first time they tried it. Of course by now you know that Michael Jordan got cut from his high school basketball team as a freshman. But did you know that Abraham Lincoln lost the first time he ever ran for office? In fact, he didn't just lose, he placed eighth out of thirteen candidates for state legislator in Illinois. Or did you know exactly one thousand people turned Colonel Sanders down before he finally found a financial backer for his Kentucky Fried Chicken restaurant? Now, if he had come to me, it would have been a thousand and one people, because I don't like the way KFC treats its chickens. But you get the point. Most people would give up after getting turned down ten times, let alone one thousand. But Colonel Sanders believed in his vision and didn't care how many times he heard no. Just like Michael Jordan didn't give up on basketball, or Abraham Lincoln didn't give up on politics. They didn't look at themselves as failures when they got turned down. They just looked at those rejections as another obstacle they had to overcome. I'll say it one more time (at least): Always listen to your dream, not the negativity people will put in your ear. Don't let them talk you into failure.

Smash the Rocks

In *Autobiography of a Yogi,* there are so many inspiring moments from Yogananda's life, but the one I want to share here is the story of one of his students who was trying to dig a well in the backyard of his Ashram, or religious school. If I remember the story correctly, the student started digging a hole until he hit a rock, at which point he stopped and started digging another hole. Once again he hit some rocks and once again, he started a new hole. Finally, he decided to keep digging in the same hole even though he hit some rocks again. Sure enough, that time he almost immediately broke through the rocks and found the water he was looking for. After the well was completed, Yogananda called all his students over and said, "That is the way to find God. Keep on digging and digging, never worrying how far you have come. Then suddenly, one day, you will find yourself *there.*" That's really so true—you're only going to find success, or happiness, or, most importantly, God, if you keep digging. To keep digging is everyone's job in life.

For Yogananda's student, the challenge was breaking through the rocks to build a well. For you, instead of actual rocks, maybe your job is to break through what you perceive to be a "glass ceiling" at your job. Whatever your challenge is, you can't let it defeat you. Please don't tell me you quit your job, or you can't get ahead at your job, because of a glass ceiling. Fuck a glass ceiling! If you think there's a glass ceiling holding you back, then you're a slave. Because we know that glass breaks very easily. Shatter that glass, brush off the shards, and get on with your vision. No obstacle is too severe for you to overcome it. Nobody reading this book is going to starve. In fact, most people reading this book are probably doing so in a climate-controlled setting. So if you ain't starving and you got heat or air conditioning, then you're already doing OK. You just have to understand that you *can* do better as long as you *don't* give up. You can make it from the ghetto to the head of the boardroom if that's where you want to go. No piece of glass can stop you. Just like you can make it from the ghetto to the silver screen or even from the ghetto to the White House. No matter where you want to go, as long as you follow your path with faith, dedication, and hard work, you *are* going to get there.

And try to have fun with the obstacles. After all, challenging obstacles are what make video games fun. Movies are interesting because of drama, which is another form of obstacles. Stop thinking of life as a series of pitfalls and try to start thinking of it as a roller coaster instead. It might it have its bumps, its freefalls, and scary moments, but in the end, everything is already in order. Everything is just the way God planned it.

Finally, it's so unrealistic to think that there won't be obstacles in your path. Like it or not, God will test you. Remember that God tested Jesus, just like he tested Lord Buddha and Abraham and so many other miracle workers. What makes you think he's not going to test you too? You're not going to just waltz through life. No one has yet, and you're not going to be the first. You're going to stumble, fall, and scrape your knee time and time again just like the rest of us. So the sooner that you accept that life is the process, the sooner you'll be able to accept all the beautiful things that life has to offer too. I'll say it one more time: You're never a failure until you're a quitter. You've got to understand that the rocks are just speed bumps. They might slow you down, but they should never stop you.

You Can't Go "Too Hard"

I also want to emphasize that even when you seem to have "made it," you're still going to run into the rocks. No matter how large the checks get, no matter how big the houses become, the rocks will never, ever go away. They certainly didn't go away the first time I found a little success. I've talked a lot already about the struggles I faced with companies like Def Jam and Phat Farm, so I want to use another, more recent venture here as an example of why you can't just start resilient, but you have to stay resilient too.

I had a tremendously difficult time getting MTV to pick up *Run's House,* the reality show starring my brother and his family. Initially, I thought it would be an easy pitch. I had a strong track record on television with shows like *Def Comedy* and *Def Poetry* under my belt, plus I had recruited a very strong team, including Puffy, Stan Lathan, and Will Griffin, to produce the show. And most importantly, I knew the show would be an inspiration to America. I knew in my heart that *Run's House* was the rare show that could uplift *and* entertain people.

Unfortunately, MTV didn't see it that way. They were used to reality shows that glorified drama, drugs, and dysfunction. *Run's House* was just the opposite. Instead of dysfunction, it was all about a family functioning under God's laws. There was drama—all families go through it—but Run's was more subtle. And it was always resolved by people trying to lift each other up, instead of trying to tear each other down. Unfortunately, the themes that drove *Run's House* were just not part of MTV's consciousness or experiences. And because of that, they had real difficulty seeing my vision. With the exception of Tony DiSanto, who was our on-set producer, I felt the people at the network were never plugged into what I had envisioned for the show.

Now, when MTV's difficulties became clear to us, we had a decision to make. We could either say, "Well, we gave the show a good shot, but there's just not a space for it right now." Or we could continue to fight for the show even harder. Obviously, I pushed for the second option. We could have taken *Run's House* to another network, but I knew that ultimately MTV was the best home for it. And I was willing to fight for that fit. In fact, I really went on the offensive and started calling everyone I knew at MTV to speak on behalf of the show. I called Judy McGrath, the head of the network, so many times she was probably afraid to pick up the phone when she heard I was on the other line. I think

I called everyone in that building at least ten times, begging anyone who would talk to me to reconsider their position on *Run's House*. I even called Tom Preston, who was the head of Viacom at that time. Tom was running like fifty channels and probably didn't even know what the hell I was talking about, but I called him too. And if that wasn't bad enough, then I called his wife, Kathy, and pleaded my case with her, too, even though she had absolutely no connection to the deal. But it didn't stop me from trying to convince her! And when there were no phone calls left for me to make, I went to meetings at MTV and screamed at the executives for not realizing the mistake they were making. And I'm sure those executives were shocked at how irate I was in those meetings.

It finally got to the point where my own partners started getting pissed at me. They began saying, "Russell, you're going too hard. What's wrong with you?" After all, Puffy and Stan do a lot of business with MTV and they don't need me running around yelling at people, burning down all the bridges they've worked so hard to build up. I understood their position, but also told them I couldn't hold back. I simply had too much faith in the show.

Ultimately the collective pressure from the phone calls and e-mails and notes built up to the point where the network started to figure that maybe I *was* onto something. They finally gave the show a shot and people responded immediately. It had one of the highest debuts in MTV history and as I'm writing this, the second season has just finished, with another season on the way. And that's very inspiring for me, because when you watch *Run's House*, instead of getting to see a family that's worse than yours, you actually get to see a family you might want to pattern your own after.

Some people were incredulous when they heard how hard I was pushing for *Run's House*. Their attitude was "Man, you're Russell Simmons. You don't have to work this hard for a TV show. Let it go." But the only reason I'm "Russell Simmons" is because I'm willing to be so persistent in fighting for a concept I believe in. Which is not to say that I sometimes wish there weren't fewer obstacles. I didn't enjoy harassing my friends. I didn't enjoy going into meetings and yelling at people. I didn't want to become so passionate that I was making my business associates uncomfortable. But I've also been in the game long enough to understand that most of the time, that's what it takes. Whenever you do something even halfway original, you're going to have to get your hands dirty to get that idea made. No matter how many "hits" you have under your belt. Even though *Def Comedy* was a smash, people still said *Def Poetry* was a dumb idea. And even after my instincts for *Def Poetry* turned out to be right, people still told me that my instincts for *Run's House* were wrong—they said that no one wanted to watch God on Thursday nights. And now that *Run's House* is one of the biggest hits on MTV, I'm sure someone will tell me my next project is doomed to failure too. It never ends. That's why you must accept that from throwing little pebbles to pushing big boulders, people are always going to try to inject their negativity in your path.

I've accepted it, so I know that there's never going to be a moment where I can lean back, put my feet up on the desk, and say, "Man, that was a good ride. I think I'm done." No, whether it's because someone's trying to force you or because you think you've done enough, you can Never Quit. When you step into the box, then it's OK to quit. Until then, you keep working. If I go around saying I'm a philanthropist and that I'm dedicated to fighting poverty and uplifting poor people, then that's a lifetime commitment. I can't write a few checks and then just decide that my job is done. I have to accept that being a philanthropist and an activist for poor people is going to be my job until I take my last breath. Just like if you're truly committed to practicing the law, there's always going to be more law to study. If you're a committed doctor, there's always another sick person to help, always more cures to learn. A *doctor* might retire. But a great *healer* is going to keep helping people until it's time for her to check out herself. Whatever you want to do in life, if you want to do it right, you can never quit working at it. Life is a practice. So be happy with your practice and never quit it.

Get Out of Your Own Way

So far, we've been talking about why it's important not to quit because of other people's negativity. Now I want to focus on why you should never quit because of your own negativity. That's really the essence of this chapter. We might point a finger at the world, or at other people, when we give up, but we should really be pointing at ourselves. That's because rather than uplifting ourselves with faith and confidence, instead we burden ourselves with worry and anxiety and guilt. So that when we do face one of those inevitable obstacles, we already feel so weighed down that the idea of pushing on seems impossible. But if you can learn to lose that weight by detaching yourself from pointless emotions like fear and worry, you'll see that you *do* have the stamina and strength and resilience to overcome whatever is in your path. You just have to get out of your own way to realize it.

The biggest thing that separates you from the success that you seek is *fear*. Not a lack of money, or a lack of opportunity, or even a lack of talent, but an abundance of *fear*. I keep saying that word because it's so important we address fear head on. If you don't address it, it will keep you off your mark your entire life. Because, as it says in the *Bhagavad Gita*: "The doubter is the most miserable of mortals."

While there are countless things we think we're afraid to fail at, the truth is we're all really only afraid of one thing—and that's dying. The fear of death is the most fundamental kind of fear, the fear that motivates most people's decision to quit. In yoga, the fear of death, or "Abhinivesha," is one of the five "Kleshas," or obstacles to human liberation. And that's the point—the fear of dying is really just another obstacle. And of course the irony is that there's really nothing to be afraid of, since no matter how hard we fight it, or try to avoid death, we're all going to die anyway. I'm going to die, everyone reading this book is going to die, and everyone we know is going to die. Sorry, but that's the truth. It's almost illogical to waste the time you've been blessed with to live worrying about dying. I don't want to seem morbid, but it's true: Death is inevitable. Or, as the ancient Buddhist scripture *The Dhammapad* puts it, "Not in the sky, not in the midst of the sea, not even in the clefts of the mountain, is there a spot in the whole world where, if a man abide there, death could not overtake him."

Obviously I'm in no rush to die. I want to ride this wave as long as I can, not even for my own enjoyment, but so that I can use my resources to help other people ride it with me. I've got some more work to do and I don't think God is ready for me to finish just yet. However, if I knew my time was up tomorrow, I can honestly say I wouldn't be afraid tonight. Not because I have such control over my emotions, but because I believe in the cycle of life, that our bodies are just a temporary home. For example, my father passed while I was writing this book, and although I love and miss him immensely, his death didn't rock me the same way that my mother's did years ago. Not because I loved him a drop less than my mother, but because I like to think that now I'm a little farther along in my spiritual development. I understand that while my father might have left his physical frame, his spiritual essence is alive and well. I wanted to explain this concept to my daughters before his funeral, so I encouraged them to think of their grandfather as a butterfly. Butterflies start as caterpillars, but after they go into their cocoons, they emerge with an entirely new body. Butterflies still have the same soul they had when they were caterpillars, just with a beautiful new frame to carry it in. So I told my daughters that while at that moment their grandfather's soul might be in a cocoon, very soon it was going to reemerge as a butterfly. I realize that's not a concept that everyone is ready to invest in, but it's helped me, and I hope it helped my daughters too. To quote the *Bhagavad Gita* again, "These bodies are perishable: but the dwellers in these bodies are eternal, indestructible, and impenetrable."

I don't want to get too sidetracked about reincarnation here, since I'm mainly interested in talking about it here as it pertains to freeing yourself from fear. But I'll end this segment by suggesting that if the concept of reincarnation feels strange or foreign to you, consider that it's a concept found in many religions, including Christianity. We all know that according to the Bible, Christ himself rose from the dead. But did you also know that Christ mentioned several times that John the Baptist was the prophet Elijah in a previous life? Or that the Christian church didn't ban the doctrine of reincarnation until 553 A.D.? Probably not. So before you write off the concept of the cycle of life, understand that it might be closer to your spiritual tradition than you've ever realized. And again, I'm not trying to put any heavy weight on you. This isn't the Catholic Church here. This ain't any of that "believe this or else" shit. This is just my way of promoting what seems to be an easier path through life.

Don't Hold On to Your Mistakes

By now you're probably wondering what butterflies and funerals have to do with this law, but I promise there's a connection. You see, when you're afraid of death, you live your entire life trying not to die. That fear becomes an excuse for you to not take risks, to embrace the mundane instead of pursuing your passions. That might seem like a safe way to live, but it's rarely a successful one. Conversely, when you detach yourself from the weight of your fears, you'll find that you'll be able to soar to much greater heights.

The concept of detachment is something I've instinctively felt for much of my life, but I really wasn't able to articulate it until I read *The Seven Spiritual Laws of Success*. In particular, I was inspired where Chopra writes, "in order to acquire anything in the physical universe, you have to relinquish your attachment to it. This doesn't mean that you give up the intention to create your desire. You don't give up the intention and you don't give up the desire. You give up your attachment to the results." As you can see, that's something we've already talked about in this book, but it's particularly relevant to this section. That's because you're only going to be tempted to quit when you're attached to the result of your effort. Or, to take it one step further, when you're attached to your physical self instead of your spiritual. That's why I believe that the more you can detach yourself from your fear of failure, the more freedom you'll have to realize your dreams.

Similarly, don't waste energy by holding on to your so-called mistakes. If you make what seems to be a mistake, say "my bad" and move on. Don't stay attached to what's already happened. Instead, eliminate that fear by letting go of your past and focusing on what needs to be done now. Trust me, it actually feels good to admit you've been wrong about something. Sitting in front of a group of people and actually saying, "Sorry, but I fucked up," is surprisingly easy (though you definitely don't want to get into the habit of doing it). Admitting that you were wrong isn't only easy, it's actually fun. It dissolves all the tension and lets you focus on your next move. What's hard is sitting in front of those same people and trying to convince them that you didn't fuck up when you and they both know that you did.

Another emotion that is very important to detach yourself from is guilt. Now, when I say don't feel guilty, I don't mean it's OK for you to go out there and harm someone else, or steal from someone without feeling any regret. When we discuss the concept of Karma in greater depth, you'll see why you should always avoid doing *anything* that is harmful. Instead, I'm encouraging you not to feel guilty about the honest mistakes you make in life. Just as many people give up because they're afraid of the results, an equal number quit because they feel guilty about their mistakes. Don't fall into that trap either. Again, understand that life is a process and you're never going to get things right all of the time. There are going to be moments where you slip up, just as there are going to be moments when you make real progress. The key is to accept this process.

I'll give you a little example of what I'm talking about. A few years ago, I was hanging out in the East Village with Glen Friedman. We were walking down the street when all of a sudden I was overcome by a desire to have a slice of pizza. That might seem like a perfectly harmless desire to most people, but as a fellow vegan (in fact, the person who turned me on to the vegan lifestyle, more about that later) Glen told me not to give in to the desire. He reminded me that pizza contains dairy, and that as a vegan I had committed to avoiding any animal products, period.

But the smell coming from the pizzeria was so good that I was having a hard time resisting. Besides, how was one little slice of pizza going to hurt anyone? So over Glen's objections, I went in and grabbed a slice. When I came outside, I had taken about two bites when some young guy with dreads rolled by on his skateboard. He looked at the slice in my hand and then said mockingly, and with obvious disappointment, "What are you doing eating that pizza, man? I thought you were a vegan!"

I mumbled some dumb shit in reply, but suddenly the pizza didn't taste so good to me anymore. I threw it out and we went on our way. But for the rest of the day, I had a hard time forgetting that guy's reaction. You see, promoting nonharmful foods, especially to young people, is something I take very seriously. While it wasn't like he had caught me eating some steak and lobster, it was clear that he was hurt by the sight of that slice in my hand—instead of seeing me as an inspiration, he saw me as a hypocrite. Maybe he had thought about being vegan, but now that he had seen me breaking the rules, he wouldn't feel obligated to follow them so closely himself. Admittedly, the idea of me worrying about a slice of pizza might sound stupid to you, but to think that I had potentially turned someone away from a more rewarding lifestyle really did make me feel like a failure. I was down on myself at first, but the more I thought about it, I realized I had to detach myself from that guilt. Because if I kept feeling guilty, eventually I'd just say, "Man, I've failed as a vegan" and I would have gone home and eaten a bag of White Castle. Of course, that wouldn't have done anything but set me back further than my alleged failure had.

That's why it's very important to accept that none of us are perfect. We can strive for perfection, or admire that attribute in figures like Jesus or Lord Buddha, but we can't become discouraged if we don't achieve it in our own lives. It's great if you're inspired by a religion or a philosophy or a particular lifestyle. But it's not great if you become obsessed with being the "perfect" Christian, or the "perfect" yogi or the "perfect" spouse. Because chances are you're going to make mistakes. You're going to fall down and find yourself very far from perfection. So instead of being so focused on living such a rigid life, give yourself a little room to breathe. As much as we sometimes want to paint it this way, the world is not black and white. It's OK if sometimes you find yourself in that gray area. Just stay focused on getting back to where you ultimately want to be.

Every year, between my birthday in October and New Year's, I give myself what I call "a holiday period." For three months, I try not to judge myself quite as harshly as I might during the rest of the year. During my "holiday," I might have a drink or smoke a cigarette or sneak a bite of fish or stay out too late at a party, even though I know those actions aren't contributing to how I ultimately want to live my life. But by giving myself that "break," I've found it relieves some of the pressure I might feel during the rest of the year every time I turn down a drink, or don't order the fish, or leave a party early. So while I might not always be a perfect yogi, or a perfect vegan, or a perfect father, I try not to feel guilty or anxious about the slipups I have during my "holiday," or frankly, the slipups I have during the rest of the year too. I've learned that there's no value in an emotion like guilt. It's like empty carbs. They might seem to fill you up at the moment, but in the end they're only going to slow you down.

Rejecting *No*

Detaching yourself from guilt and anxiety is way to break free from the chains that you've been holding *yourself* back with. The world didn't put those chains on you. *You* did. However, once you have won this "battle with yourself," you still need to be resilient in your dealing with the world. That's why now I want to address another phenomenon that causes many people to quit: hearing the word *no*.

If you are looking for a new job, or backing for a new venture, and hear no from nine people, still ask the tenth person anyway. And if they say no, then go back and ask the first person again. Because even if someone tells you no, they might not really mean it. They just might require more convincing. Or they might be testing you to see how much you believe in your idea. Whatever you do, don't get defensive. Embrace their rejection and instead of walking away in a huff, or slinking away because you're embarrassed, stand your ground and then politely, and without a trace of bitterness, ask them what made them say no. When you do that, several positive things can happen. Maybe you'll call their bluff. Or maybe through their answer you can get some insight into what will make them say yes. Listen closely to what they tell you—you may have a winner that they just don't understand, and their insight might actually make it a bigger winner down the road. By articulating what they don't understand, or don't like, they're actually helping you fill in the gaps. Another benefit of accepting their critique and then working on it is that when you come back to them the next time, you won't be giving them the same idea in the same way. Most importantly, never be self-conscious about being persistent. Because a real leader will see your persistence as a strength, not as a weakness.

I certainly appreciate it when people are persistent with me. There might be someone out there who I legitimately want to speak with, but I haven't gotten around to it because my schedule is so hectic. If that person is persistent in calling me, eventually we'll make it happen. But if she calls me once and then gives up when she doesn't hear back from me, then we'll never get started. And that would be a loss for both of us. But whatever the reason, I'm not going to hold your persistence against you. Because I know that being persistent, and not passive, is what made my own dreams come true.

The art is to be persistent without being a pest. A good way to be persistent is calling or e-mailing a person. You don't have to make it a big pitch, all you need to say is "I'm just checking in and wanted to make sure you didn't forget about me. Because I'm ready to serve." That's such an effective way to stay on someone's radar. If you do that once every couple of weeks, without seeming whiny or defensive, I promise eventually that person will not only get back to you but will also be impressed with your persistence.

Conversely, bugging someone day in and day out won't make him change his mind. If anything, being a pest will just make him become biased against your idea. Be persistent in looking for a different answer, but only when you have something new to share. If someone tells you no, don't come back the next day and ask if that's still the answer. Instead, go away for a while, put in the work that will make your idea stand out in a new way, and then come back looking for a yes. The person who does that is being persistent. The person who looks for a new answer without putting in the work is a pest.

Let's say you want to pitch me on a business venture. Chances are I might listen to you for a minute, but my normal response will most likely be no. It's nothing personal, it's just that I get approached dozens of times every week, so it's going to be very difficult for your pitch to stand out and really grab my attention. So how do you get me to change that answer? Well, the first step is not to walk up to me the next day with the identical pitch (believe it or not, a lot of people do that). For me, that's the equivalent of quitting. Instead, go to work on a new pitch. If I had financial concerns about your idea, don't come back until you have ten money backers. If it seemed I thought your pitch was unorganized, don't come back until you have the entire pitch clearly articulated. If you were trying to pitch me verbally the first time, come back the second time with a business plan on paper. If I didn't seem excited about your designs, don't come back until you have some new ones. Do all of that, plus take the thousands of other little steps you need to take to make your idea better. And *then* come back to me. And when you hand your typed-out business plan to me that second time, tell me, "Before I was pitching an idea. Now I'm bringing you property and it's worth money and I own it. So are you interested now?" And if you really do take all those steps, chances are the second time around I'm going to say yes.

But you're only going to have the confidence to come back that second time if you realize my first rejection was only a test. You have to see every so-called failure as a test of your resilience. Just like you must accept that the universe is always going to say no at first when you come up with a new idea. That's why your job is always to make the universe say yes.

CAN'T STOP, WON'T STOP

I want to end this chapter by talking more about hip-hop, since I feel much of the culture's success is due to its resilience. It's almost as if hip-hop has a "don't quit" mentality burned into its collective DNA. Obviously I'm a little biased, but I don't think

I'm overstating the case here. Hip-hop *had* to have a resilient attitude because so much of the culture has come, and continues to come, out of the struggle. In fact, just recently someone asked me how hip-hop has changed over the last twenty-five years. I replied that only the faces have changed—otherwise hip-hop's heart is still where it started, in the struggle. If there's a slight difference, it's that now hip-hop is pulling people out of the struggle on a global scale. Whereas before it was lifting kids up in Brooklyn, Queens, and Philly, now it's uplifting young people in England, Japan, and Pakistan too.

It's so inspiring how hip-hop has prospered despite having so many obstacles put in its path. From the very first day some kid in The Bronx picked up a mike and started to spit rhymes, the world has been telling hip-hop no. Whether it was the cops, the radio stations, the record labels, or even other artists, the first thing so many rappers heard was no. That's why we have to celebrate the persistence of people like DJ Kool Herc, Eddie Cheeba, Grandmaster Caz, Kurtis Blow, and so many other pioneers. These people refused to quit because they knew hip-hop was their best opportunity to share their struggle with the world.

I know I've already talked about hip-hop's struggles, but I can't help but do it again, since we're addressing the Law of No Failures, Only Quitters. Not to make light of the struggles people face today, but so many rappers out there have no idea how many barriers have already been torn down for them. Today, a lot of rappers become frustrated if they can't get their song on the radio, or their video on TV. They see other rappers getting exposure, so they ask, "Why not me?" But you must understand, for many years, stations weren't playing any hip-hop, *period*. It wasn't like the next man was getting his shine on while you were getting shut out. No one in hip-hop was getting a real opportunity. I remember when Run DMC finally got on MTV, the only other black person they were playing was Michael Jackson. And he was only OK because that was when he had a broken nose and straightened hair. I had to *beg*

MTV to play "Rock Box," and they still were very resistant. And remember, we're talking about a video that had rock 'n' roll guitars and little white kids running around in it. Jam Master Jay, God rest his soul, even winked at the little white kid in the video! We did everything we could (without compromising our basic vision) to make that video palatable for MTV, and they still weren't interested for a very long time. To say nothing of the fact that BET *never* played that video.

Today, the tables have turned and it's the stations doing the begging. They're begging to premiere Kanye West's new video, or to be the first station to go behind the scenes on the set of Beyoncé's new movie. Now there are countless outlets for hip-hop videos, hip-hop songs, TV shows and vehicles that promote the culture. But that's only possible because the pioneers refused to quit back in the day. They kept spitting rhymes whether MTV was interested or not. It would have been easy to say, "Well, we better stop rhyming because stations aren't going to play rap. Let's start an R&B group instead." But they didn't say that. They kept fighting so that you can enjoy hip-hop today.

When I talk about the obstacles faced by the pioneers, I'm not trying to take anything away from today's artists, or to suggest that rappers worked harder back then. I'm just trying to remind today's artists of their past, so that they never forget what their culture is capable of. In fact, I actually think many of the artists today are just as resilient, and just as allergic to quitting, as those pioneers were twenty-five years ago. From Ludacris to Jay-Z to TI to 50 Cent, so many of today's hot rappers faced obstacles early in their careers. Jay or 50 most certainly didn't hear yes the first time they tried to get a record deal. In fact, they heard no so many times that they decided to release records on their own rather than let the industry's ignorance force them onto another path in life. But they never gave up. Because they understood success isn't going to happen overnight.

If you want a great example of a "don't quit" attitude in hip-hop, then you don't need to look any further than Sean "Puffy" Combs. Puff has a lot of powerful attributes that have propelled him to success, like creativity, vision, passion, energy, and charisma. But I think the one quality that has really separated him from the pack is his refusal to ever give up. When Puff says, "Can't stop, won't stop," he really means it. And he's been like that from the day I first met him, which must have been back in the early nineties. I feel like I've told this story a thousand times, but I'll tell it one more time because it is such a tangible example of his persistence. I was in a gym, working out on a StairMaster when Puffy walked in with Andre Harrell. I had never met him before, but within a few minutes, Puff was talking trash about how he could stay on a Stair-Master longer than I could, even though he'd never tried one before. I was working out on them all the time and knew how hard they were, so I agreed to a bet on who could stay on the longest. If I won, he owed me fifty dollars. If he won, I'd give him seven hundred dollars he said he needed to fix his Volkswagen. Well, Puff's Volkswagen must have been in pretty bad shape, because he stayed on that StairMaster for an hour and a half to make sure he beat me. Most people would have quit long before that, but not Puff. He was going to stay on that StairMaster until he was sure he had won his bet. It's a small example, but to me it exemplifies his resilience.

I really love persistence in a person, sometimes even more so than talent. I think that's why I probably feel so strongly about Jinx, who I was talking about in the last chapter. Jinx certainly has plenty of talent, but what I really love about him is his resilient nature. His career hasn't progressed as quickly as he might have liked, but the setbacks haven't slowed Jinx down a bit. Every day he finds time to be in the studio making music, and every night, he's still standing outside of the radio stations in New York, trying to get a Funkmaster Flex or a DJ Clue to play his songs. Every night like clockwork, he's out there promoting himself, looking for an opportunity. A lot of people wouldn't do that, especially people who already had a deal but never saw it go anywhere. They would probably just blame the label, or blame their management, and then give up. But not Jinx. Whether he has a deal or not, he's going to keep pushing his music. And I really believe it will work out for him as an artist. But even if it doesn't, even if he never gets a hit single, or never sees himself on TV, he's still going to be fine. Because by refusing to quit, he's kept moving forward in life. I know that even if he doesn't make his first million as a rapper, he might make even more than that as the creative director of one of my companies. Because the world always rewards people who don't quit. That's why I encourage Jinx to remember Yogananda's story. As long as you keep digging at the same hole and refuse to quit, you will be rewarded. What you find at the bottom of that hole might not always be what you were looking for when you started digging, but it will be something worthwhile and useful. However, if you stop digging every time you hit the rocks and start another hole, then you're only going to be rewarded with more rocks.

RECOGNIZE THE REAL:

Success takes time. Young people need to know that nothing's going to happen on your timetable. There are going to be unforeseen disappointments. That's why you need to take a steady approach to entrepreneurship.

None of this is luck. The world is a science, and God will only show the results that you deserve.

LAW NUMBER EIGHT:

THE SCIENCE OF SUCCESS: PLANT THE GOOD SEEDS

When we do wrong, we come to suffering. When we do good in the world, we come to happiness.
—BHAGAVAD GITA

IF YOU PLANT GOOD, healthy seeds in the world, the world will give you a good, healthy harvest in return. I know that sounds very elementary, but so many of us still live our lives wondering why some people "make it" and others seem caught in a perpetual struggle. What I hope to explain in this chapter is that there's really nothing to wonder about. The science is simple: When you give the world love and respect, the world will give you love and respect back. When you give the world negativity and contempt, the world is going to return that negativity to you. Granted, it's very a simple science, but that doesn't discount that it's a science that is applicable to everything you do. Remember, there is a direct connection between what you put into the world and the level of success you achieve in your personal or professional life.

Again, I'm not suggesting that this science is radically different from what you've probably already been taught. Every religion and culture around the globe teaches a version of this law. I like to call it the law of "Karma," which is a Hindu term meaning "cause and effect." Others describe it by saying, "You reap what you sow." Or maybe you've heard it described as "What goes around comes around." It's truly a universal concept. That's why no matter what you look like, where you live, or what flag you stand under, this law applies to you—you're only going to get out of the world what you put into it.

If there's a difference between yoga and other traditions, it's that in Karma the results from your actions aren't just limited to this lifetime—rather, they will follow you from one lifetime to another until you finally "get it right." Each time you give the world a negative or harmful action, you're planting the seeds of bad Karma. Conversely, every time you do something good or helpful, you're burning away one of those seeds with your good Karma. As long as you're planting bad seeds, you'll never become fully in union with God. And that's going to be true for not only this lifetime, but a thousand lifetimes, or a million lifetimes, however long it takes until you do burn all that negativity away.

I do want to try to clear up one misconception I sometimes encounter when I talk with people about this concept. In their eyes, the logical extension of bad Karma is that we are responsible for the bad things that happen to us in life. In other words, if we get cancer, it's because we've sowed so many bad seeds. Or if a loved one is killed in a tragedy, it's because of those bad seeds too. But I don't believe that's the case. Bad Karma might stand in the way of your enlightenment, but it's not going to bring down punishment on you. If you get cancer, it's not because of bad Karma, but because you caught cancer. Just as Martin Luther King, Jr., didn't get shot because he was an evil person. He got shot because someone else was evil and wanted to eliminate his positivity. Jam Master Jay wasn't gunned down because he led a selfish, greedy lifestyle. He was gunned down because he tried to live a giving, helpful lifestyle by staying in the hood and working with the people who needed his help. As Reverend Run says, when Jay passed, "He really just passed the test." In other words, he's not gone. He just moved on. We can miss Jay, but we shouldn't worry about him, because he's just fulfilling his Karma.

So try not to lose faith when you don't see an immediate response to other people's actions. People want to see the lying CEO lose all his money and go straight to jail. They want to see the person who cut them off in their car get pulled over by the cops at the next intersection. A world like that would be fun, but, sorry, success requires more faith than that. Karma follows on its own schedule and moves at its own speed. So don't worry about why the laws of Karma are not affecting other people when you think they should. It's not your job to understand anyone else's Karma. That job belongs to God, and he (or she) will get around to it when they see fit.

Instead, put all your focus on the good work you can do in this lifetime. Because we're all going to be stuck in this cycle until we finally get it straight. And once you do get it together, you'll just turn into a beam of light and enter a state of pure enlightenment. That's the state we all have to strive for.

Hopefully I'm not losing anyone here. I recognize that a lot of you probably bought this book for worldly reasons—you're looking for tips on how to start your own record label, or advice on how to multiply your money. You probably weren't looking for advice on how to turn into a beam of light. So for our purposes, I'm going to focus on Karma as it pertains to *this* lifetime. As I've said before, I understand that the concept of reincarnation might not be in step with how you view the world. However, I want to be very clear here—the language I'm using might sound different, but the concept I'm talking about directly addresses those issues. Because creating good Karma is how you're going to start that label and make it successful, just like good Karma is how you're going to keep your money tree growing. In fact, good Karma is going to be the foundation for everything positive and lasting that you're able to build in life. At the very least, Karma is the science of happiness. At the very most, it's the secret to becoming one with the universe.

In order to improve your Karma, first you have to accept that everyone in this world is connected. You might live in Brooklyn, but you're just as connected to a person living in Bel-Air—or Baghdad, for that matter—as you are to the person next door. Everything you do in this life affects someone else. Even when you breathe, you're compromising someone else's airspace. It's very tempting, especially when you're younger, to only think about how your choices will affect *you*. But that selfish, shortsighted attitude will bite you in the ass time and time again. You must understand that your actions don't only affect you, they affect *us*.

And when I say "us," I mean every creature that lives here on Mother Earth. In my book, being harmful toward a cow or a chicken is no different from being harmful to another human. I admit that not everyone else shares that belief, and a lot of people tell me, "Russell, why are you worrying about chickens when people are dying out here?" Well, my concern for our community—and for all communities—is exactly *why* I promote vegetarianism! In my heart, I know that as long as we continue to support the brutal killing and torture of animals on a massive scale, then we're never going to realize our true potential. When it comes to the obstacles facing our community, it's right up there with guns, drugs, lack of education, and racism. Yet out of all those struggles, it's by far the easiest for us to overcome. Because by simply putting down a hamburger and picking up a veggie burger, you're taking a real step toward uplifting yourself.

Like everything I promote in this book, learning how to consistently plant the good seeds is a process. Hopefully you'll start burning through your bad seeds right away, but it's probably going to take some time. That's certainly been the case in my own life. I might preach about planting good seeds, but as anyone who knows me could tell you, I'm still a very long ways from turning into that beam of light. It's going to take all of us a long time before every seed we plant is good. Just keep working toward that goal, because the more good seeds you plant, the more you'll realize how rewarding it is to pick their fruit when it's ready.

THE GOOD SEEDS

Initially, I wanted to use a term other than *Karma* in describing *The Science of Success,* since that word seems to carry a lot of baggage. To many people, *Karma* connotes Eastern mysticism, a concept that doesn't necessarily apply to our Western lifestyles. However, in the end I decided to stick with *Karma* not only because it's the term I use in my own life, but because I want people to understand that there's really nothing foreign about it at all. I might have only started using *Karma* when I got into yoga, but I realize that it's a concept that I've been familiar with my whole life.

And you're already familiar with it, too, as we've all been taught that for every action, there's going to be a reaction. Simply try to view Karma as the spiritual component of that truth. Granted, hearing that all your less-than-perfect moments are going to come back to you can seem intimidating at first. However, I feel that Sowing the Good Seeds is actually a very uplifting concept. While it's true that your bad Karma will come back to you, it's also true that you can burn away all that negative baggage through your good deeds. To put it even more bluntly, you might have fucked up yesterday, but by doing better today, you can still get closer to God tomorrow. And obviously for someone like me, who's fucked up plenty of times, that's a very appealing concept.

One of the first steps toward doing better today is accepting that you have a choice in every decision you make in life. Understand that any bad Karma you create will be by your own doing. We tend to blame other people, or the conditions we live in, for our negative acts. But that's bullshit. No matter where you live, no matter what people are saying or doing around you, you still can make the right choice every time. If someone disses you, you don't have to dis him back. If someone cheats you, that doesn't give you the right to cheat someone else. If you're broke, that doesn't give you the right to steal. There's never only one way to react to a situation.

Your ability to always make a choice can be both a gift and a curse. The gift is that when you respond to a negative situation with positivity, you lift that situation up and yourself along with it. The curse is that when you respond to a negative situation with more negativity, you just push that situation, and yourself with it, down even further. So when you choose between the positive and negative response, you're really choosing whether your life will be happy or unhappy. No one else is responsible, because only you control your actions. As Patanjali once said, "You are your own best friend as well as your own worst enemy."

There's a lot of responsibility that comes with that statement, but would you really want it any other way? Who else would you prefer control your fate? The politicians? The corporations? The preachers? Or you? The answer should be obvious. That's why I find the concept of Karma so liberating. It puts your future squarely in your own hands. Your actions will determine your future. Those actions will either move you toward that beam of light I was talking about or toward darkness. Which direction is up to you.

What Is the Right Choice?

Of course, it's easy to tell people to always make the "right choices" in life. What isn't as easy to tell them is what those right choices are. Some are obvious—we know we're not supposed to kill, rob, cheat, steal, etc.—but many are more subtle. That's why I find it's helpful to try to follow some sort of code that can guide you on which choices to make. There are certainly plenty to choose from out there. If you're a Christian or a Jew, you probably follow the Ten Commandments. If you're a Muslim, you try to live under the five pillars of Islam. If you're a Taoist, then you most likely try to follow "the Way." And I could keep going, as there's a parallel code in every other faith or philosophy as well.

Personally, I try to base my decisions on the five "Yamas," or "restrictions," as they were described by Patanjali over two thousand years ago. The five Yamas (some traditions list ten) are:

- "Ahimsa," or the abstention from harmful actions
- "Satya," the abstention from lying
- "Asteya," the abstention from theft

- "Aparigraha," the abstention from attachment to possessions
- "Brahmacharya," or the abstention from gratuitous sexual activity (my least favorite)

I really believe that if you make your decisions based on these Yamas, particularly on Ahimsa, then you'll consistently plant the good seeds that you need to reap real success. Again, the Yamas are just my way of describing a universal concept. Someone following the Ten Commandments is just as likely to plant good seeds as someone operating in accordance with the Taoist tradition, Islamic laws, or the science of yoga. But if there is one major difference between the various paths, I think it has to do with the Yama's particular definition of nonharming. To my admittedly limited knowledge, almost all spiritual practices preach the importance of human beings' not harming each other. In yoga, the practice of abstaining from harmful actions, on the other hand, takes that concept and applies it to *all* living creatures. So if you're like me and truly believe in abstaining from harmful actions, then you'll realize that one of the biggest obstacles facing our collective Karma is the way our society views eating meat.

I WON'T EAT ANYTHING THAT TRIES TO RUN AWAY FROM ME

At this point, some of you are probably saying, "Oh, no, here comes another vegetarian rap." I understand people don't like to be told what they should eat by some pushy "celebrity," so I'm going to try not to hit you too hard over the head here. The last thing I want is for you to start to tune out when we're talking about an important subject like Karma. My goal is to simply explain my own reasons for choosing to cut meat out of my diet. If that influences you to set out on a similar path, then great. If the vegetarian thing doesn't resonate with you, hey, that's fine too. Just try not to let it put any distance between you and the ultimate goal of this chapter, which is to remind you to always plant the good seeds.

Even though I don't want to be pushy with my beliefs, I can't avoid an obvious truth like that eating meat creates bad Karma. I'm not trying to criticize you if you're a meat eater, or say you're a bad person. I'm just stating the fact that once you begin to work meat out of your diet, your karma, and your success, will begin to improve right away.

My personal decision to become a vegetarian was based largely on my desire to be less harmful in my actions. I used to eat all kinds of meat—spare ribs, chicken wings, pig's feet, elephant's ass—you name it. But as I became more conscious of what I was putting into my body, I also became aware of how harmful the system we use to raise and slaughter the animals we eat in this country is. For example, consider the life of the chicken you buy in the supermarket. That chicken might come in a clean, neat package but, don't kid yourself, there was nothing clean or neat about how that chicken lived and died. That chicken came from a huge plant where it was stuffed in a cage for its entire life, living in its own shit, getting pumped up with steroids and other toxins until someone slit it throat and dropped it alive into a vat of boiling water. And unless you're killing your six-pieces yourself, that's very likely the back story every time you eat a piece of chicken. If you traced the life of that chicken backward from your plate to its birth, I suspect you'd push that six-piece away and ask for a salad instead. I know that description was intense, but, sorry, that's how it's going down. That's why I've decided I don't want my Karma promoting those sorts of actions.

Another reason I embraced vegetarianism is because I believe the meat industry is particularly harmful to poor people. I'd be a hypocrite if I spoke out about what is or isn't going into poor people's pockets, but didn't say anything about what's going into their stomachs too. The truth is that both physically and spiritually, the people in the struggle are the ones who can least afford to ingest all this negativity. If you're struggling, understand that a lot of that health care that you can't afford, *including* mental health care, is connected to your diet. So while fast food and fried chicken might be cheap on your wallet, they're going to be *very* expensive for both your health and for your Karma.

Conversely, vegetarianism really improves your health. The biggest benefit is the increased energy that you'll feel. Let's say I go out to lunch and order a veggie burger, while my friend has a big, fat greasy hamburger. After lunch, my friend is going to feel full and be fighting the urge to fall asleep. But I'm going to feel fresh, reenergized, and ready to go back to the office and do more work. You won't believe how much your energy picks up once you give up meat. You see, meat is very hard for your body to digest. Normally, it sits in your intestines for at least four days until it is digested. And when you eat a lot of meat, it can get backed up for months. All that meat, just sitting there and rotting in your digestive track, will really slow you down. But once you replace that meat with a vegetarian diet that's heavy on vegetables, grains, and soy, your energy will shoot way up. I don't want to go too far into the medical benefits of vegetarianism, but if you want to learn more, I highly recommend John Robbins' *Food Revolution* (the book that changed my thinking about what I eat) and Gary Null's *Get Healthy Now*. Both books will force you to take a long look at how eating meat is affecting your life.

Finally, I also promote vegetarianism because I believe too many of our natural resources are wasted on raising animals for the slaughter. There are still so many hungry people living in this country (not to mention the six thousand people dying every day from poverty in Africa), yet we still squander millions of valuable acres that could be used for vegetables and grains on cows instead. Why do I say those acres are being wasted? Consider this—I once read that one acre used to raise a steer will produce about a pound of protein. But an acre that's planted with soybeans will produce seventeen pounds of protein! That means growing soy, instead of raising beef, is a much more valuable use of land, not to mention healthier and less harmful. So we can talk about ending world hunger, but as long as we're supporting a system that wastes so many resources, it's only going to be talk. If we could just stop wasting all this land, water, and grain on these animals and plant some soybeans instead, we could feed the entire world and stop starvation. To me, that's a pretty good reason to stop eating hamburgers.

Those are the main reasons I'm encouraging you to consider vegetarianism. If you decide you want to try it for yourself, don't be scared—jump right into it. People will tell you that it's so hard, but it really isn't. I've heard the whole rap about how there's nothing good to eat if you're a vegetarian, but that's BS. There are plenty of soy or gluten products that will help you make the transition. You can get soy wings that taste just like chicken wings, or veggie burgers that taste just like a hamburger. But you'll find after a while that you don't even want a fake burger or fake wings. They're going to remind you of all that poison you used to eat. You'll be so happy with your new diet that you won't even want to think about, let alone eat, the types of food that were slowing you down in the past.

If you don't have a problem with eating meat, I respect that too. I'm not on some kick where I think all meat eaters deserve to have horrible things happen to them. I'm sure that many meat eaters are actually more conscious and more uplifted than I am. The only thing I would ask if you're a meat eater is that you become more conscious about the quality of the food you're putting in your body and, more importantly, putting into your children's bodies. Right now, there's a big disconnect with consumers in this country about what we eat and how that food is produced. Even if you think all this talk about Karma is bullshit, and you think eating meat is as natural as breathing air, at least be aware of what you're ingesting. I'm not asking *you* not to eat animals. I'm just asking you to know what you're ingesting.

Finally, we need to encourage the big companies to find less harmful ways to kill the animals they serve to us. That's really my fundamental message here—the suffering of animals does not have to be as intense as it currently is. If nothing else, we have to find a way that these animals can lead a productive, healthy life before they're eaten. I know these companies could kill their chickens, cows, turkeys and pigs in a humane way and still make money. KFC, or McDonald's or Burger King or Tyson's or Purdue, or any of these companies, *could* do it, but *won't* do it unless we *force* them to do it. We put billions of dollars into their pockets every year, so we have the right to demand a more humane practice. I don't think that's too much to ask.

I know vegetarianism is still a subject that makes some people uncomfortable, but learn what you can. Read *Diet for New America* and *Get Healthy Now*. If you haven't already, you should also check out Eric Schlosser's *Fast Food Nation*. Learn the facts and then make your own decisions. Because society is only going to tell you that meat tastes the best and that most vegetarians are weirdos. But society is wrong. You don't only have to listen to society. It's OK to look inside yourself and find an answer that's different from what society says. Make your own choice on this topic. And if you listen to your heart when you're making it, I'm confident you'll start a journey that will not only lead to a healthier lifestyle physically, but more importantly will help you burn through all the bad Karma you've been building up.

JUDGE NOT

Hopefully that last section didn't strike you as too severe, because I was sincere when I wrote that I'm not judging anyone who chooses to eat meat. Even though I feel strongly about the effect meat is having on our society, I don't think it's helpful to be an angry vegan. So while I support the basic mission of a group like PETA (People for the Ethical Treatment of Animals), I can't support them throwing paint on Mary J. Blige or some other celebrity because they're wearing fur. To me, that's not the way. I'd love for everyone to give up meat and fur tomorrow, but I'm not going to give them a heavy judgment if they don't. That's because I believe being judgmental is just as harmful to your Karma as eating a hamburger. Just as I think we eat too much meat as a society, I also think we're also way too quick to judge the actions of other people.

Practicing nonjudgment is actually very good for your Karma. That's because when you *stop* judging other people, you'll be able to *start* focusing on what you need to do to correct your own issues. To continue with the PETA example, Kimora used to use fur in her Baby Phat line and I used to have leather on some of my Phat Farm products. So even though I support PETA, how could I criticize someone else when my own actions needed so much improving and refining? That's true for all of us. We need to stop worrying about who's bad and who's good and start worrying about ourselves. I spend a lot of time taking politicians and corporations to task for their lack of sensitivity, but I know that I'm still sexist, racist, classist, homophobic, and all these other things in my own heart. And we all are—we all struggle to hear our high notes. In fact, our struggle to realize the divine in ourselves is why we often have such a struggle seeing it in others.

Sowing Success Seeds

We've been talking a lot of about planting the good seeds in your personal life, but I do want to stress that this science directly applies to your professional success as well. Just as your actions have to be positive, the services you provide to the world also have to be positive if you want to reap any lasting professional success. If your products are inspiring and truly make people happy, then you're moving toward the light. But if you cut corners and try to trick people with your product, or give them something that is actually harmful, then the world is going to give you hard times back. A lot of things you can sell will create temporary happiness and success, but to be truly happy, you have to give things of *lasting* value.

Look at drug dealers. Let's be real—dealers do make people happy at first by selling them drugs. But what they're really selling is short-term joy and short-term happiness. That's why the success and happiness they derive from that trade is always going to be temporary too. Of course, when they start, every drug dealer says he's only going to stay in the game for a second. But how many really do that? Almost none. Most get caught up in the lifestyle, and then eventually that same lifestyle catches up with them. I'm not trying to judge anyone here, I'm just reporting what I've seen time and time again. Every hustla I've seen come, I've also seen go. They don't want to admit it, but the truth is that drug dealers usually die long before the drug addicts do. That's Karma at work.

That's why it's so important to never go for the shortcuts. When you do that, you can literally be digging your own grave. To be successful, you always have to sell things that are useful. Don't compromise yourself just to make money, because I am telling you that until you put something good into the world, you're not going to get anything good back from it.

If you want a little example of how planting good seeds can create success for you in the business world, let me share an experience that reaffirmed my own belief in this law. In the summer of 2005, I was in London when I got a call from Bono, who was organizing the Live 8 concerts to help wipe out the debts of African countries. He said, "Russ, this is what I need from you. I need you to produce the Live 8 concert in Philly and fix it to make sure it does a better job representing the hip-hop community." Of course I said, "OK," put down the phone, and went right to work. For the next two weeks, that's all my staff focused on. Not

Phat Farm, not Rush Card, not anything else that had been on the burner, but Live 8. Simply because I thought it was such an important cause. So we busted our asses and did what we could to get the message out there. And the concert was a big success, raising a lot of awareness about the plight of poor people in Africa. After the concert, I went back to New York and a few days later I got a call from one of my sales reps. "Damn, Russell," he told me. "Phat Farm's selling like crazy in Philly!" Now, I can honestly say that neither Phat Farm, nor any other of my ventures, was ever part of my motivation to get involved in Live 8. I was strictly motivated to help wipe out poverty in Africa. But if that motivation helped create a little bounce for my clothing line in Philly, then to me that's Karma. So for anyone who's still looking for that worldly motivation, there's an example for you. If you do good by the world, the world will do good by you.

Besides any little material reward that might come your way, it's just a lot of fun to create good Karma. I'll give you another example. Not too long ago, it occurred to me that I wasn't doing a good job sharing the resources I've been blessed with. I might write a few checks for charity, or encourage young people to vote, but I don't do enough for the people who are close to me—the people who made those resources possible in the first place. So I decided to spend a week doing a better job at sharing the cool things I get to do every day but usually take for granted. The week started with me taping an episode on *The L Word*, which is my longtime assistant Simone Reyes' favorite show. Normally, I would have just flown to the set, shot my scene, and then flown home again. But for what I decided to call "Karma Week," I brought Simone with me to the set so that she could meet the stars of the show and hang out backstage. Simone ended up having a fantastic time, and her happiness in turn made me happy. And what normally would have been another busy day on my schedule turned into an experience Simone and I will remember for a long time. The same thing happened again when I had a meeting with Bono later that week about the Live 8 concerts I was just talking about. I knew that Ellen Haddigan, who's done so much incredible work for Rush Philanthropic, was a huge U2 fan, so I invited her to sit in on the meeting. For Ellen, meeting one of her heroes in Bono was a fucking phenomenal experience. But it was rewarding for me, too, because I got to share a happy moment with someone who's done so much good work for me. But the day that week that really blew me away that was when I brought my longtime security guard Brother Leo to a meeting I had with Minister Farrakhan. I knew the Minister had always been an inspiration to Brother Leo, but I had no idea how much of an impact the meeting would have on him. When Brother Leo entered the room with me, he literally fell to the floor at the sight of the Minister and started crying. It wasn't an act for him—Leo was literally overcome at the sight of the Minister, whose service to the community was such an inspiration to him. Luckily the Minister is used to reactions like Leo's and even though he was on crutches at the time, he got down on the floor and hugged Leo—it was a very touching scene.

Not to pat myself on the back, but I felt this series of actions created some good Karma for me that week. Just those three small investments in other people made my week much more meaningful. What normally would have been just a regular week became one of the most memorable of my life. It had started with me sharing some of my resources, but ultimately I got so much more back in return. And that's really the lesson of Karma—that by lifting up others, you lift up yourself.

Granted, I was fortunate in that my resources allowed me to introduce Ellen to Bono, or Brother Leo to Minister Farrakhan, but don't forget that we all have resources we can share. We all have ways that we can lift each other up. It might not be money or relationships with celebrities or other high-profile things that many of us think are so important. That's OK, though, because the worldly things are not the things that make you happy anyway. If your resources are limited, maybe you could just help some people by working in a church or a community center. Or maybe you could just spend some time with a kid in your neighborhood who doesn't have one of her parents around and probably could use a little love and guidance. And even if you don't have the resources to do any of those things, you can always share with people by simply smiling. Remind them that the sun is out and they should smile too. Just by being positive in your own life, and with your own actions, you're creating an energy that's going to uplift the people around you too. Really, sharing any of your resources is great for your Karma.

Be Part of the Solution

I hope you don't interpret all this talk about doing good work as my way of suggesting that I'm a little bit more uplifted, or conscious, than the next man. I wish that was the case, but I know my consciousness is actually pretty low. Which is exactly why I push the Karma rap so hard! Look, I'm basically the same guy who used to hustle fake cocaine on the streets in Queens, trying to find a way to happiness. The only difference is now I accept that I won't find that happiness through money or drugs or material things—that I can only stay on that path through planting the good seeds. What I'm suggesting isn't that I'm so spiritual, but more so that I'm *selfish*. I want to be happy. I want to have lasting success. I want to keep working on getting it together until one day I'll turn into that beam of light. All I'm doing is encouraging you to be a little selfish too. To create that same happiness and lasting success for yourself through creating good Karma.

Sometimes—like when it comes to taking Simone with me to *The L Word*—I'm able to make the sacrifice because it's easy. But other times I look back and realize that I missed the mark. The critics don't need to tell me that I'm full of shit sometimes, because I already know it. I'm a guy who speaks in front of young people about doing more to help the environment, but when I'm done I'll jump in my big gas-guzzling car and drive off. I know that it would be more helpful to drive a hybrid than an SUV, but I like the way my gas guzzler feels. I'm still too selfish to make even that minor sacrifice. Or sacrifice a thousand other little things that I should give up but don't have the discipline or the patience to let go of. I'm not perfect, but in time hopefully I'll realize that good Karma is more important than those other things.

Unless you're a Gandhi, or a Yogananda, or a Mother Teresa, you're not going to get everything right. It might be the goal, but you might have to live with less. That's why, to me, the practice is to focus on doing as much good as you can while also doing the *least* amount of harm. That doesn't mean you have a blank check to run around breaking laws and when you get caught say, "Hey, I tried." Instead, it means that you have to make a sincere effort to be more connected and more conscious of your actions than you already are. If you're not changing, at least be *aware* of the changes you need to make. Awareness is always a great start, because at least you'll be moving in the right direction.

Once you're aware of the effects of your actions, you'll start to make those changes. In your personal life, maybe instead of eating meat all the time, you'll only eat it for special occasions. Or instead of pumping all that gas into your SUV, maybe you'll finally move toward the light and go buy a hybrid. And when you get to the lot to pick it up, you might even see me there getting one too. Or maybe you'll take it even a step further toward the light and start riding a bike to work every day. I know that changing cars, or riding a bike, might seem very small in the big picture, but they actually do matter. Because again, when you take one step—or in this case one peddle—toward God, he'll always take two steps toward you.

Finally, I'm always hearing people say, "Karma's a bitch," or "Karma's going to bite you on the ass one of these days." While it is true that everything you do will come back to you, if you take one thing from this chapter, let it be that Karma doesn't have to be a bitch. As I said, the influence of Karma on your life is totally up to you. You only have to worry about Karma when you sow the bad seeds. When you plant the good seeds with your actions, Karma won't be a bitch, but a goddess. A goddess who will help you reap some of the sweetest fruit you've ever tasted.

RECOGNIZE THE REAL:

Don't get caught up with always needing to see instant results from your work. Instead, have faith that there will always be a reaction, because that faith is what allows you to make a lifelong commitment toward goodness instead of always looking for the shortcuts.

Understand that giving is just
receiving inside out.

LAW NUMBER NINE:

YOU CAN NEVER GET BEFORE YOU GIVE

*The possession of material riches, without inner peace, is
like dying of thirst while bathing in a lake.*

—YOGANANDA

I **WANT TO START THIS CHAPTER** by sharing two stories that illustrate what I believe to be the most fundamental law in this book, which is You Can Never Get Before You Give.

A few years ago, I went back to my old neighborhood of Hollis, Queens, with a film crew that was doing a little piece on me. They were taping me walking along Hollis Avenue when the younger brother of an old friend of mine came up to me and said, "Yo, Russell, I'm starving. Can you bless me?" I didn't quite understand what he meant, since usually folks in Hollis aren't afraid to ask you straight up if they want something. So I said, "What do you mean, bless you?" "You know, hit me up with some money," he said. "It's really tough out here."

So I peeled him off a couple of bucks and kept it moving. But as the day went on, I kept coming back to that encounter in my mind. Here was this guy talking about "I'm starving," but he was damn near three hundred pounds and was eating a Twinkie! He was talking about how "it's tough out here," but it was the middle of the afternoon, and it looked liked he'd just rolled out of bed after partying all night. Conversely, I've got too many commitments to sleep late. If I'm not up early for yoga, my day is shot. He looked like he was about to take the money I gave him and go get lifted with his friends, but I can't get down like that either. I've worked too hard to break my attachment to drugs and alcohol. The Twinkie he was eating looked good, but I can't eat that sort of junk anymore.

So here's a guy who's already sleeping till noon, eating junk food, and getting fucked up whenever he wants. To most people, that's the lifestyle of the rich and famous. And he already had it. What could I give him? On the surface, he already had everything.

But obviously he wasn't happy with his condition. He saw himself as starving and needing a handout. In my opinion, his problem was that every day, he was waking up trying to figure out what he can *get*, instead of waking up and trying to figure out what he can *give*. Instead of asking for a blessing, he should have practiced *being* a blessing. Instead of asking for a favor, he should have walked around looking to do a favor for someone else. Instead of asking me for a gift, he should have been trying to give a gift to me! Understand, I'm not talking about a material gift. If he had come over and told me something inspiring, or had said something interesting, then that would have been his gift. And when he told me he was struggling, then maybe I would have given him something more meaningful than just a few bucks. But instead, his first question was what could he get. And because of that, he didn't get much.

Now, compare that story with an encounter I had when I spoke at a Global Diversity Summit in Miami a few years ago. During the summit, I was approached by a woman named Teneshia Jackson, who, in a very polite manner, introduced herself and explained that she had just quit her job at IBM and was planning to move to New York in order to pursue her love of hip-hop. She explained that she was inspired by my career and wanted to know if she could serve any of my initiatives. Though I was impressed by her attitude, it turned out that her experience wasn't really appropriate for what we needed at that time, so nothing really came out of the conversation. A few months later, I was at the Detroit summit when Teneshia approached me and again asked if there was any new way in which she could serve the organization. And again, I told her there still weren't any appropriate positions, but I really appreciated her enthusiasm and support.

Normally, that's where the story would have ended. But to my surprise, when I showed up for work in New York a few weeks later, Teneshia was standing out in front of my office waiting to speak to me. I went over to see what she wanted, and once again, she asked if there was any way she could support any of my initiatives. Even after two rejections, she still wanted to know how she could serve.

And for the next few days, whenever I got to work, Teneshia would be standing out there on the street, looking to serve. Finally on the fourth day I went over to her and said, "I can't believe you're still out here. We still don't have any positions open, but if you want to work for free, then come on upstairs and you can work with Brother Gary." So Teneshia came upstairs with me and started volunteering for Gary Foster, a political analyst who works in my philanthropic and social initiatives. Gary is one of the most intelligent and resilient people I've ever met, but he ain't an easy person to work for! He can be very demanding and I figured Teneshia would get tired of volunteering for him after a few weeks. But that never happened. Instead, she did such a great job for Gary that he eventually came to me and said, "Listen, we have to find a job for this woman. She's giving so much and she deserves to get paid." So we decided to put Teneshia in charge of the Hip-Hop Summit's Get Out the Vote Tour. And she did such a great job with the tour that once it was over, we had to find her a permanent job in the organization. And since then she's worked her way up the ladder in our office. Currently, she's the head of Human Resources and Organization Development at Rush, but I know there's much more for her to do, because she's one of the true leaders in our company. Yet she would have never been able to lead if she hadn't stood in front of my office for four days in a row looking to *serve* first.

With her persistence, commitment to hard work, and faith in her vision, I could have used Teneshia's story to illustrate several of the laws in this book. But above all else, her story really reflects that You Can Never Get Before You Give. That's because Teneshia understood what that brother in Hollis couldn't grasp: If you see someone with something *you* like, instead of asking for some of it, help *them* make some more of it. Don't ask for a blessing—be a blessing. Contribute to their process and help it grow, until eventually you become part of that process yourself. In other words, you can only get ahead by giving back first. That's the essence of everything I want to promote to you in this chapter.

And please understand that no matter who you are, or what you do, or what sort of title you have, your main job in life is to give. If you're a rapper, your job is to give people happiness through your music. If you're a doctor, your job is to give people a cure to whatever is ailing them. If you're a politician, your job is to give service to your constituents. If you're a drug dealer, as we said in the last chapter, your job is to give people that high they're chasing. And from the arms dealer to the social worker to the bus driver, everyone's basic job is to give. Even if your only ambition is to be filthy rich, understand that before you can be rich yourself, you have to help someone else make money first. The law of giving is unbreakable.

It took me a very long time to realize that truth. In fact, I spent my first thirty-five years worrying about consumption. When I went to work every day, I thought my sole purpose was to acquire things. But with some help from Reverend Run, I eventually realized two very important facts. The first was that money alone won't ever make you happy. That's such an important point and I want to discuss it in much greater depth later in this chapter. The second was that instead of acquiring things, my real purpose had always been to serve. In fact, any "success" I'd experienced up to that point had actually come from my service. Def Jam was only successful because we gave rappers the exposure they deserved. *Def Comedy* was a hit because I gave comedians a forum to share their talent with the world. Phat Farm was successful because it let me share a Nu American Dream with hip-hop. And right on down the line, everything worthwhile I'd done was fueled by giving.

In fact, I didn't write this book necessarily to encourage you to overhaul your lifestyle. A lot of you are practicing these laws already but might not be aware of it. You might be in a space similar to where I was, actually giving though you think you're taking. So if you're happy and successful, it's probably because you're giving already. I'm just promoting that you be more aware of this law, to reaffirm it on a daily basis. Instead of practicing it instinctively, make it a conscious part of your lifestyle and aspirations. Accepting the power of this law has helped me realize that for the rest of my career, my only purpose is to serve. Whether it's through business ventures or through philanthropy, I'll only be successful as long as I'm serving. And I'm fine with that, because serving is really one of the most rewarding things you can do with your life. According to Gandhi, "The best way to find yourself is to lose yourself in the service of others." What Gandhi was saying is that God is inside all of us, but we'll never hear that voice as long as we only worry about ourselves. We've been programmed to put "me" before "we." Yet as long as you put "me" first, you'll miss out on all the blessings life has to offer. Conversely, giving is the only process that will help you be happy and more inspired. Or, as I like to say, when you let go and give, you let go and let God.

UNDERSTANDING ABUNDANCE

Before we go any further, I want to make it clear that I'm not suggesting that there's anything wrong with making money. How could I? I'm a businessman by trade and I work hard to try to make sure that all my businesses are successful. And if you've seen my home on MTV, or read stories about me in the press, you know I've been blessed with a very comfortable lifestyle. I'm not trying to imply that there's anything wrong with owning things and living in abundance. As Reverend Run says, "It's OK to be materialistic. God's materialistic. He owns the earth."

However, piling up zeros in your bank account, or cars in your driveway, won't in and of itself make you successful. Rather, true success is based on a constant flow of giving and receiving. In fact, if you look up *affluence* in the dictionary, you'll see its root is a Latin phrase meaning "to flow with abundance." So in order to be truly affluent, you must always let what you've received flow back into the world. Because when you hoard what God has given you, your energy becomes stagnant, and that's when you become sick.

How much abundance you want to promote is something you'll have to work out on your own. There are some, like Reverend Run and his mentor Bishop Jordan of the Zoe Ministries, who suggest that you should make as much money as you can without harming anyone. They believe that making money is actually one of the best ways you can serve people. "It's hard to help poor people when you're one of them," Run always says. Another one of his favorite sayings is "People say that money is the root of all evil. If you take a walk around the ghetto, maybe you'll begin to think that the *lack* of money is actually the root of evil."

Bishop Jordan breaks it down even further in his book *Cosmic Economics,* where he writes, "How can you be perpetually in want and reach out to help poor people? How can you be poor and bring people out of poverty? Oh, you might be able to help out at a soup kitchen, but how can you make a difference? You can't. Rich people are the ones who create foundations and charities that provide food and job training and health care and make people's lives better. There is no virtue in poverty. None. Rather, it's God's desire that we prosper. . . . God's purpose for placing financial substance into your hands is for you to manifest increase in your life."

Admittedly, not everyone is comfortable with such a heavy prosperity rap coming from preachers. There's a perception that "men of god" shouldn't get paid well for their work, that it's somehow unseemly to hear them talking about the importance of making money. Personally, I don't have an issue with Reverend Run's or Bishop Jordan's approach. I know dentists get paid well to fix teeth. So why can't a preacher get paid well to fix souls? In fact, I smile when I see them rollin' around in Rolls-Royces like they do, because I know they got those cars from helping to uplift people's souls. Besides, I don't believe building up your bank account has to necessarily come at the expense of your spiritual investment.

In fact, there are plenty of religions that promote getting your money right. Did you know that are over 2,300 references in the Bible pertaining to financial responsibility? Obviously the church fathers weren't mad at people for making money. Similarly, if you were to look inside my meditation room, you'd see a big picture of Laksmi, the Hindu goddess of prosperity and generosity. I love that picture because it shows Laksmi sitting on a lotus flower, showering her disciples with a constant flow of gold coins. That might sound like an inappropriate image for meditation, but millions of very devout people worship images of Laksmi every day. I find it inspiring because it reminds me that the gold is only good as it comes from the natural cycle of giving and receiving.

That's why, when it comes to money and spirituality, I probably fall somewhere in between Bishop Jordan and the renunciants, or those who reject any sort of material attachment. For me, the best approach is what the yogis call "the middle way," a path between indulgence and austerity.

I'm never going to give away all my possessions, but I do want to downsize. I like to say that as big as my house is, I've learned that I can only sit my ass in one chair at a time. That means that while you might find possessions you like, there's a limit to the amount of enjoyment they can bring you. You might have a hundred chairs, or a hundred cars, or a hundred houses, but you can only put your ass in one of them at a time. Unfortunately, many people don't understand that and instead of realizing that all chairs feel pretty much the same, they think that the *hundred and first* chair is going to be the one that really makes them feel great. And when they do that, they're making one of the biggest (and most common) mistakes people make in this world, which is equating money, or toys, with happiness.

MONEY NEVER EQUALS HAPPINESS

People have been fooling themselves into thinking money equals happiness for thousands of years, and they'll probably keep on fooling themselves for a thousand more years too. Luckily, you don't have to be one of those people. You can avoid that fate by understanding that while it's fine to have toys, never invest yourself in those toys. Never become obsessed with toys to the point where you actually think they can make you happy. That's an empty dream, because only *you* can bring happiness into your life. A toy can never do that. At the very best, toys are simply a celebration of your aspiration, a symbol of your victory over the struggle. At the worst, they're a cancer disguised as a cure, a faulty foundation that will crumble under the weight of your expectations.

I've seen too many people get depressed chasing money and toys. They think that all it will take to be happy is a few more dollars, or a faster car, or a bigger house. Damon Dash likes to call these people "cake-a-holics," because they're addicted to making money the same way a drug addict is addicted to dope. Just like the junkie endlessly chasing the next high, the cake-a-holic is stuck in his own same futile pursuit of happiness. I was never quite a cake-a-holic myself, but I understand the urge, because in a sense, we all chase the toys. I certainly used to hustle my ass off, always thinking that everything was going to change for the better once I got just a *little* bit more money. But nothing ever did change for the better. That change only happened when I realized that giving was the only key that could unlock the happiness I was looking for.

Now, some of you might be thinking, "Shit, give me the toys and the money, I'll figure out a way to be happy." Well, I'm not discouraging you from going out there and getting paid. But while it's tempting to think that money is going to solve your problems, please believe me, it won't. I know plenty of millionaires and I tell you that most of them aren't happy. Forget millionaires, if I know fifteen *billionaires*, then I know thirteen unhappy people. These people's lives might be filled with mansions and yachts and private jets, but their medicine cabinets are also filled with antidepressents.

They're depressed because despite all their toys, the material things aren't making them any happier. These billionaires keep hustling for the next check, never understanding that no matter how many zeros are on it, the happiness it will bring is as fleeting as the smoke floating out of the junkie's pipe. They never understand that they can be surrounded by fame, luxury, and wealth, but unless they have God in their heart, at the end of the day they're still going to feel empty inside. Because when you eat alone, you won't enjoy your meal.

And it's not just the very wealthy. There is one person working for me, who I've known for a very long time, who thought money would solve all their problems too. The person was a little depressed and thought a big bonus would make them happier. So I gave them the bonus, but the next day they were just as depressed. The money, which they were so sure was going to make them feel whole again, didn't make a fucking bit of difference.

Whether it be getting a big bonus, signing your first movie deal, or selling a million records, the greatest obstacle for some people is what society might refer to as success. I've certainly worked with many artists who made a lot of money, but it left them feeling emptier than they did when they were broke. So many of the "success stories" I've been involved with have played out like that. I've watched very talented artists get the money and the fame but then almost immediately go into a tailspin. Not because they were depressed by nature, but because their natural process had been interrupted. One moment they were creating out of love, and the next moment they found themselves creating for money. And as bad as you want the money when you're broke and struggling, when it comes, the transition can be very jarring.

In these artists' minds, the money and toys had taken on more weight than they deserved. Which is why when many artists get paid for the first time, they mistakenly believe that they've accomplished a very big part of their mission. But that weight ends up hurting like hell when it drops on them. Because after they buy that $100 thousand car, after a while they realize that all they do is drive it. And while they were expecting to feel like, "Yeah nigga, what?," the first time they drive around the block, when they finally park it they actually feel more like, "OK, now what?" It's very anticlimactic. They start feeling depressed, because instead of driving a dream, they realize they're driving a car just like everyone else. It might have plusher seats, or bigger rims, or a more powerful engine, but at the end of the day, it's still just a car. Ultimately, their life is no better or worse than it was without that car.

Sometimes they still don't want to admit that they've been wrong, so then they run out and buy that $100K watch everyone's talking about, thinking maybe *that's* going to make the difference. On their way home from the jeweler they keep looking at the watch, but once they know what time it is, there ain't much more the watch can do for them. They realize that they can't look at a diamond, as beautiful as it is, for very long without getting bored. That's when they know they've been running down the wrong path.

Whereas before they were asking the car salesperson, "How much is that car worth?" or the jeweler, "How much is that chain worth?" now they start asking *themselves*, "How much is life worth?" Because they've realized that their definition of success and happiness has been way out of whack.

This often happens to rappers in particular, since so much of their poetry focuses on the material aspirations of the struggle. When they finally do get paid, they feel obligated to get those toys, even if the toys had only been a way of expressing their ambition. I saw this happen to one rapper in particular, and his story is an excellent example of the disappointment that comes from confusing money with happiness.

Before he became a star, this rapper's happiness came from creating good songs. Sometimes he'd write about getting paid, but it was only part of his vision. His larger gift was articulating the struggle, and people loved him for being able to lend a voice to their experience. However, as his popularity grew, he started drifting away from the streets. His songs became more about all the money he was making and the fly lifestyle he was living.

But even though he was rapping about money, in reality he was finding out that the money did not make him happy at all. Before he had money, he thought getting it would be a huge buzz. But when he finally held the cash in his hands, it was more of a fizzle. He realized the only real buzz he got came from writing songs that touched people. The only time he was really thrilled, when he really felt alive, was when people were cheering for him when he performed.

Unfortunately, by the time he had that epiphany, his status in the industry had changed significantly. In an effort to defend his new image and lifestyle, he had gotten into a beef with another rapper. But that rapper dissed him so badly that soon he wasn't hot in the streets anymore. And when you don't have the streets in hip-hop, you don't have any true love either. That realization made this rapper as sad as he had ever been. He went into a dark space and it took him a while to emerge from it. However, I'm very proud to say that he's not only back, but better than ever. Because now he's reconnected with his true mission, which is spreading love through his poetry instead of chasing money.

Stories like that is why I always tell the artists to never lose sight of what they're really working for. They're not getting paid because they walk around in the most expensive gear, drive the nicest car, or are surrounded by beautiful women. They're getting paid because they've made hot songs, told hot jokes, or designed hot clothes that have brought love to the world. They're being *rewarded* with love and happiness for *giving* love and happiness through their art. The toys might accentuate the happiness, but they're not the cause of it. What they *gave* to the world is why they were *given* all the other stuff.

THE BUSINESS YOGI

Not too long ago, I was talking to a reporter who wanted to know if it was difficult for me to find a balance between my business pursuits and my spiritual beliefs. "Is it really possible to be a business yogi?" he asked, to which I responded, "I sure as hell hope so." That's not to say that I consider myself a yogi. At my very best, I'm an aspiring yogi. But I do view myself as someone who's looking to create a space where profit and giving don't have to be mutually exclusive. I believe that any future success I experience will be built on promoting products that don't only build up bank accounts, but build up the world too. If I can use my businesses to create helpful, lasting services for the world, then I'm moving in the right direction. When I watch a Bill Gates and a Warren Buffet use their money to fight poverty and improve education on a global scale, or a George Soros use his wealth and influence to promote freedom through democracy, then the idea of being a "business yogi" doesn't seem so farfetched anymore. Some of you might look up to me, but those kinds of people are *my* heroes.

Another person who's been a major influence on how I view giving is Bono. As I mentioned earlier, I was extremely proud to be part of Live 8 and I've also viewed his battles for human rights with admiration. But I'm particularly interested in Product Red, a brand he created with my friend Bobby Shriver. If you're not familiar with the concept, Bobby and Bono signed up major companies—including American Express, Giorgio Armani, Gap, and Motorola—to license "Red" versions of their products. What that means is that when consumers buy a "Red" shirt from the Gap, or a "Red" phone from Motorola, a portion of the profit from that sale will be earmarked for the Global Fund, to fund AIDS programs that focus on women and children in Africa.

The idea is that when they're looking for a phone or a T-shirt, consumers will seek out "Red" products if they perceive that some of the money they're spending is going to a good cause. The corporations will still make their money, since there's no difference in cost and quality between a "Red" phone and a regular Motorola, but people in the struggle will be served too. Instead of just operating for profit's sake, initiatives like "Red" will show business the advantages of becoming more connected with the cycle of giving and receiving.

I hope to prove that giving can be an effective business model in my own ventures too. For instance, I didn't launch the Simmons Jewelry Line so I could put a hot watch or a hot chain on your wrist. Rather, my goal for Simmons Jewelry is ultimately to be able to use the company's resources and relationships to build factories and schools in Africa. Instead of just exploiting the African people for their diamonds, Simmons Jewelry can help create new jobs and opportunities for them. I want to help create a cycle of giving and receiving in Africa, so in the future, the majority of money going into Africa comes from local enterprises, and not from foreign aid. This concept is at the front of my consciousness these days, as I've just returned from a trip to Africa. We traveled to South Africa and Botswana, ostensibly to learn more about how Simmons Jewelry could help empower Africans through the diamond trade, but the experience taught me so much more than that. The first thing I learned is how humble, intelligent, giving, and regal the African people are. It was so inspiring to see that despite all their struggles, they are able to carry themselves with such pride and dignity. They were some of the most beautiful people I have ever met and after even just one short visit I can honestly say that my love for the African people is unconditional.

My trip taught also taught me how crucial it is that we keep fighting for initiatives that can make a real difference in ending poverty and disease in Africa. The people of Africa need more than a handout; they need a helping hand that promotes empowerment, trade, and investment. As I'm writing this, my views are creating a little controversy here in America, but I have complete faith in our mission. I know in my heart that the path we want Simmons Jewelry—and ultimately all companies—to follow in Africa is the one that will be the best for the African people. Having just returned, I feel like I'm not capable yet of articulating all the emotions I have toward Africa and the African people. But it's a conversation I need to start, because I really believe that helping Africa will be one of my most important jobs from here on out. It's a daunting job, one that certainly requires more resources and talents than I individually possess, but I think it's one of the most important ones I can undertake. It's not an overstatement to say that the future of Africa is the future of humanity. The paths we follow in Africa over the next fifty years will have a tremendous impact on the path mankind will ultimately take in the coming generations. So I pray that in the near future my own journey will become much more intertwined with Africa's journey.

Another example where I've tried to use business to promote change is Atman, a men's fragrance I developed last year with Kimora. Because we're always looking to contribute to the cycle of giving, we decide to donate one hundred percent of our profits from the fragrance to charity. Atman (which means "higher self" in Sanskrit) is about to launch as I'm writing this, and if it performs the way we hope it will, we're going to put some serious money back into the streets that have supported us for so many years. American charities are going to get the lion's share of our profits but I'm especially proud that we're going to earmark twenty-five percent of those profits for Alicia Keys' Keep a Child Alive charity, which helps African children get the drugs they need to fight AIDS and other diseases. Let's be clear—I'm not trying to suggest that selling perfume is in itself an important service. Obviously, nobody *needs* a fragrance and I've never been a fragrance type of dude. But when I realized we could take the money a fragrance would generate and put it back into the streets, then it became more than just a vanity thing. It became a giving thing. And when I realized how much I could give, then suddenly I became a fragrance guy after all. So whether it's Simmons Jewelry, or Atman, or my new RWS clothing line, which also donates a percentage of its profits to charity, I'm always looking to give something back. I know our blessings are going to come from our giving. So if we don't give back to the community, we're going to block our blessings. And blocking blessings is bad business.

Hopefully, if enough people see what I'm doing, or see what Bono is doing, or see what Bill Gates is doing, then maybe they'll start to pattern their own business plans on a giving model. We might not be able to change the definition of business, which is to make money, but maybe we can change the motivation behind it.

Just recently I attended the Clinton Global Initiative in New York City, in which former president Clinton brought together politicians, business leaders, and activists to fund solutions to the world's most pressing problems. It was an incredible event and I felt very honored to walk among people like the Bill Gates, Bishop Tutu, Warren Buffet, and Virgin's Sir Richard Branson (who alone pledged $3 billion toward ending global warming). To see so many businesspeople committed to using their resources to uplift others was one of the most inspiring things I've ever seen. It made me feel hopeful about the future.

Maybe in the not-so-distant future we can make the concept of sharing cooler than the concept of hoarding. Maybe we can promote an environment where moguls won't be lionized for their yachts or mansions but for the good work they're doing with their money. We're certainly starting to see it happen already. When someone says "Bill Gates," you don't automatically think "rich dude" anymore. Instead, maybe you think about the great work his foundation is doing in the war against poverty. And hopefully you'll even be a little more appreciative of his products because of it. When you hear "Bono," maybe you'll think "activist" as much as "rock star," and be even more inspired to hear his music. Or, when you think of George Soros, maybe you don't think "billionaire investor," but think of a man who's using his money to peacefully promote democracy across the globe. And hopefully, one day that will be how the world thinks of me too— as someone who used his resources to give back. I want my success to be measured not by how much money I've made, but by how much service and inspiration I was able to give back. I'd be happy if, when I pass, my tombstone reads, "Here lies Russell Wendell Simmons. A person who started to understand that the only purpose in life is giving back to the world."

GIVING FOR A LIVING

I want to talk specifically about philanthropy now, which is becoming my true passion. I don't think simply writing checks is a good indicator of whether you're a true philanthropist or not. True philanthropy requires a lifetime commitment to the cycle of giving. And that's what I hope to achieve.

I know that no matter how much I'm able to give, whether it be through Atman, or Rush Philanthropic, or through HSAN, there's still so much more work to be done. I can hear that voice of God inside of me and, trust me, it's not congratulating me on what a great job I did giving my money away. Instead, it's saying, "You gave away a small amount of your money and bought a lot of bullshit with the rest. And you did a lot of bullshit with what you bought." I don't want to hear that from God, so my challenge is to do better in finding more ways to serve. I know it won't be easy, because I often say my toughest job isn't making money but spreading it around properly once I've made it. Whether it's the kids from Rush Philanthropic, the young people I meet through HSAN, Jinx, family members and friends who need my help, strangers who approach me on the street, or even children dying in Africa who've never heard of me, my job is to use my resources to try to make all of their lives better. That's a tall order, and sometimes it does feel like "Mo money, mo problems." Ultimately, though, there's no other job I'd rather have.

I do want to make it clear that you don't have to be "rich" to make a commitment to giving in your own life. If you only have a little, then only give a little. If you happen to have a lot, then give a lot. But remember, God's going to be as happy with the quarter you give to a homeless person as he is with the billion dollars Bill Gates gives to fighting poverty in Africa. Bill Gates is sharing his resources and you're sharing yours. The size of your resources might be different, but the intention is the same. And that's all that matters.

A final note: Don't get tricked into thinking that a gift has to come in a material form for it to have value. At the end of the day, you can give and receive so many wonderful things without spending any money. Even if you're down to your last dollar, you can still afford to give someone a smile, a little encouragement, a compliment, or a hug. All those things have tremendous value and you can always share them with the world no matter how hard you're struggling. Remember, when Confucius was asked to define *charity*, he replied, "Love one another." So you might not have money, or you might not have time, but you always have love that you can share.

Ninety percent of the battle to become a happy, uplifting person is waged in your heart. And when you win that battle, and become committed to giving fearlessly to the world, your success will be unlimited. One of the most important things I can tell you in this chapter is that a smile and giving attitude alone will make you ten times the businessperson you already are! I promise you will be ten times more likely to make money and receive toys when you live a giving, compassionate life. They will be a direct benefit from your heartfelt commitment to giving.

HIP-HOP'S GIFT

I can't talk about philanthropy without acknowledging the incredible job hip-hop has done in uplifting people in the struggle. The culture has a reputation for being materialistic and self-centered, but I'm here to say that hip-hop is actually an incredibly giving community. In fact, I believe that hip-hop is the most giving community in the history of American pop culture. The jazz, the blues, and rock 'n' roll never gave back to their communities the way hip-hop has. That's why we need to recognize what a great job these rappers have done.

The majority of rappers have a foundation or a local charity they support. Certainly more rappers have foundations than pro basketball players (though I am inspired by all the incredible work Dikembe Mutombo is doing in his native Congo), and ballplayers make a hell of a lot more money than rappers! Whether it's through organizations or just through personal initiatives, most rappers try to use their money to make positive changes in people's lives. They might not talk about it much, but they're doing it.

I'll talk about it, though, because I think it's important to celebrate this aspect of our culture. Having come from the streets themselves, rappers know how the streets are often overlooked by "traditional" philanthropy. There's a reason no one in hip-hop was surprised by what happened in Hurricane Katrina. Angered, yes. But surprised? No. Rappers understand that if they don't give back to the streets, the streets might never get the help that they need. That's why artists like Puffy, Eminem, Jay-Z, TI, Ludacris, 50 Cent, Kanye West, Nelly, Ice Cube, Damon Dash, LL Cool J, Chingy, Wyclef, David Banner, Cash Money, Mos Def, Snoop Dogg, Dead Prez, and many, many others are seriously involved in philanthropy.

I'll share a few examples so that you can appreciate their commitment. I happen to know that Ice Cube does a lot of work with diabetes and autism groups. He doesn't seek publicity for it, but it's still a priority to him. Or look at Nelly. He tragically lost his sister Jackie to cancer, but that just made him more committed to fighting the disease through his 4Sho4Kids Foundation. Or take Eminem. A little while back, there was a lot of nonsense going around about how he was a racist. During all that drama, I did a little digging and found out that he had anonymously given money to a shelter for battered African-American women. I tried to share that with the world, but not many people listened. Similarly, even though media commentators like to talk about what a bad role model he is, I never hear them talk about the fact that his Shady Foundation is out there every winter in Detroit giving coats to kids and feeding the homeless.

I've already talked about the good work Alicia Keys is doing for Africa, but we also need to acknowledge how much Wyclef Jean has done for his native Haiti. His Yéle Haiti Foundation is dedicated to fighting poverty in that country, which as much as we try to ignore it, is the poorest in the Western Hemisphere. Thankfully Clef isn't ignoring anything—his foundation is providing scholarships to 3,600 children and rebuilding twenty flood-damaged schools, not to mention distributing food and cleaning up garbage in some of the country's worst slums. And he's not only committed to giving to Haiti. Whenever we ask him to come out for a Hip-Hop Summit or a rally, he never says no. In fact, when we rallied against the education cuts in New York City, he lay down in front of the police and told them to take him to jail, because he wanted to publicize the issue. That was his gift to our cause. To me, he's a servant and a soldier.

Finally, I want to say this message isn't an attempt to change the mainstream's opinion of hip-hop. Rather, my message is directed to the people who *already* believe in hip-hop's goodness, since they're the ones who are going to change the world. Not the critics.

All I want is for the hip-hop nation to understand that it's not enough to only emulate Nelly, Eminem, or Alicia Keys when it comes to the worldly things they promote. If you emulate how they dress, how they talk, what watch they wear, or what car they drive, then you should emulate their commitment to giving as well. Because that commitment to giving is a larger part of who they are than what they wear or what they drive. Maybe you don't think I'm so cool anymore, so when I talk about giving, it goes in one ear and out the other. But you know Nelly is still fly. You know Alicia Keys is still hot. You know TI is a cool motherfucker. And they're all telling you exactly the same thing I'm trying to promote in this chapter—that giving is the key to life.

Once the hip-hop nation embraces this commitment to giving, we're going to dramatically change the face of philanthropy in this country. Just as hip-hop made Tommy Hilfiger or Cristal or Range Rover cool, we're going to help make philanthropy cool too. It's already getting there, but we're going to ride the crest of a new wave of consciousness and help put it over the top. We're going to find a way to take the millions of dollars we pump into the market every year and redirect some of it back into the struggle. So instead of having the rich old guys hoard it and let it become stagnant, we're going to put that money back in circulation through giving. So that it can help change the root causes of poverty and inequality.

A More Giving Government

My concern is that while we're seeing this amazing change within our young people, our government is becoming even *less* compassionate in its policies. Instead of encouraging us to give, it's encouraging us to be afraid. Afraid of terrorists. Afraid of immigrants. Afraid of gay people. Even afraid of hip-hop. And when people become afraid, they become insular. They begin to worry about hoarding and protecting what they have instead of sharing it with others.

This lack of giving isn't only evident in our domestic policies—we need to become even more compassionate on a global scale as well. As long as we have the most resources, then I believe we have the most responsibility to give as well. It's our job to help people wherever they need help. To me, that's the cost that comes with being the boss.

The fact is we spend way too much money on weapons and war. In 2006 alone, the United States' defense spending exceeded $500 billion! That's more than every other country in the world combined spends on defense! For example, North Korea and Iran, two of the countries that are allegedly such a major threat to us, only spend roughly one percent of that amount.

In comparison to military spending, our government spends roughly $49 billion on children's health care, $7 billion on job training that could help lift people out of the struggle, $7 billion on Head Start, the early-childhood education program for the poor, $2 billion on programs that could help reduce our dependency on oil, and a pathetic $10 billion on humanitarian foreign aid.

But if we could give just a little bit more in those categories, then we wouldn't need such a disproportionately massive military budget. Because the more we lift people out of poverty and ignorance, the less there would be to fight about. If we spent as much on aid as we spent on bombs, eventually people would forget about the bombs. So while spending a few more billion dollars promoting peace might seem to cost a lot, war is always much, much more expensive.

In particular, we have to do more for the poor people who are dying needlessly every day from poverty. According to President Clinton, if we were to increase our foreign aid even a tiny percentage, from .01 percent of our Gross National Product to .07 percent, we could change the world dramatically. So why isn't that a priority? If there were six thousand Americans dying from mosquito bites every day, it would be fucking impossible for us to stomach that. If there were thousands of Americans dying from drinking dirty water, we wouldn't accept that either. So how come we can accept it happening in Africa? Or Haiti? We have to do better.

As a society, we were rightfully outraged when thousands of innocent people were killed in the 9/11 attacks. Yet I've read that the equivalent of seven 9/11s takes place every day from preventable deaths around the globe and we act like it isn't happening. Just as we correctly set aside resources and money to fight those who want to bring us harm, we have to also set aside a similar amount of resources and money to reverse the terror that poverty is creating all over the globe as well. So no matter how much we're already giving, we have to give more.

I know the policies I'm promoting might sound idealistic, or naive, but those are the principles I really believe in. And besides, when I see that men like Gandhi and Martin Luther King Jr. were killed for promoting similar ideas, then I really know that they could work. If they had only been promoting fanciful, impossible ideas, then they wouldn't have been considered threats to the status quo. But because their ideals of nonviolence and giving really were very pragmatic, they were threats. I'm not even remotely suggesting that I'm in the same league as a Gandhi, MLK, Mother Teresa, Yogananda, Pantanjali, or any one of the other amazing superheroes who promoted peace, but I am going to try to use my resources to promote the principles they believed in. I really want to promote the idea that giving love, compassion, and support can be the foundation of a successful domestic and foreign policy. I really want to promote that there is no social program greater than love, just like there's no national defense greater than love.

I believe that giving always leads to success. And I believe that's as true for people as it is for cities, states, and even countries. When we give the world good, the world will give us good back. When we give the world violence and anger, that's what we can expect back from the world. It's that simple.

Our country in particular has been blessed with incredible resources, so that we can do good all over the world, not just in countries where there's a lot of oil in the ground. Instead of being satisfied with what we've got, let's insist our government promote compassionate policies that will help people everywhere they need help. Because as long as some people are struggling and we choose to do nothing about it, then no matter how good we've got it, we'll never be truly successful.

RECOGNIZE THE REAL:

Giving, not trading or selling, is the basis of success. The most rewarding thing you can do is just to give the world something good. And ultimately you will be paid so much more for that gift than if you had tried to trade it for something else.

If there's one message I can get out,
it's how could anybody believe that
their god is different, let alone better?
They all can't be nothing but great.

LAW NUMBER TEN:

SUCCESSFUL PEOPLE STAY OPEN TO CHANGE

*We are here to awaken from the
illusion of our separateness.*
—THICH NHAT HANH

WHEN YOU EMBRACE DIVERSITY and stay open to things that seem different from you, you can always take advantage of new opportunities as they arise. The rise of hip-hop is such a powerful example of this law. You didn't have to be Nostradamus back in the late seventies to know that hip-hop was the future. In fact, the future was *already* taking place on the streets of Harlem, Queens, The Bronx, and Brooklyn. Those old white guys literally could have come down from their offices and seen it with their own eyes. But they didn't, because they didn't respect the streets. They couldn't believe that street kids could create something as meaningful, as powerful, and as lasting as the rock 'n' roll their own kids were listening to back in the suburbs. It was so alien to them. All they saw was a bunch of thugs in gold chains shouting over loud music. They never understood that those "thugs" were really artists. That mistake cost them a chance to make millions—even billions—of dollars. The major labels should have been snatching up all the good rappers back in 1979, while I was still living with my parents and throwing house parties. But they didn't, and that mistake opened the door for me. And I was more than happy to walk through it.

Some people might think *I'm* being racist when I talk about those old white guys, but I don't think there's anything wrong with that statement. I'm not saying they were bad businessmen because they were white. I'm saying the were bad businessmen because they didn't respect diversity. And trust me, I realize respecting diversity is something that black folk need to work on too. There were plenty of black executives at the time who hated hip-hop just as much as the white executives—maybe even harder! The black guys should have been more receptive, because a lot of them were from the streets themselves. But the streets were exactly what they were trying to get away from. They had gone to college, gotten nice jobs with expense accounts, and the last thing they wanted to do was to let a bunch of ghetto niggas mess shit up for them. So they shut out the streets and, in doing so, blew a once-in-a-lifetime opportunity. Any one of those black executives could have done what I did. And since they were already inside the system, they could have done it with a *quarter* of the effort and in *half* the time. But they didn't, and again, I was more than happy to do it for them.

It would be hard for them to make the same mistake now. That's because the hip-hop nation is teaching the world that respecting diversity doesn't tear communities apart—it actually makes them stronger. Hip-hop has created a dialogue that allows poor people to realize that their problems *are* the same. The kids in the trailer parks who can't get out generation after generation are starting to realize that they're fighting the same battle as the kids in the ghettos. It's not a battle of black against white or Latino against Asian. It's a battle against a lack of quality education. A battle against a lack of services. A battle against predatory lending practices. A battle against a lack of vision, a lack of high notes, and a lack of compassion. They're all fighting the exact same battle.

EMBRACE DIVERSITY

The question executives need to ask themselves today is, how can I avoid the kinds of mistakes those executives made back in the seventies? How can I make sure that the next big thing isn't taking place forty blocks uptown while I'm sitting in a fancy office completely unaware of it? Or even worse, ignoring it? The answers to those questions will be part of your company's winning formula.

The first answer is, build a *real* commitment to diversity in your organization. There's been a lot of lip service paid over the last twenty years to making businesses more diverse, but it takes more than talk. Holding a diversity seminar twice a year where most of your staff is asleep is not going to do it. And neither is patting yourself on the back after you hire a black guy for some midlevel position. That type of "commitment" is bullshit. And your staff is going to know it. A real commitment to diversity has to come from the top. If your company is going to win, the CEO and executives have to lead the fight for diversity.

That's why I want to speak directly to all you employers about the interview process. The first thing you have to do as an employer, whether you run a Fortune 500 corporation or an indie record label, is have an *open mind* before you start talking to potential employees. You have to accept that culturally not everyone is the same as you and just because they look different, or dress different, doesn't mean they *are* different.

That's hard, because it's human nature to hire people that you're comfortable with. It's natural to feel a connection with someone if she went to the same college as you, or if your families used to vacation on Martha's Vineyard together. But you can't cling to those things when it's time to make a hire. Instead, open up your spirit and consider people for spots that aren't traditionally reserved for them. If you're a white male, then you might think the position you're looking to fill is a white male's job. You might not think it consciously, but it can be there subconsciously. Maybe you just don't expect to see this Indian-American, this African-American, this Mexican-American, even this woman, in that spot. But the truth is the Mexican-American, the African-American, or the Indian-American is just as competent as anyone else. They just need the opportunity to prove it.

The interview process has to be about people's passion, not

their "pedigree." Look a little deeper into people's spirit and don't worry so much about their cultural statements. You might be looking at a young black kid for a job and think he's disrespecting you by wearing jeans instead of a suit to the interview. But you also might not realize that he spent $150 on those jeans and that he considers them the flyest thing in his closest. He's actually trying to show you respect by wearing those jeans.

Don't get caught up on someone's pants, his accent, his skin color, or his experiences. Instead, look for his willingness to work and willingness to give. If he can do those things, he's going to be a real asset to your company, even if he doesn't look or talk like you. I'm not saying you're racist if you hire someone largely because he reminds you of yourself. Again, that's just human nature. But try to get past that urge. Even if you're not consciously being racist, you *are* costing your company money. That person you overlooked might have brought your company the perspective it needed to find "the next big thing." And in the business world, missing out on "the next big thing" is even worse than being racist.

Of course, hiring is only the first step. After you bring in people with different perspectives, you have to respect their vision. Find out what they think. Find out what they can bring to the table that's different from what's already there. Make it known that you're always open to new ideas. I want my employees to feel comfortable coming to me with any idea, even if at first it doesn't seem like the type of thing that a "rap mogul" would be into. The moment I dismiss an idea because it sounds "too suburban" or "too white," then I'm setting myself up for failure. Don't hire people with different visions and perspectives and then lock them out. Give them autonomy, which means the opportunity to make mistakes.

A culturally diverse workplace will also help your employees get out of the ghettos of their own minds. If you're only exposed to one thing culturally, then you live in a ghetto. It could be a WASPY ghetto, a Jewish ghetto, a black ghetto, or an Asian ghetto, but without diversity, it's still a ghetto. And you bring that ghetto mentality with you to the workplace. But if you come to work and deal with different people with different perspectives, your lenses clear up and you can see all the opportunities that are out there. That's why you always want to bring the melody of different experiences to your company and then let them join your chorus. When you do that, everyone sounds much better.

THE SELLOUT THING

I've spent a lot of time, both in this book and in my life, encouraging "mainstream" America to do a better job of respecting hip-hop culture. But now I want to switch gears and encourage the hip-hop nation to do a better job respecting some of the mainstream's rituals, especially in the business world. Because the same way those old white men cost themselves a lot of money by refusing to move outside of their cultural comfort zone, you can miss out on a lot of checks by making a similar mistake.

For instance, let's say you're one of those people who I just spoke about, someone who goes to an interview dressed in baggy jeans instead of a pair of slacks, or at least some nice chinos. If you didn't know any better, well, now you know. But if you wore those jeans because you didn't want to be perceived as doing the "sellout thing," or being a "sucker," then you need to reevaluate your priorities. If you feel like putting on a suit makes you a sucker, then, hey, don't do it. You won't have the reputation as a sucker, but you won't have a job either. You have to make choices in life, and sometimes those choices involve adjusting your attitude depending on the situation. I'm not saying sell out or kiss ass or stop Doing You. I'm just reminding you to be aware of how you come across.

People really play themselves in the business world by speaking the wrong language, particularly body language. I see it all the time. For example, not too long ago I was having a meeting with some young entrepreneurs who wanted me to invest in their venture. They had a good idea and a strong product, but the whole time we were talking, one of them had his feet up on the chair and was either staring into space or typing on his two-way. When the meeting was finally over, I told the guy (let's call him "Pat"), "Just so you know, your whole body language is basically telling me, 'Fuck you.' I know that's not what you really mean and I'm not insulted. I understand you. But I also understand that a lot of people in the business world are going to hate you because of that attitude." Of course "Pat" started protesting, telling me, "Naw, son, it's just that—" But I cut him off and explained, "I'm not looking for excuses. I'm just telling you because I love you and I want to help. The attitude you have right now is not going to work. You're not going to survive if you do that in the wrong environment. They're going to smile in your face during the meeting, but the minute you get out of the room they're going to say, 'Fuck that kid.' And you won't even know, because they won't tell you how they feel. But the next time you see them and try to generate some business, they're just going to look at you like you're crazy."

I hope "Pat" got that message, because he has a lot of talent and vision. But he wasn't giving off the type of energy I wanted representing me in the corporate world. I'm looking to hire people who are courteous, who understand what they want from the corporate structure and then present themselves in a way that makes that possible. Because your body language, your clothes, and everything you share with the world should inspire people. So if you do something that you think is personally inspiring but fails to inspire your boss or your clients, then your mission was unsuccessful.

That's why I don't need on my team people who can only play one note. When it's time to go over to Motorola or to Chrysler and pursue new initiatives, I need people who are educated and can shift gears. They need to represent hip-hop culture, but they need to be able to speak the King's English too. So if you think you're playing yourself by putting on a suit and speaking the King's English, then don't bother trying to work with me.

Maybe you think it's hypocritical that I give all the judgment but never have to put on a suit myself. And it's true, when I go over to AOL, or meet with HBO, they'd probably throw me out if they saw me wearing a suit. My uniform is some Phat Farm gear and a fitted cap and that's what they expect from me. But I promise, if one day those expectations changed and I thought my partners would be comfortable if I wore a suit, then every day you'd see me in a Phat Farm suit. If that's what my partners want, then that's what they'll get. Because I can't be a good leader unless I'm a good servant first.

I don't need to prove a point with the clothes that I wear. That's not the battle I need to fight. I need to protect my vision, to protect my artists' vision, to protect the integrity of my product. I could care less about the street integrity of my outfit or my grammar. Because whoever I'm talking to, I try to talk like that person. I want to become them. I want to teach them from their perspective. That doesn't mean I'm selling out. That just means that I'm buying into the concept that the end of the day we're all the same.

Obviously when it's time for you sit down in that meeting, I hope it won't matter to the people on the other side of the table what you're wearing, or what language you're speaking. I hope you can sit there and not feel like you have to subjugate any part of your personality. Ideally, you can be positive, inspiring, and considerate while completely being yourself.

But the reality is, most people aren't as open-minded as we would like. So a lot of the time, you're going to have to work harder to make people comfortable. Instead of pushing who you are, and where you come from, so hard, you're going to have to be more selfless. Instead of being hardheaded and making a big point out of only wearing what you want to wear, and only speaking how you want to speak, put a little bit of yourself on hold for a minute. Let them know that you want to be part of their team, even if their team wears a suit. The people on the other side of the table can be the petty, close-minded, provincial ones. You can be universal.

I want to be clear here that in no way am I promoting corporate culture over hip-hop culture, or "King's English," over "real talk." To do that would be denying the part of my makeup that makes me a little unique. I'm simply encouraging the hip-hop nation not to take it too far in one direction. It's not about wearing a suit or not wearing suit. It's about balancing what you feel comfortable wearing or doing with what's expected of you. When you can find that balance, you'll always find success too.

Remember, respecting diversity is a two-way street. When you're so rigid in the way that you see the world that you can't connect with other people, then you are severely limiting your ability to succeed. You need to find a way to open yourself up without diluting who you are. When you can do that, you'll be able to push ahead in business and in life. But when you're close minded and rigid, then you'll always be stuck in the same place.

Ignorance Ain't Bliss

I've been guilty of being culturally closed-minded and rigid myself. In fact, that attitude almost cost me *Def Poetry Jam,* a show I help produce for HBO. I'm so inspired by *Def Poetry*—it's in its fifth season and has helped make poetry cool again. But I'll be real. When I first heard people talking about poetry slams, in my ignorance, I wasn't interested. I made rap records and hip-hop comedy shows. Poetry was something soft, something for white people in coffeehouses. Luckily, my brother Danny, who is not only older but also wiser than I am, kept pushing for me to check one out. When he finally dragged me to my first slam, I knew right away I'd been making a huge mistake. I realized instantly that many of the voices I was hearing were authentic and that the streets would respond to them. Getting behind poetry would not only make sense financially, it would also provide young people with a new way to express themselves. And anytime I see an opportunity to provide a positive service while improving my portfolio, that's always going to be something I want to get involved in.

So I hooked up with my *Def Comedy Jam* collaborator Stan Lathan and started working on the show immediately. But if I had clung to my preconceived ideas about poetry, there would have never been a *Def Poetry Jam*. Someone else would have realized the marketability of poetry and they would have been collecting and cashing all those HBO checks. That's why before you say no to something, take a moment and try to reflect on what you're really feeling. Are you saying no because the idea doesn't have value? Or are you saying no because the idea seems alien to you and you don't understand it? Be honest with yourself. Always check out new things for yourself before you judge them. Otherwise, you're going to miss out on some incredible opportunities.

Ride the Changing Tide

Even as I write those words, I can look around and see that there are still so many people, especially in corporate America, who don't understand that truth. Take magazines—they still haven't embraced the idea of diversity. Sure, maybe each issue of *People* has a picture of Puffy or Jay-Z chillin' on a yacht, but that's not enough. I love Puffy and Jay, but there's so much more to hip-hop than them. People in America want to see pictures of Snoop Dogg as much as they want to see Tom Cruise and Brad Pitt. The people aren't as hung up on race anymore. Only the establishment is. I don't care if you run a TV network, a magazine, or a bookstore. Your business will improve when you embrace diversity through hip-hop. You're not segregating or diluting your product—you're expanding your base to include tens of millions of people between the ages of twelve and forty-five. We know that roughly forty-five million people worldwide spend $12 billion annually on hip-hop products. And don't think it's just black folks I'm talking about. When I worked at Def Jam, the RIAA figured out that eighty percent of the people who bought our records were non-African-American. That's why I laugh every time I get called an African-American mogul. Most of the people who buy Phat Farm are white too. People want to call it an "ethnic" company, but that's a misnomer. I make pink argyle sweaters, for goodness' sake.

We have a long way to go, but things are changing every day. I just want them to change faster. And if you run a business or are looking to start one, you have to embrace the changes that hip-hop has made. If you don't accept that, you're going to find yourself on the outside looking in. If you can't talk the language of young people, your product can't grow. And the language that young people speak today is hip-hop. America is a diverse country, but until now, that diversity hasn't fully been reflected in its popular culture. That's changing and the successful businesspeople are going to be the ones who go with the change. That's why I always say that if you want to be succesful in the entertainment business, don't see color, see culture.

Ethnic Understanding

One person who's really helped me embrace the power of diversity is Rabbi Marc Schneier of the Foundation for Ethnic Understanding. Rabbi Schneier approached me several years ago and invited me to be part of his efforts, particularly in improving relations between blacks and Jews. It was a mission very close to my heart, since I not only work with so many Jews but have also admired the ways blacks and Jews worked together to lift up American consciousness during the Civil Rights Movement. So I eventually agreed not only to join the foundation, but now I'm actually chairman of the board. I made that commitment because I think communication can help clear up some of the misunderstandings that have kept people apart.

I know that some people wonder why I'm so passionate about

this kind of work, but my motives are transparent. I just want to encourage as much outreach as possible. Because I believe outreach is what will help black people and Jewish people get past any perceived differences. Just as I believe it can help black and Asian people, or Jewish and Latino people, get past their differences too. Look, as a foundation we understand we're not going to change the world overnight with a few fund-raisers. We know it's going to take more. What we're trying to do is create dialogue that promotes diversity to young people, so that they can effect those changes themselves.

I'll give you an example. One year, the foundation decided to honor Jay-Z at a fund-raiser. When I approached Jay about it, at first he was a little hesitant, because he didn't feel he'd done anything worthy of being honored. But I told Jay that in his own way, maybe without even realizing it, he had done important work, because one of his closest friends in the industry, Lyor Cohen, is Jewish. And Jay has been very public in acknowledging the impact Lyor has had on his career. To the millions of kids who follow Jay's every move, the message they're getting is that even if you were raised in the projects, there's nothing weird about calling a big Israeli guy with a funny accent your friend. That might not seem like much on the surface, but it can't be underestimated. Because everything, and I mean *everything*, someone like Jay says impacts youth culture in this country. When he started wearing throwback sports jerseys, kids all over the country started wearing those jerseys too. When Jay switched his look to button-down shirts, millions of kids stuffed those throwbacks way into the back of their closets and bought button-down shirts. So if Jay speaks about the importance of improving relations between blacks and Jews, it will have a real impact. If Condoleezza Rice went to a fund-raiser and spoke on the same topic, no one would question it. Well, I've got news. In American youth culture, Jay-Z has twice the influence of Condoleezza Rice. Just like Puffy has more influence than George Bush. So if I can use my connections to have a Jay-Z speak about the importance of accepting diversity, then that's what I'm going to do. Because it *will* effect a change.

But before you think I'm being too idealistic, understand that part of my motivation in promoting diversity is also creating a good business environment for people in the struggle, particularly African-Americans. When you don't embrace diversity, you are going to cost yourself money. It's that simple. Maybe the old white men who shut me out could afford to make that mistake, but most black folks can't. We simply can't afford to isolate ourselves economically. We can't afford to miss out on business opportunities, or any sort of opportunity for that matter, because of superficial issues like class and culture. Thankfully, I learned early in my career, and have been reminded so many times since then, that embracing people who might seem different is a great business practice. At the end of the day, even though your language might be different, or your clothes might be different, or your skin color might be different, or your religion might be different, your aspirations are most likely the same. When you study the various spiritual scriptures, even as superficially as I have, you begin to realize that nearly everyone is the same. We all want to live in a state of peace. We all want to be able to provide for our families and, if we're fortunate enough, build nice houses and go on vacations. We all want happiness on our own terms. We all want the freedom to be able to follow our own vision for our life. From Baltimore, to Baghdad, to Beijing, that's what we all want.

And I've seen it time and time again in my own career. I've made most of my money in the music and fashion industries. You know what many of the executives in those industries are? Jewish. In the fashion biz, I've almost become an honorary Syrian Jew, I work with so many. I could never be successful in these industries if I wasn't comfortable dealing with those guys. But I am, because I've come to learn that they're no different from me. Despite all the surface dissimilarities, we're more alike than we are different. I know now that it's possible for me to have as much in common with the Syrian Jews, or the Pakistani Muslims, as with the guy who grew up around the corner from me in Hollis. And once you have that knowledge, you lose so much weight. When you drop the racial and religious baggage that holds us down in this country, and also the world, you'll be free to start moving forward with the people who truly share your dreams and aspirations.

Demand Dialogue

One of the most effective ways of promoting diversity is through promoting dialogue. In the absence of dialogue, people tend to stand in their separate corners and build walls based on their perception of differences. But once the conversation starts, then those walls fall down. And once those walls fall down, then we're free to build something meaningful and lasting.

I know dialogue is the key to better personal relationships, better business relationships, and better politics. My belief in the power of dialogue is why I'm so committed to working with Rabbi Schneier. Similarly, my belief in the power of dialogue is why I'm equally committed to working with Minister Louis Farrakhan of the nation of Islam. That might sound like a contradictory statement to some people, but to me it's really the same thing. It's about promoting discussions that will draw people out of those dark corners and bring them back into the light, so they can see just how similar we really are.

As to Minister Farrakhan, I know that there are some who still call on me to publicly denounce him. But that ain't ever going to happen. That's because we're never going to find real success in this country if we try to isolate one another. One of the things that yoga has taught me is that it's more useful to bring people together than to divide. If I were to denounce Minister Farrakhan, that would just push people apart. But by continuing to work with him, I know that I'll have a better chance of bringing more people *together* in the long run.

Like many of us, I'm sure the Minister has said some things that didn't come out the right way. But I happen to know Mr. Farrakhan is also a person who wants all of us to do better in life, not just Muslims. And I know that like the rest of us, every day *he's* striving to be a better person *himself.* Besides, I've *seen* the good he's already done. I know that people went home after the Million Man March and changed for the better. Just like I know so many people were deeply moved by the Million Family March and the Millions More Movement as well. To say nothing of all the social and spiritual initiatives he's created that have had an incredibly positive impact on people's lives.

And I am definitely one of those people. I don't think I've ever heard a religious leader speak so eloquently about religion's ability to free people up rather than limit them. Just as I've never heard a leader speak so eloquently about the truth that all the scriptures are one, and that all people are one. That's why it pains me that as I'm writing this, Minister Farrakhan's physical form is struggling so much. Yet I'm also inspired that even during this struggle, he continues to promote love and unity of all people.

That inspiration is why I continue to promote dialogue with Minister Farrakhan, but promoting dialogue is really something I want to do whenever I think my resources can bring people together. That's why I tried to mediate an agreement between PETA and KFC. That's why I've tried to mediate so called "beefs" between people in the hip-hop community. That's why, when everyone was calling for troops to be sent into the Sudan to solve the situation in Darfur, I was one of the few people who stood up at the rally in Washington, D.C., and called for more *dialogue* instead. Not because those other people were wrong, or had bad intentions, but because I really believe that dialogue is the greatest tool we have in bringing people together. And I refuse to accept that there's any situation, no matter what's been said, or how diverse the participants are, or even how much blood has been spilled, that can't be solved through dialogue.

Support Diversity All the Time

I do want to make one important note here: You can't only support diversity and freedom when your rights are at stake—you should fight for those concepts for everyone, *all* of the time. You should speak out against prejudice whether it's directed toward African-Americans, Asian-Americans, Latinos, Muslims, Christians, Jews, blacks or whites, gay or straight, women, whoever. Because an attack against any group is an attack against you.

This is a particularly important message for the hip-hop nation. Now that we've tasted so much success, it's very easy to get complacent and stop fighting for everyone's rights. But we can't do that. We have to do even better.

Take the issue of gay marriage. Like the rest of the country, it seems the hip-hop nation is divided on this issue. Personally, I don't have a problem with it. If two people are in love and want to get married, why should we stand in their way? I'm not here to tell you what you should think, but if we truly support equal rights for everyone, then I think we could do more. I don't really see the hip-hop nation as being as far out in front on this issue, or on issues like women's rights, or immigrants' rights, as we could be. I'm not saying we're standing in the way, but I think we could do better. We fought, and continue to fight, very hard to secure our rights. But we can't get satisfied. Because you don't just swim to the other side of the river for yourself. You do it so you can help bring other people across with you.

And it's important we make that commitment to diversity not only in our words and actions, but in our hearts as well. Let's be real. Many of us get upset when some public figure makes a derogatory comment about African-Americans, but then in private we laugh at jokes about Asians or Mexicans or whoever. We need to get that kind of negativity out of our own heart if we expect other people to get it out of theirs.

One of the reasons people don't accept differences is that they spend too much time judging each other. I know I'm repeating this judgment rap a lot, but if there's one thing that bears repeating, it's that judgment will poison your dreams. That's why you should try to be aware of how much time you waste every day judging other people. Judging their hair, the way they walk, their clothes, everything. At some point today, tell yourself, "For the next hour I will not judge anything or anyone." You'll see how hard it is. And then you'll realize how much energy you waste worrying about other people when you could be using that energy on improving yourself. One of the mantras I like to meditate on is "Today I shall judge nothing that occurs." And when I'm not meditating, I just say, "Judgment is BS!"

PATHS TO GOD
(NOTICE THE PLURAL TENSE)

We've been speaking about race, which is one area where a lot of people still have a problem accepting diversity. Now I want to address another space in which people still have difficulty respecting diversity, which is religion.

I believe very strongly that there are as many paths to God as there are people. Therefore, there is no need for religions to be competitive. Look at my brother Reverend Run—he's a funny kind of reverend. He wears a collar and a cape, but he also goes to yoga and has been heavily influenced by its spiritual teachings. So I always call him a Christian yogi, whatever that means. I must be one, too, because I'm as quick to quote the *Bhagavad Gita* as the Bible. That might sound like a contradiction to some people, but it's as natural as breathing to me. Like I said before, there are many paths. And I want to walk down all of them. I might turn around after a while, or even make a wrong turn, but I know that as long as I'm heading toward God, then I must be going in the right direction.

They're All Good Because They're All God

Since I've gotten more in touch with my spiritual side, the teachings of all religions sound good to me. That's because the great prophets all taught the same thing, which is love. They might have come at different times, and spoken different languages, but they all revealed the same truths. It's very important that we recognize that, and instead of retreating into the doctrines we're most comfortable with, we stay open to all these important messengers and messages.

I believe that anyone who thinks only his or her religion is right is actually *wrong*. No disrespect, but you're *wrong*. You have to remember that Jesus wasn't a Christian, Muhammad wasn't a Muslim, Abraham wasn't a Jew, and the Buddha wasn't a Buddhist. In other words, these great prophets didn't look to separate themselves through labels or titles. They were only interested in promoting ways to stay in union with God. The gangs and the rules and the organizations didn't come till much later. Instead, they all looked to unite the people around them through finding God and spreading love. And only when you accept that fact can you receive the true gifts of their teachings.

That separatist attitude is at the heart of the violence in Iraq, in Israel, in the Sudan, in India, in the Philippines, in Nigeria, in Ireland, in Bosnia, in Chechnya, and so many other places in the world that I don't even know about yet. And, as much as we don't want to admit it, it's starting to be the case more and more in this country too. All these so-called religious leaders want to claim that only their prophet was right and then point their fucking fingers at the next man's religion! But that's the worst thing any religious leader can do, because that finger-pointing just leads to violence.

Think about it. If you could sit down Lord Buddha, Jesus, Muhammad, and Abraham in the same room, do you think they would start picking up chairs and fighting each other? Of course not. They'd have nothing but love for each other. Because they all preached nothing but love. So why is it that so many fundamentalist Christians, Jews, Hindus, and Muslims want to fight in the names of those great teachers?

If you're a Muslim extremist, do you really think that God is sitting somewhere saying, "Great job killing those Jews!" Or if you're a Jewish extremist, why would you think that God would be happy with you for killing Muslims? It's the dumbest thing I've ever heard. Anyone who thinks God wants you to kill for him is acting out of ego, not faith. God doesn't need you to kill in the name of a gang. The truth is, if God really wanted the world to be Islamic, or Christian, or Mormon, then that's what would happen. No matter how much humans tried to fight against it with their little guns and bombs. Remember, God doesn't want us to convert anyone for him, or to "protect" any faiths. He just wants us to work hard at fulfilling our own potential.

When it's all said and done, I think God's going to be happy with the person who spent his or her life trying to give and leading a nonharmful existence, even if that person never went to church. Conversely, I don't think God will be pleased with a person who went to mosque, or church, or synagogue every day, but also killed in God's name.

That's why if you want to be extreme about something, be extreme about loving. Or be extreme about giving for a living. Be extreme about following your vision. Be extreme about surrounding yourself with positive people. Be extreme about practicing good Karma. Be extreme about counting your blessings. Be extreme about always being present. Be extreme about starting today. Be extreme about empowering yourself. Be extreme about spitting truth to power. These are the principles you should always try to be passionate about. Not shutting people out, or putting them down, or harming them because they seem to be different.

RECOGNIZE THE REAL:

If it were up to me, I'd burn all the flags in this country, not because I'm unpatriotic, but because I want to get rid of all things that let people separate themselves from each other.

Hip-hop is about empowering people to end poverty and ignorance. No matter who we are, we need to create opportunity for those who are locked out.

LAW NUMBER ELEVEN:

BE POWERFUL, BE HEARD

Nobody can give you freedom. Nobody can give you equality or justice or anything. If you're a man, you take it.

—MALCOLM X

FOR ME, one of the best perks of so called celebrity is getting to travel around the country, speaking to young people. It's very inspiring for me to hear what's on their minds and learn about their perceptions and aspirations. And while I'm always eager to hear their stories, I have a fundamental message that I want to share with them too—the message of always knowing your own worth. That's why many times when I speak at colleges or universities, the events are billed as a lecture on "Empowerment Through Hip-Hop." While "lecture" might be a generous description (my appearances are a lot more informal than that), it is true that empowerment is always one of the major themes.

Specifically, there are two kinds of empowerment I try to promote. The first is personal empowerment, in which individuals who have been so worn down by the struggle that they begin to doubt themselves find the courage to wipe off their lenses and see that they *can* control their own destinies. The second is community empowerment, in which communities that have been locked out *collectively* lift themselves out of the struggle and assert their aspirations. I know those might seem like lofty goals, but I believe they can be achieved once we all have an appreciation of our physical, mental, political, and financial worth.

EMPOWER YOURSELF THROUGH
EMPOWERING OTHERS

Until recently, I probably would have described myself profession-ally as a promoter of youth culture. I saw my job as promoting the hot new shirt, the hot new rapper, the hot new poet, or the hot new comedian. However, I've come to realize that my job entails much more than promotion. My job is really to find ways I can use my resources to help people *empower* themselves.

I was reminded of that truth recently at the Clinton Global Initiative, which I mentioned earlier. One of my favorite memo-ries of that week was watching Chris Tucker work a room filled with world leaders, promoting ways we can fight AIDS in Africa. Chris got his big break on *Def Comedy,* so to see him standing alongside President Clinton while talking about helping Africans was a very powerful moment for me. I almost never use the word *proud,* because there's too much ego in it. But I was *proud* to see Chris using his celebrity so wisely. To think that one of my TV shows had empowered Chris not only to help himself, his family, and his friends, but to then do something as meaningful as help fight poverty in Africa, was an incredible feeling. It made me feel like maybe my life's work *has* had some value. By helping empower Chris, I felt I had played a small role in many others' being em-powered as well.

I'm not suggesting that my desire to empower people is completely altruistic. Again, it's very important to understand that when you empower other people, you're really empowering *yourself* as well. That's one of the fundamental messages of this chapter. Just like practicing good Karma, or Giving for a Living, empowering others will have a positive impact on your spiritual well-being and on your worldly success. So even if you think you don't give a shit about the next man, or the next woman, empow-ering others is still in your best self-interest. Because the more people you can empower, the more blessings you will generate for yourself.

In terms of personal empowerment, there are many different roads that will lead you toward the fulfillment of your own worth. Some people get a sense of self through religion. For others, the empowerment comes through intellectual pursuits or physical prowess. Personally, I've managed to find a little bit of all those empowerment tools through the practice of yoga. But yoga doesn't only empower you, it does so in a way that makes you more sympathetic to the needs and the struggles of the people around you. So by empowering people through yoga, I'm actually creating a more caring environment for me to live in.

Another great example is voting, which I'll also discuss later in this chapter. I believe that my life definitely improves when young people are empowered by the political process. I believe young people are more compassionate with their votes. In fact, I've seen the polls and studies that *prove* that young people are more tolerant and open-minded in how they view the world. That is why when they vote, on the average they don't vote for policies that promote exclusion, fear, hoarding, and war. They vote for policies that promote inclusion, trust, giving, and peace. So if they became more empowered, it would create not only a better world for me to live in, but for my children to grow up in as well. And promoting that sort of world is definitely in my best interest.

Similarly, I certainly come into more blessings whenever I'm able to empower young people through the Hip-Hop Summit's "Get Your Money Right" Tour. As someone who sells toys like clothes and jewelry, encouraging young people to save their money might not seem to be in my best interest. In fact, just the opposite is true. When young people handle their money wisely, it only makes my brands stronger. Remember, I try to build classic, lasting brands that don't cater to the trends. So when young people use their money wisely, instead of blowing it on the trendy shit, then they'll be more likely to seek out classic, lasting styles. They'll be more likely to grow with my brands. I'd rather young people save a little money now and build a meaningful portfolio. That way we can have a relationship that will last for decades, instead of for a few years, or even just a few seasons.

And a final word to the employers out there—it is definitely in your best interest to empower your employees. I know that when the people who work for me feel empowered, they become much more effective employees. When they feel empowered, they seek out new challenges and opportunities on their own accord without having to be told what to do. So rather than having to spend most of my time micromanaging, I can use my energy concentrating on the big picture, which I'm much more effective at. That's why I always remind my employees of the old Chinese proverb (with my own take on it), "Give a man a fish sandwich and you feed him for a day. Teach a man to fish and we'll all eat fish sandwiches for a lifetime." So remember, when you promote a culture of collective empowerment in your company, then everyone eats better.

GET YOUR BODY AND
MIND RIGHT FIRST

One of the first steps toward empowerment is having confidence in your physical form. That doesn't necessarily just mean being able to run fast or jump high, or lift a lot of weights. Those abilities can make you feel great for a short while, but the effect they'll have on your life is limited. What I'm really promoting is being comfortable in your own body, of having confidence in your physical relationship with the earth. Some people find that comfort through sports, for some it's dance, for others it's simply watching what they eat. As you know by now, I've found that sense of well-being through yoga.

The Asana, or physical component, of yoga is what initially got me addicted to the practice. I wasn't expecting it, but sweating like a slave and working my ass off while trying to remember God with each breath gave me a sense of physical connectedness that I hadn't felt before. And after each session, I'd feel like I had stretched out all my muscles and ligaments, realigned my system, improved my circulation, and regained a little bit of the balance that had been missing in my life. Instead of feeling tired, I felt completely rejuvenated. And to this day, whenever I come out of a yoga class, I still feel inspired, similar to the rush I get when I'm immersed in a new business project, or social program. And that sense of energy and purpose can inject a sense of empowerment into your day.

Having said that, I try not to get too caught up in the whole physical thing. Just like you can't take your money with you when it's time to check out, you can't take your looks or your health with you either. So as important as it is to be comfortable with the condition of your body, it's much more important to be comfortable with what condition your mind is in. That's why I must stress that the physical practice of yoga is actually only one of eight steps involved in the process. The other seven are spiritual steps designed to bring you closer to God. As a student of yoga for over ten years, I have seen that yoga has led me to feel healthier, more aware, and empowered in all aspects of my personal and professional life. Essentially, it's helped me manifest my dreams.

Smile and Breathe

The physical practice of yoga might seem to be about putting your body into crazy poses. But in fact, its real purpose is to help remind you how you can overcome any physical, mental, or spiritual sense of disempowerment through the simple act of smiling and breathing.

For example, let's say that you're trying to do a physical pose called "Salamba Sirsasana," or, in layman's terms, a headstand. Essentially, it requires you to kneel, setting your forearms on the floor shoulder-width apart. Join your hands, then lean your head forward so that all your weight is on your head. Next, you must straighten your legs so that your toes touch the floor behind you, then lift your legs up over your head in a straight line and keep them there for fifty breaths. On paper it sounds next to impossible, but people who practice yoga can do it without much trouble. How? By smiling and focusing on their breath. That's how you overcome *every* difficult pose in yoga, by smiling and breathing.

The physical practice is a reminder that those poses are an extension of life itself. Each pose represents one of the many difficulties we all face in life. And just as you can get past the physical obstacles by smiling and breathing, in the same manner you can get past the *emotional* obstacles you perceive to be in your way. That hour-long class is really just an intense example of what you have to do during the rest of the day. So if your boyfriend breaks up with you, instead of cursing him out or crying, try to smile and breathe instead. Focus on your breath and it won't seem as painful. If you're about to take a test and you don't feel prepared, instead of panicking, just smile and breathe. Get yourself in a positive space and get a much better score, even if you're not prepared. Or if you're about to leave your job for a new opportunity and you're worried about whether it's the right decision, just smile and breathe. All the anxiety will fall away and you'll live up to your potential. Remember when earlier in the book I said "smile and breathe" is the most common piece of advice I give to people? Well, that is a truth I learned from yoga.

If you can wake up every day and approach your work with a smile and a breath, I really believe you can lead a healthier life. When you know your mind can take whatever the world throws at it, you'll be much happier. I know my life is much healthier, both physically and spiritually, now that I've embraced the Asana practice.

Erase the Anxiety

Yoga is also a crucial tool for empowerment because it helps get rid of our old friends self-doubt and anxiety. Yoga can teach you to harness the power that's inside of you, instead of constantly diluting that power with worry. So many times in life, we fight the same struggles over and over again. And in the process, we end up disenfranchising ourselves as much as any racist politician or greedy businessman could ever hope to.

I certainly used to disenfranchise myself. I had money, traveled the world, ate in the finest restaurants, stayed in the best hotels, and was always surrounded by powerful people. But I struggled with fame and success as much as I had struggled with obscurity and so-called failure. I had money in my pocket, but *still* worried I wasn't smart enough. I still worried that I wasn't talented enough. I *still* worried that my next idea was going to fail and that people would laugh at me. I *still* worried that it was all going to end one day and everyone would say I was just a fluke. I still worried that people only wanted to be around me for my money and for what I could get them, instead of truly liking and caring about me.

And to be honest, I *still* ask myself those same questions. The difference is now, I might *ask* those questions, but I don't *struggle* with them as much. They come into my mind, but through yoga, I'm able to push them right out again. Through yoga, I can hear God's voice telling me that *I am* talented. I can hear it reminding me that I am smart. That I will realize my dreams with hard work and focus. Reminding me that it won't end tomorrow, and if it does, I'll still be OK. Yoga has helped me believe that people love me for who I am, instead of who I appear to be. Yoga helps you realize that nothing is out of your reach, that no bar is too high and no race is too long. That's the gift that yoga gave me.

I was reminded of this recently when I was speaking to some students about the power of yoga. After my lecture, one of the students came up to me and said, "Russell, you kept saying how meditation has been one of the keys to your success. But you weren't meditating when Run DMC was big. You weren't meditating when Def Jam first blew up. You got paid all of those times without yoga."

On the surface, he was right. It's true that I was able to manage Run DMC without the benefit of yoga. Just like it's true that I helped build Def Jam before meditation was even on my radar. But I also had to tell him he was overlooking a key fact: You see, without that focus and the confidence I gained through yoga, Def Jam would have been the zenith of my success. Let's be real, I wasn't the first black guy to make a little money in the record business. My initial success was nothing that Berry Gordy, Quincy Jones, or many, many other talented people hadn't done before me. If I've done something that's fairly unique, I like to think it's being one of the few guys who were able to build on their initial success. I like to think that what separates me from the pack is that I made some money and, as hard as I might have tried, didn't piss it all away on cocaine, parties, and cars. I avoided being another guy who had it all and then lost it all just as quickly.

BE POWERFUL, BE HEARD

We've been talking about yoga, which is a fantastic tool in promoting personal empowerment. Now I want to promote a tool that can do a similar job in uplifting you and your community. A tool that can empower you by making it impossible for the powers that be to ignore you any longer. A tool that will help you establish a real connection between you, your community, and the world at large. And that tool is voting.

We've already established that the hip-hop nation moves as an army, an army that determines what's hot in this country. That's a tremendous amount of power to wield. Which is why I want to encourage our army not only to flex our muscle in the artistic and commercial worlds, but in the political and social process as well. Those are the spaces where we can do the *most* good work with our power. Not only for ourselves, but for the entire country and ultimately the entire world.

This lack of political empowerment is why voter registration and political activism is the fundamental mission of the Hip-Hop Summit Action Network. It's very important that young people, who often perceive themselves as being locked out and disenfranchised, embrace the political process. They might feel like they don't have a say in politics, but the fact is that no matter where you come from or live your vote counts every bit as much as Bill Gates's vote. Just like its counts every bit as much as my vote, or Donald Trump's vote or President Bush's vote too.

Thankfully, the message of political empowerment has been well received by the hip-hop nation. In just five years, we've held over sixty summits, which helped register hundreds of thousands of new voters. Just as importantly, wherever the summits are held, rappers come out and help us share this message with their fans. So it's really just a matter of time before young people realize that the key to unlocking many of their frustrations is already in the palm of their hand. Through the efforts of the rappers and the Hip-Hop Summit, young people are becoming more aware that by exercising their right to vote, they're recognizing a law of success that will empower them for a lifetime.

Feel the Connection

I'll admit that I haven't always promoted voting this strongly. The truth is, I didn't even register myself until I was well into my thirties. Like many people in this country, I felt disconnected from the political process. I was aware that the civil rights movement had fought very hard to ensure my right to vote, but I still didn't appreciate its value. And when you don't feel connected to the process, it's very easy to sit back and complain, or sit back and just watch things happen. You watch unfair drugs laws get passed, bills that only benefit big business get signed, and wars get started, but you still don't feel a responsibility to do anything about it. It starts to feel like you're *watching* history happen, instead of *making* history happen.

We know many young people don't have that sense of responsibility, but it's not because they're callous, or don't have an opinion on things. The lack of responsibility is rooted in a sense of powerlessness. You don't feel responsible because you don't feel like you could ever really make a dent in the world. It's a lack of connectedness more than a lack of caring. And one of the easiest ways to connect is through voting.

You're Already Paying for It

There's also a more straightforward reason to take advantage of your vote—you're already paying for it. Even if you say you're not "down" with politics, I've got some news for you—you *are* already down. No matter what you think about politicians, or how much politics turns you off, if you're earning a check, then you're already part of the process. That's because the government is taking a slice of every check you earn and using that money to fund its policies. You can stay at home on Election Day for the rest of your life, but Uncle Sam is still going to take his cut. So wouldn't you rather have a say in how he uses it?

If your wife, or your husband, came back from shopping with your credit card, wouldn't you ask what she or he bought with it? Of course you would. So you need to ask your politicians the same thing when it comes to how they spend your money. It's your right to ask them what policies they're paying for with your money.

Remember, you're not only paying for those policies with your check, you're paying for them with your Karma as well when you don't vote. You create bad Karma for yourself when you don't weigh in on policies that harm innocent people. If you don't vote and your indifference helps elect a gangster government that abuses its power, then that abuse is on *your* Karma. But when you vote for candidates that don't seem as eager to lead our country into negative situations, then at least you've tried to promote a more positive path. The candidate that you've supported might not win, but at least you've done your part. And doing your part is the responsibility that comes with being empowered.

I'm encouraged by how seriously the hip-hop nation took its responsibility during the last presidential election, but we weren't able to effect enough of a change in that race. Because we took such an active stance, some people interpreted President Bush's reelection as a sign that young people still haven't emerged as a political force. But I saw something different. I saw young people voting for themselves, internalizing the idea that they had made an investment in themselves and their future. It was a first step in personal and communal empowerment of young people and I was inspired to be a part of it.

Even though the Hip-Hop Summit continues to register new voters in record numbers, the establishment still looks at hip-hop's activism as just a fad. But remember, those are the same kinds of people who said that hip-hop itself was just a fad. We've proved that mentality wrong before, and we're going to do it again. Even back in the seventies, I knew hip-hop was going to last because it empowered people by giving a voice to the voiceless. That's the same reason the political empowerment of the hip-hop nation won't be a fad either. Because now that they've been empowered, the hip-hop nation knows voting is another way to make its voice heard, another way to help shape the world. We didn't stop then and we aren't going to stop now either.

Transcending Parties

I don't represent any party. I only represent hip-hop, which not only transcends race, ethnicity, class, gender, geography, religion, and national boundaries but transcends political parties as well. I know when I talk about "gangster governments" and voting President Bush out of office, it might seem that I'm implicitly endorsing the Democratic Party. However, while I've been very vocal about my disappointment with President Bush's response to September 11, the subsequent war in Iraq, and his lack of compassion for the victims of Hurricane Katrina specifically and poor people in general, I don't want anyone to interpret this chapter as either an attack on the Republicans or as an endorsement of the Democrats. The truth is, when I encourage you to vote, it's never just for one party or for one issue. Once you register, I don't care if you cast that vote as a Republican, Democrat, a Libertarian, a Communist, an Independent, a member of the Green Party, or whatever. I just want you to be part of the process.

I know the media calls me a "Democratic operative" sometimes, but I think I've demonstrated my impartiality by endorsing Republican Michael Bloomberg for mayor of New York City and Republican Michael Steele in last year's Maryland Senate race. Admittedly, the Steele endorsement in particular shocked and disappointed a lot of my liberal friends. But they shouldn't have been surprised, because I'd been impressed by Mr. Steele's integrity and vision for some time, especially his vision for economic self-empowerment for poor people in America. That he was a Republican was never a big issue to me. Instead, I saw someone who was committed to empowering people in the struggle.

When it comes to politics, I try not to focus on labels—instead, I try to focus on finding the high notes in politicians and then working on pushing those notes to the forefront. Therefore, if a Democrat wants to do something about empowering poor people, I'm going to support that person. And if a Republican is truly committed to helping lift people out of the struggle, that person can count on my support as well. At the end of the day, I don't give a care about political parties or polls or the public perception. All I care about is finding ways to make this system uplift poor people. And whoever can help me in that quest is going to have my support.

That's why if the Democrats think that they can take the hip-hop vote for granted, they are mistaken. I'll admit that philosophically the Democrats are more in tune with the aspirations and the needs of people in the struggle. In recent history, they have done much more to empower poor people than their opponents. (Conversely, the Republicans haven't only failed to empower people in the struggle, they've made disenfranchising them part of their policies.) But despite the Democrats' positive legacy, lately they seem too preoccupied with polls and perception to truly fight for the changes that could make a difference in poor people's lives.

I attribute the Democrats' lack of will to the fact that their leadership is still too far removed from the people they want to help. Essentially, it seems Democrats want to help people without knowing them. When I go to Democratic fund-raisers, I'm often alarmed by how few black people are there. Or by how few Asians or Latinos are there either. I once walked out of a very big Democratic strategy meeting in New York City because of the nearly one-thousand people there, almost all were white. They were talking about empowering people, but none of the people they were going to empower were present to hear them. A barbecue at Dick Cheney's house would probably look more inclusive than that fund-raiser!

I know I'm giving the Democrats a hard time here, but only because I really want them to do better. I've invested a lot of resources in the Democratic Party, because out of the current options, I believe they can do the best job to uplift America. I just don't want them to take hip-hop in particular, or African-Americans in general, for granted. The Democrats need to compete for our interests and our votes, instead of assuming that we're going to follow them blindly every November.

Ultimately, we shouldn't rely on the Democrats or the Republicans to invite us to their parties. Instead, hip-hop needs to unify the voices of all people who want politicians to focus on fighting poverty and ignorance and promoting love. No matter what flag those people happen to stand under. And when those voices, which might be singing alone right now, become a hip-hop chorus, then we're going to see a dramatic change for the better in this country.

I'm Not Running

I want to end this section by addressing the myth that my political activism is designed to set the stage for my own eventual run for office. While it's very flattering that someone would even think I was capable of holding an office, I can promise you that the speculation is wrong. First off, I don't have any political aspirations outside of empowering people. Secondly, even if I did decide to run one day, I'm too messed up to ever be elected. I enjoyed myself way too much in the eighties—I can't even imagine the photographs and stories that would emerge if I ever did subject myself to that sort of scrutiny. That's why when I hear the pundits predicting that I'm going to run for city council, or mayor, or governor, I just laugh. Because I know it's not going to happen.

But I am trying to set the stage for a day when some of the young people reading this book will feel empowered enough to run for office *themselves.* I like to think I helped ignite a cultural revolution with hip-hop, and I want to help effect a new social movement through hip-hop's political empowerment as well. Hip-hop is the best generation we've ever had. But it can be so much greater with a stronger commitment to the political process.

GET YOUR MONEY RIGHT

We've been talking about spiritual and political empowerment, but I also realize that many of you picked up this book in order to learn about concrete steps you can take toward financial empowerment. Far from being separate, these issues are actually closely related. The most important step you can take toward financial empowerment is the spiritual investment of empowering someone else first. That's *always* the best investment you can make.

Having said that, I want to speak directly on financial empowerment, since there's a real hunger out there for this sort of information. That hunger is why the Hip-Hop Summit has is so focused on its Get Your Money Right Tour, which features rappers speaking directly to hip-hop fans about how to get their financial house in order. It's been a huge success, mainly because we've been blessed to be able to pick up the phone and call a Nelly, an Eminem, or a Beyonce and have them come out and speak about this issue in a way that's credible, and in a language that their fans can understand. And for young people not only to hear this message of fiscal responsibility but to have it sink in, is incredibly empowering.

This message is particularly important because the schools aren't teaching young people how to have a stable financial relationship with the world. The schools aren't teaching our youth about credit. They're not teaching them what a FICO score is. They're not teaching them about how to rebuild their credit if they've gotten into trouble. They're not teaching them about predatory lenders, or about how to get a legitimate loan either. They're not teaching them about building equity. Even though we know our young people are going to be bombarded with offers for credit cards and loans while they're developing financial habits that could hurt them in the future, we still don't share this information with them. And because of that lack of instruction, too many young people fall into a cycle that promotes spending (and debt) instead of saving (and strong credit). Many end up making mistakes with their money, mistakes that they then spend a lifetime trying to make up for. That's why we're working so hard to change their perception of personal finances. If you want very specific advice on how to avoid those pitfalls, then I highly recommend you visit the Hip-Hop Summit's Web site at HSAN.org. We're going to deal with the larger issues of financial-literacy empowerment in this chapter, but the Web site will provide you with specific information you can use to start getting your money right today.

Make Money to Make More Money

When it comes to financial empowerment, the first thing the hip-hop nation must realize is that it's *already* empowered. Every year, it pumps billions of dollars into the economy. That's real power, but only if it's used wisely. The problem is that hip-hop just isn't using that purchasing power to invest in things that tend to increase in value. Instead, the majority of that money is spent on toys like televisions, cars, clothes, and jewelry. And while those kinds of toys are fun, they don't grow in value. That's why we're encouraging young people to spend their money on things that can grow into even *more* money, like real estate, stocks, and even small businesses. You might feel great after you buy a forty-inch TV for your apartment, but you'll feel even better when you buy a smaller TV instead, then put the money you saved toward *owning* your apartment. So while it's cool to buy a CD from your favorite rapper, if you save a little every month and get your money right, maybe you can start your *own* label. And one day your favorite rapper might be recording for you.

Emphasize Owning

As a community, we still focus too much on renting and leasing. I know those often seem like the only options, but if you clean off your lenses, you will see that you can obtain anything when you're smart with your money. You'll see that you can empower yourselves by putting more emphasis on *ownership.*

Rightly or wrongly, the world caters to people who own things. It doesn't cater to people who rent things or lease things or put them on layaway. If you own your home, you get a tax break. If you make your mortgage payments on time, your credit score goes up. And then you can buy even more property. If you own your own home, you get more respect from your neighbors, from the cops, from the politicians, from everyone. It might not be right, it might not be fair, but it's a reality that we can't hide from. When you own the things that are a priority in your life, you're a player in this game. But when other people own them, and then sell them back to you, you're usually going to get played.

Thankfully, an emphasis on ownership is already becoming a bigger part of hip-hop's message. So many artists are now talking about being a CEO instead of "just" being a rapper. That's a great cultural shift. Previously, rappers usually talked about how they deserved a deal from a record label. But now they're focused on owning their own labels. They've seen the examples set by people like Jay-Z, Damon Dash, 50 Cent, Master P, and Cash Money and they know that *they* can be the ones handing out the deals, instead of the ones looking for a handout. And that's another important sign of empowerment.

Past the Bling

I want to take a moment to address the perception that somehow rappers aren't appropriate role models for fiscal responsibility. In the eyes of some critics, hip-hop promotes a world that's filled with fancy cars and bling—the kind of lifestyle that's unobtainable for most people. Therefore it's hypocritical for rappers to come to the summits and encourage young people to save and be smart with their money.

Well, to those who say we're promoting an unobtainable lifestyle, I ask how the hell is it unattainable? I achieved that lifestyle and I don't come from privilege. Ludacris got it and he doesn't come from privilege either. Just like 50 Cent, Snoop Dogg, Nas, TI, Eminem, and so many other artists who came up in the struggle have managed to obtain it too. The cars and the jewelry aren't meant to make you feel bad about yourself, or to drive you into debt. Instead, they're meant to inspire you. They're a way of saying that you can do it too. That with hard work, dedication, and faith, anyone can do it.

But while we understand the aspirational significance of those toys, at the Hip-Hop Summit, we're also encouraging young people to look *past* the bling. Because when most people watch a hip-hop video, they only see the cars and the jewelry. What they don't see is the accountants and managers working behind the scenes to make sure that there's enough money to buy those toys. So while rappers *seem* to be spending unlimited money in their videos, in real life many of them are very responsible with their money. Certainly LL Cool J wouldn't be where he is after twenty years in the game if he was reckless with his money. Jay-Z wouldn't make *Vanity Fair*'s Power List if he didn't have a financial plan. Puffy wouldn't be able to simultaneously run companies like Bad Boy and Sean Jean if he was blowing all his money on toys.

It's very important for these young people to understand that many rappers are using their minds to find ways to make even more money. It seems like almost every rapper that attends a summit has an amazing story to tell about the business ventures he's involved in. When Paul Wall came to one of our Houston summits, he talked about how he actually just raps for fun. His real money comes from ventures like designing custom-made gold teeth, or grills, for celebrity clients. Similarly, Ice Cube broke down how, while he played around with a little bit of money as a rapper, he made his real fortune producing his own movies. It's very important for young people to realize that their heroes aren't one-dimensional when it comes to finances. It's important for them to understand that 50 Cent is making so much money off his energy drink, his clothing line, his sneakers, and his video games that he never has to sell another record as long as he lives. So even if 50's videos seem to promote lavish spending, the reality is much different. He's actually a disciplined businessman who doesn't play around his money. That's the real message that these heroes are sharing at the summits. It might not be a message that's been promoted as loudly as the bling, but it's definitely getting louder.

My Own Money

When it comes to handling my own money, I'm probably as conservative as you can get. I'll take risks when it comes to new businesses, because I'm comfortable banking on myself. But as far my actual investment portfolio, I play it very close to the vest. The financial plan laid out by my friend and advisor Tracy Maitland isn't designed to make me any richer, but to protect the little bit of wealth I have. Specifically, I've put a great part of holdings in AAA convertible bonds, which are a pretty safe choice. They may not be as fruitful as real estate or stocks, but at least I know they're not going to lose any money.

That doesn't mean I'm encouraging you to run out and buy some bonds. I'm not an expert on this subject by any means and I would never pretend to know enough about the financial market to tell you specifically what to do with your own money. If you want to know what kind of bonds to buy, or how to play the market, there are a lot of other books and TV shows that speak to that. The sole reason I'm sharing this is to show you that I do have a long-term goal for my money. I want you to understand that even though I wear a baseball hat and sneakers, that even though maybe I don't speak so well all of the time, that even though I come from a culture that some think is shortsighted and materialistic, I actually am fairly conservative with my money.

And even more importantly, I'm far from alone. Every successful rapper, no matter how many cars are in his videos, or chains are around his neck, has a similar plan as well. I'm not saying he is the next Warren Buffet—plenty of rappers have blown, or come close to blowing, their fortunes. But so have plenty of doctors, or stockbrokers, or lawyers, or actors, and even so called moguls. That's why we need to stop holding rappers up to a different standard than the rest of society, and instead start saluting them for being a support system for their fans. From movies to TV to the rest of the music industry, I don't see any other artists who do as much to try to empower their fans. The rappers who support the Hip-Hop Summit aren't promoting a dream— they're promoting a tangible support system that all their fans can access.

I don't think it's an exaggeration to say that financial literacy, economic empowerment, and wealth building is going to be the last leg of the civil rights movement. Because one step toward financial literacy takes you two steps toward personal empowerment. Just like voting and yoga take you closer to empowerment as well. And when I sit at the Hip-Hop Summits and watch the rappers talk to their fans about financial literacy, talk to them about voting, and talk to them about knowing their physical and mental worth, I really feel that this generation is not so far away from getting it right. Because I know they're looking to improve the quality of life for all people. They want to help raise the consciousness of the masses. And if they can do that, then we'll all have the empowerment that we seek.

RECOGNIZE THE REAL:

The people in power love to see poor black, white, Latino, Asian, and Native Americans stay separated. Because when they're separated, they can't harness the incredible power that they posses collectively. The power they would have if they voted together on a common agenda. The power they would have if they made a financial commitment to supporting companies that supported them back.

Always speak from your heart, even if what you're saying isn't popular. Dissent built this country. There's no one good idea that we have to subscribe to. We can never be afraid to add our voice to the American voice, which is a collective voice.

LAW NUMBER TWELVE:

SPIT TRUTH TO POWER

Do not believe in anything simply because you have heard it. Do not believe in anything simply because it is spoken and rumored by many. Do not believe in anything simply because it is found written in your religious books. Do not believe in anything merely on the authority of your teachers and elders. Do not believe in traditions because they have been handed down for many generations. But after observation and analysis, when you find that anything agrees with reason and is conducive to the good and benefit of one and all, then accept it and live up to it.

—LORD BUDDHA

I'VE SPENT A LOT OF TIME celebrating the good work hip-hop has done in this country, particularly through promoting diversity, empowering young people, and reminding them to Do You. But I want to end by this book acknowledging one of hip-hop's greatest accomplishments, which has been giving a voice to the voiceless. An amplified, articulate, and adamant voice that can't be ignored. You can't shut your ears to the truth when hip-hop has the microphone.

Thankfully, this commitment to spitting truth has remained a constant staple of the culture over the past twenty-five years. From Melle Mel to KRS-One to Chuck D to Dead Prez to Eminem, hip-hop has never been afraid to spit truth to power and tell the country what's *really* happening in the streets. Of course, you may hear some of the struggle, particularly the raw poverty and ignorance, in the voices of rappers, but we can't forget that voice is expressing their reality. That's why while I encourage the high notes, at the end of the day, I'm more worried about cursed *actions* than curse *words*. The bigger problem is that the negativity exists, not that the rappers are expressing it. Instead of attacking rappers for expressing our reality, we should applaud them for forcing us to address the wounds of poverty and disenfranchisement that continue to fester in this country.

The challenge we now face is to spread hip-hop's example throughout society. We have to spread the message that in order to find true success, we can't ignore the truth. So whether you're a rapper, a real estate agent, or a retiree, your priority should always be to address the truth rather than sweep it under the rug.

DON'T BREAK THE MIRROR

In all the years I've been involved in hip-hop, one of the most thrilling moments for me came in 1989 when NWA released their song "Fuck tha Police." Of course at the time, a lot of people, especially those in police departments, were less than thrilled about that song. In fact, they were outraged by what they considered an attempt to incite violence against them. The police didn't just want the song banned from the radio, they wanted NWA thrown in jail. They thought if NWA was allowed to promote that song's message, it could challenge the police's authority.

But I heard something different. I heard a group of young people from South Central Los Angeles who had the courage to speak the truth about the police brutality that was a huge issue not only in their city, but in African-American communities all over the nation. NWA wasn't saying "Fuck tha Police" just to be controversial, or as a call for revenge. Instead of creating more violence, they were trying to end it. They were hoping that by talking about the problem loudly enough, they would finally provoke someone do something about it.

And while I do believe that "Fuck tha Police" did make the atmosphere a little bit better in Los Angeles for a time, people in power still didn't listen closely enough. Instead of doing something about that raw frustration, they kept looking the other way until the Rodney King riots finally forced them to address the situation. But all the suffering and loss that came with the riots could have been avoided if we had listened a little closer to NWA's warning. Not everyone might have agreed with the language they used to sound an alarm, but in retrospect we have to appreciate how prescient that warning was.

Unfortunately, almost twenty years later, we're still not listening closely enough, as evidenced by Hurricane Katrina. For years, New Orleans rappers like Master P, Juvenile, and Lil' Wayne have been releasing powerful, graphic songs depicting the poverty and despair in their communities. But once again, society didn't listen. When the Hot Boyz rhymed about "bling-bling," society heard *that* message loud and clear. Society heard it so clearly that they even put "bling-bling" in the *Webster's* dictionary! But when the Hot Boyz rhymed about the social conditions in New Orleans, that message didn't get the same kind of attention. It wasn't until Katrina ripped the lid off New Orleans's incredible poverty and hopelessness that society threw up its hands and said, "How could this be? How could people be living like this? It doesn't look like America." And it was frustrating to hear those sorts of comments. Because society wouldn't only have known about the real conditions in New Orleans, but could have actually started doing something about them, if it had listened more closely to what the rappers had been saying. But society didn't hear, not because the truth wasn't being shouted at them, but because they closed their ears to it. When I say society, I'm referring mainly to the organized powers in this country. The politicians, the corporations, the schools and the media as well. I believe the *people* hear the truth very clearly when it's being shouted. But institutions shut it out, because many times that truth is critical of them. The truth often comes in the form of young people calling out old people in the establishment for their lies and hypocrisy. Obviously, that's not a message the establishment is interested in promoting.

I'll give you an example. Several years ago, I was invited to speak before a congressional panel reviewing Senator Joe Lieberman's Marketing Accountability Act, which was investigating the marketing of violent material to children. At the start of the hearing a senator, I think it was Senator Thompson from Tennessee, took the mike and shared his vision of how art could help influence society. "I think that every young American, especially teenage boys, should see *Saving Private Ryan*," he intoned. "I believe that movie builds character. I believe it helps them understand the sacrifices that come with war."

I found the senator's comment ironic, as it was very similar to the message I was trying to share with these politicians about hip-hop. Just as the senator felt there might be a greater message behind all the violence and killing in a movie directed by Steven Spielberg, I wanted to stress that there's a similar message in a record produced by someone like Dr. Dre.

So when it was my turn to testify, I told the committee that instead of seeing *Saving Private Ryan*, maybe teenagers should have to listen to Snoop Dogg. Instead of trying to teach them about a war that happened over fifty years ago, we need to teach young people about the war that's going on down the block *today*. We can't forget that people are dying on the sidewalks of our cities just as terribly as our troops did on the shores of Normandy. But while we rightly pay tribute to that past battle, we're not paying nearly enough attention to the battle that's waging today. I didn't say that to in any way disrespect the sacrifices of our veterans, but only to remind those politicians that they can't keep ignoring the truth that's taking place right here on our streets. I wanted to remind them that if they walked out of Congress and kept going for just a few minutes instead of getting into their chauffered cars, they'd see a real life war going on in the streets of D.C. A war that hip-hop has been reporting on for many years.

The problem is that when politicians hold these panels, it's usually to ask, "How is it that 50 Cent is allowed to say these terrible things to our young people?" But what they should be asking is "How can we prevent another young person from having to grow up in the same conditions as 50 Cent?" They should ask how we can stop another child from having his mother killed when he was a young boy. How can we change the conditions that led to him getting shot nine times. We need to ask *those* questions. And until we do, I don't think a rapper like 50 Cent owes us shit but the truth.

Whether it's by 50 Cent, Snoop Dogg, NWA, or whoever, there is not *one* record that I hear on the radio that I think *shouldn't* be on the radio. I want to make this clear. There's not one record that I find offensive. That's because one of the things I've learned from yoga is that God is everywhere and in everything. If there's interest in these records that some people find offensive, it's because they are telling the truth about their environment. We can't break the mirror. We have to look at and address these conditions that are reflected in it.

And instead of being afraid of that truth, we should use it as a road map for what we can do to fix these problems. Instead of worrying about cleaning up rap, we need to worry about cleaning up the communities that a lot of these rappers are talking about. Neighborhoods that don't have enough services, enough jobs, enough good housing. If we do that, rap lyrics won't seem so negative anymore.

Spitting Truth All Over the Globe

When people hear hip-hop all day long . . . it is no surprise that they [become angry] as soon as they walk past policemen.

A quote from one of the senators on that panel I was just telling you about? Nope. It's actually a quote from a French politician who wanted to ban hip-hop in France after riots broke out in Paris's *banlieues,* or African immigrant suburbs, in 2005. The politician tried to claim that the rappers were inciting violence by criticizing the police and the government in their lyrics. But of course, what was true in Los Angeles in 1989 was also true in Paris in 2005. The French youth weren't rioting because of hip-hop. They were rioting because the rest of society wasn't addressing the conditions and situations that French rappers had been warning them about for years.

So even if we don't always hear the truth that rappers spit in America, it's very inspiring to remember that their commitment to truth and honesty has already spread across the globe. Everywhere that hip-hop is popular, which is to say almost the entire world at this point, it has become the voice of the voiceless. Inspired by the honesty of rappers like NWA, Public Enemy, and Dead Prez, these rappers might speak different languages, but they share a belief in using hip-hop to give a voice to the voiceless.

That's why in Paris, it was the rappers who were speaking the loudest about the struggles of the African immigrants in that city. It was the rappers who warned that these young people from Algeria or Senegal or Cameroon might be living in France, or even have been born there, but still feel completely locked out of French society. Just as in Brazil, it's the rappers who are speaking the loudest about the incredible violence and poverty that can be found in the *favelas,* or ghettos, of São Paulo and Rio. Just as in the Ukraine, it was a rap song called "Together We're Many" that became the anthem of that country's "Orange Revolution." And from England to Germany to the Gaza Strip to South Africa to Taiwan, you can find rappers spitting truth to what is happening in their worlds, too, warning us to pay attention to their conditions before it's too late. So if in America sometimes it seems like the message has drifted away from protesting and toward partying, then maybe we need to look at what we've created and remind ourselves what we're capable of. Spitting Truth is a tradition we need to not only respect, but protect!

Standing Up for the Dixie Chicks

We have to be more vigilant in protecting our right to free speech and dissent, which we sometimes have a tendency to take for granted in this country. And I'm not just talking about hip-hop— I'm referring to everyone's right to spit truth. We can't forget that when Natalie Maines of the Dixie Chicks, a white, southern country group, stated she was opposed to the planned invasion of Iraq and that she was ashamed that President Bush came from Texas, it almost cost them their career. They faced boycotts, were called traitors, had to endure all sorts of personal attacks, and actually received some very serious physical threats, simply because they spoke their minds. I'm no country music fan, but I am a fellow critic of the war, so I found the situation very alarming. I was concerned that if these voices were able to intimidate and shut out the Dixie Chicks, it would create an atmosphere where any sort of dissent against the president or the war would become very difficult.

That's why at the height of the outrage against the Dixie Chicks prior to the Iraq invasion, I called up my friend Arnold Schwarzenegger and asked him if there was any way he could use his connections to get the conservative media to back off the Dixie Chicks a bit. While Arnold was sympathetic to what I was saying, he told me that if people want to attack the war, that's certainly their right, but they should also expect to be criticized. "Besides," he told me, "all those years I was criticized in Hollywood for being a Republican, I never heard the Dixie Chicks or any other artists stand up for my rights. So why should I stand and protect the Dixie Chicks if I don't agree with what they said?" I saw Arnold's point, but I was still determined to do something about the situation.

So next I arranged a conversation with then Secretary of State Colin Powell, in which I tried to convince him to get the president to help defuse the situation. I suggested that the president say something like "The Dixie Chicks have a right to their opinion and no matter what they think about me, I'm proud that they're from Texas." I thought it would have been funny, and reminded America that it's OK for people to have opinions and say what they want to say. Secretary Powell listened intently, but to my knowledge the message was never conveyed.

Eventually the invasion took place, at which point most people became even more muted in their support of the Chicks and attacks on the war. Even Bobby Shriver, whose opinion I value so much, told me that once the troops were on the ground, they needed our unconditional support and it wasn't appropriate to be so critical anymore. And while I respected his thinking, I couldn't subscribe to it. I felt that once the troops were on the ground, I had even more of a duty to speak out. And I went on television the next day (I believe it was *Good Morning America*) to support the Chicks and attack the war once more. It wasn't because I didn't respect the troops, but because I believe that in times of war and crisis it's even more important that we have a free exchange of ideas and opinions in this country. Even though I know men like Arnold Schwarzenegger and Colin Powell to be truthful and open-minded, not everyone in politics shares those qualities. When there's no open exchange of opinions, it gives those in power too much freedom to pursue their iniatives without any regard for what's in the best interest of the people. I believe the success of America was built on dissent, and when we enter into a climate where dissent is shut down, then we risk losing everything that we've gained in the country.

That's why we have to speak out when anyone's right to free speech is threatened, not just our own. And I mean *everyone's*. I might represent hip-hop, but I've got to speak up if I see a country music group get censored. They might not seem to have anything to do with me, but if the Dixie Chicks get shut down today, then there's a much greater chance Snoop Dogg is going to get shut down tomorrow.

And just as we can't allow what we *say* to the world to be censored, we can't censor what we *hear* from the world either. In other words, if you're a liberal, don't automatically shut out the conservative voices. If you're on the right, don't automatically reject everything that comes from the left. I really believe that almost everyone has a strand of truth in their message. So don't be bullheaded and think you've got all the answers. The successful people are the ones who *listen* to every opinion. As much as I'm frustrated by all the junk they promote on Fox News, I'll still sit down with Bill O'Reilly or on *Hannity & Colmes* and try to engage them in a discussion (even though it drives my liberal friends crazy). To be truly effective in spitting truth to power, you have to listen to what power has to say first. And once you've digested their truth and their perspective, then you can make your own argument much more persuasive.

Spitting Truth in Business

I know we've been talking about spitting truth in a social context so far in this chapter, but it's important to understand that Spitting Truth can been applied to a business model as well. Most companies shy away from making political statements out of fear that it will affect their bottom line. But I've found that addressing issues doesn't preclude you from profit-making. Certainly a lot of people have suggested that it would be better for my businesses if I kept my political views to myself and didn't try to tie them into any of my business ventures. But I feel that if I didn't speak out, I'd lose my integrity. And integrity is why people respect my brand in the first place.

Phat Farm was launched with a politically charged emblem, an upside-down American flag symbolizing a "Nu American Dream" that includes people of all races. Similarly, when we launched our Phat Farm Classic sneaker, we put up billboards that read, "Isn't it time for change? Economic justice now. Reparations now. It's an American justice issue." Normally, reparations for slavery is the type of issue most companies wouldn't touch with a hundred-foot pole, let alone a ten-foot pole. But I couldn't see any danger in interjecting that message into our marketing. I figured interest in that subject would just make our audience look at those billboards a little more closely than they would for a normal sneaker ad. I must have been right, because we ended up selling close to $250 million worth of sneakers while talking about economic justice. And more important than the sales, while most kids couldn't even spell *reparations* before that campaign, but now they're much more aware of the issue. So whenever I have the opportunity, I'm going to try to create a dialogue while I'm making money. It's just part of the way we do business, as well as the way we live.

Having said that, I will admit that the marketplace is one space where you have to be a little bit more selective in spitting truth. In other words, you just can't attach a cause to every product you sell and expect your audience to embrace it. You must take the time to assess the reaction you're going to get on a case-by-case basis. Try to put your passion aside and be honest about whether your message will turn your audience on, or turn it off. If you think it will turn it on, then don't be afraid to inject that passion into your product. But if you think it's going to turn your audience off, then you might want to go in another direction. My instinct was that reparations was a subject people who support Phat Farm wanted to have a conversation about. But I also realize that people might not want to hear about the situation in Darfur, or about police brutality, when they're buying a polo shirt. So sometimes it's better to hold back. When you're trying to inspire someone, whether it's in business or politics or in any field, you can't just speak *at* them. You have to make sure you're speaking *with* them.

Following My Father

I learned the importance of spitting truth to power at an early age from my father, Daniel Simmons. My father wasn't part of the "hip-hop generation," but he had what today we would call a hip-hop attitude (he helped create that attitude: In addition to bringing Reverend Run, Danny, and myself into the world, my father was a great poet who also wrote a couple of Run DMC's early songs) and was never afraid to speak his mind. That's not to say that my father operated outside of the system—he worked for the government, believed in following the rules and holding down a nine-to-five job. But he wasn't afraid to speak out against what he perceived to be any abuses by that system either. My father spit truth on many occasions, both in his poetry and in his actions, but the time that really stood out to me was a day during the mid-sixties, when my family was taking a drive out to the beach at the edge of Queens. We were driving through South Jamaica when my father saw some neighbors protesting outside a construction site. When he got out to investigate, he found out that they were upset because, while the building was being built in a black neighborhood, the contractor hadn't hired any black construction workers to work on the site. It wasn't right to only bring in white workers from outside the community when there where plenty of skilled black workers living in that neighborhood who could have used the opportunity.

Well, after my father heard that, that was the end of our trip to the beach. My father joined the picket line that very afternoon and kept coming back every day, even after he was arrested for protesting, until the contractor finally caved in and hired some black workers. And it wasn't just raising his voice—I even saw my father risk his life by lying down in front of a bulldozer that tried to break the picket line. That made a very deep impression on my brothers and me. It would have been one thing if my father was a construction worker looking for a check. But he wasn't—his own livelihood wasn't going to be affected by what happened on that job site. Instead, he joined the strike and spoke up (and even lay down) because he believed in what the workers were fighting for. That alone was enough.

Watching his example taught us that if you see a truth that's being ignored, you have to speak up for it. Even if it's hard, even if it's dangerous, or even if on the surface it doesn't look like it's going to effect your life directly, you still have to speak up. It helped us realize that spitting truth to power isn't a luxury, but a duty.

Grassroots and Shining Stars

When my father joined the picket line, he provided an example of a true grassroots protest. He saw a problem in his community, joined his neighbors in speaking out against it, and made sure his voice was heard until the problem was solved. And that is a very effective way to change a situation.

But while I've always tried to follow my father's example, I've also developed my own strategies when it comes to spitting the truth. While I readily admit that mobilizing people on a grassroots level is the best way to build a strong foundation, I also think it can be helpful to add celebrity and media attention into the mix as well. I know that some people think that having a celebrity endorse an issue dilutes its message, but I think a little star power can go a long ways toward helping inspire a change.

I like to believe that combination was effective recently when I helped build a coalition of grassroots groups and celebrities in speaking out against New York State's Rockefeller Drug Laws, which enforce mandatory jail time for drug convictions. Our opposition to the laws was based in the belief that there is no need to waste millions of tax dollars on incarcerating people who haven't hurt anybody but themselves. Even worse, ninety-five percent of the people jailed under these laws are black and brown, which made it the worst case of racial profiling we've ever seen. As I've said, it makes more sense for us to try to help people who are caught up with drugs than try to find new ways to throw them in jail.

So with the help of incredibly committed grassroots groups like the Drug Policy Alliance and Mothers of the Disappeared, plus celebrities like Puffy, 50 Cent, LL Cool J, and Mariah Carey, who were newer to the cause, we pressed the New York State Legislature to make a change. We met with New York governor George Pataki and several legislative bodies, held rallies, and made as much noise in the press as we could about the issue. And after considerable debate, drama, and heartache, we finally did convince New York's legislature to reform the laws. Admittedly, some of the grassroots groups were frustrated with the compromise we reached and felt we could have done much more. I certainly understand their frustration—I wish we could have completely wiped the laws off the books too. But I still believe the deal we reached was a major accomplishment. We might not have gained everything we were looking for, but a lot of people did come home early because of our fight, so I don't think it was in vain. The whole experience was definitely a wake-up call for me on how politics works behind the scenes, and maybe next time I will do some things different. But I ultimately believe the combination of grassroots activism and celebrity pressure did effect a change. Because when we first started protesting, a handful of people would come to the rallies. But when Jay-Z, Puffy, 50 Cent, the Beastie Boys, and Mariah were there, suddenly a hundred thousand people were at the rally, not to mention all sorts of media. So I don't see how that's a negative. Sure, a percentage of those people were probably only there to see Puffy. But while they might have come just to see Puffy, hopefully they left with a better understanding of the issue. An understanding that in turn they could share with their families and friends. And that's a victory unto itself.

It's always good to find strong partners when it's time to spit truth. The key is understanding that recruiting celebrities for your cause is also a cultural step, not only a political step. It's in style for the celebrities to be at the rallies. It's in style for them to give back. It's in style for them to speak out. So personally, I'm going to try to maximize that mindset. The Jay-Zs and the Puffys of the world have a gift for promotion that we can use to help get ideas to young people around the world. We'd be foolish not to exploit that resource, especially since these artists are givers who are happy to be exploited for a positive purpose.

The truth is, if you're a politician, you can't ignore the light that high-profile rappers can shine on a situation. That might frustrate the grassroots groups who might have already done so much incredible work on that issue, but it's a fact of life. It's a fact of life that when 50 Cent and Mariah Carey start talking about an issue, and then Puffy starts talking about it, too, there's a snowball effect. From a politician's perspective, when before there were a few voices in the chorus, suddenly it seems like the whole world is pointing their fingers at you. And that's the type of pressure that will motivate even the most selfish politician to finally do some good work for the people.

Don't Make the Struggle Harder

Mandatory drug laws are definitely one of the biggest issues I've encouraged the hip-hop nation to speak out against. But there are plenty of other issues that we also need to tell the truth about too. We need to spit truth about raising the minimum wage, increasing education budgets, protecting the environment, ending racial profiling, protecting immigrants' rights, and countless other problems. Each of those issues probably deserve their own chapter, if not their own book. But for the purposes of this chapter, I want to promote spitting truth at one issue in particular that I feel is taking a terrible toll on this country—and that's gun violence.

I've made a lot of lists over the years, some flattering, some not so flattering. But one list that I was particularly happy to be included on was a "blacklist" put together by the National Rifle Association, featuring celebrities, corporations and organizations that the NRA labeled "antigun." The NRA usually gets things wrong, but they got that one right. Because I am one hundred percent antigun!

Not surprisingly, I'm also a big critic of the NRA. It's very rare for me to be so negative about an organization, but I have hard time hearing *any* high notes from the NRA. No one has explained to me why there's a legitimate reason to manufacture tools that take lives but don't do anything to uplift lives. I don't see any value in guns and I don't want them around me.

The irony is that lot of the politicians who support the NRA are the same politicians who are quick to attack hip-hop for its violent lyrics. These people are the worst kind of hypocrites. They'll attack 50 Cent or Jay-Z for *talking* about the violence they see all around them, but then they'll turn around and defend people who are supplying the weapons behind the violence. It would be a joke if this weren't such a serious situation.

I know the NRA describe themselves as lobbyists, but to me they're straight gun gangsters. They might wear suits, speak in a civilized manner, and fly in corporate jets, but they're still gangsters who are pushing a product that kills people. And they're getting away with it because the politicians are getting paid from the NRA's money. The politicians should be the first ones to stand tall and say something. After all, their biggest priority should be protecting their constituents. But too many politicians either depend on the lobbying money or are just plain old soft and don't have the backbone to speak out against this system. So we're going to have to do it ourselves.

Some of you think you need a gun to survive the struggle, but trust me, you don't. Owning a gun will most likely make the struggle harder for you. That gun is going to bring a lot of negative energy your way. You can follow every single law in this book, but if you walk around with a gun in your waist, or drive around with one in your glove compartment, then you are going to severely dilute your power. You run a strong risk that the negativity a tool like a gun creates will pull you down. I believe there are very few material things that can threaten your success as much as a gun does.

I want to make it very clear that I'm not judging you if you do have a gun. I've been around enough guns in my life, and associated with enough people who talk about guns and own guns, that I'd be foolish to try to make a judgment on anyone else. I'm just trying to promote a different mentality. A mentality in which we stop being manipulated by predatory industries like the gun manufacturers and start handling our business in a more peaceful and productive manner.

This comes back to the idea that you should always be looking for ways that you can give, instead of for ways you can take. Especially taking a life. That's the worst thing you can do. Too many children are dying. Too many families are being destroyed. And too many gunmakers are sitting back, stacking their chips, while we're killing each other. It has to stop.

RECOGNIZE THE REAL:

We believe that we must continue to tell the truth about the street if that is what we know and we must continue to tell the truth about God if that is who we have found.

EPILOGUE

You must be the change you want to see in the world.
—GANDHI

IF I COULD END THIS BOOK on one high note, I couldn't think of a more appropriate one than those beautiful words from Gandhi. That's the essence of what I've tried to promote—by listening to your higher self, or Atman, you can return to the truth that's already inside of you and in the process change not only yourself, but the entire world, through positivity and love.

So while these laws are truly unbreakable, please don't leave this book thinking that the laws are here to tie you up—rather, they're here to free you. And the more you remember to operate under them, then the less you'll be interested in living outside of them. I promise that you'll see that freedom and lasting success are already in your heart and there's no need to spend your life searching for something else.

Once you find yourself consciously operating under the laws, or even just in close proximity to them, you can begin to effect the same change that you feel in your heart throughout the world at large. Living under these laws, you won't feel like you have to compromise what you believe in just because people around you are compromising themselves. Living under the laws, you'll look for a peaceful solution to problems that have everyone else calling for violence and revenge. Living under these laws, you'll be excited about sharing with the world, instead of plotting on how much you can take from it. Living under these laws, instead of insisting that only your particular faith knows the path to God, you'll accept that all the faiths are one. Living under these laws, if a so-called leader tries to stick people in ovens, you'll stand up and say, "That's wrong." Living under these laws, if a government tries to enslave human beings for profit under the guise of religion, you'll spit truth to that power. Living under these laws, if you hear about genocide being committed halfway around the world, you'll stand up and say, "What can I do to help stop that?" And through your example, people who previously acted like sheep, and followed whatever foul path they were led down, will see that they do have the ability to make the right choice. And through your example, you'll not only be moving closer to sustainable success, but you will be becoming a leader who will lead others to a similar state.

I don't think what I've said is that shocking or different. In fact, I think most of it is very simple and obvious. But I'm committed to sharing it because I want to be part of the dramatic shift in consciousness I feel taking place in the world right now. I want to be part of the change from selfishness and greed to happiness and sustainable success. I can only recommend the right road. Whether we end up taking it or not, it's the one I think is right.

Finally, I want to say that writing this epilogue has taken on an added significance for me, as literally just days ago I received an urgent call that Jinx, the young rapper I was speaking about earlier in this book, had been shot after attending the wake of a friend in Brooklyn. Thankfully Jinx survived, but I will admit that for the last several days his situation has been weighing heavily on me. Here is a young man barely twenty-one, who has been through so much, yet remains completely focused on pursuing his dreams. He returns to his old neighborhood to bury a friend way too early and, in doing so, once again finds his own life threatened by the struggle. I could barely comprehend the pain and uncertainty he must be feeling lying in a hospital bed with holes in his arms and legs at an age when most young people are filled with excitement and enthusiasm for the future.

Last night, Jinx and I had a long conversation, during which he spoke not only about the pain from his wounds, but also his worries about the future. And even though, when the conversation started, I was unsure of the right words to share with this incredible young man, the more we talked, the more I found myself drawing on the truths that we've been talking about in this book. We spoke about the importance of ignoring the low notes and focusing on your higher self. We spoke about why surrounding yourself with the right people is so critical. We spoke about the need to have faith in your vision even when it seems your vision is so far from becoming a reality. We spoke about how, even when faced with seemingly overwhelming obstacles, you can never quit following your dream. We talked about how, even when it seems like all the world is doing is taking from you, it's just that much more important to count your blessings and then try to share them with the world. And soon a conversation that (because of my anxiety and worry over Jinx) had started in a dark place was uplifted into the light. Jinx has many months of rehabilitation ahead of him, but I told him that when he does get back on his feet, I want to give him a book that hopefully will help him to remember to remember the things we talked about that night while he was lying in a hospital bed. And that book is the one that you're reading now.

To my lovely daughters,
Ming Lee and Aoki Lee,
and their fabulous and wonderful mother, Kimora Lee.

ACKNOWLEDGMENTS

Living Inspirations:

Daniel Simmons Sr., Evelyn Simmons, Shirley Simmons, Danny Simmons, Jamel Simmons, the Honorable Minister Louis Farrakhan, Gandhi, Martin Luther King, Sri Swami Satchidan and Paramahansa Yogananda, Reverend Run and family, the Dali Lama, Dr. Ben Chavis, Sharon Gannon, David Life, Eckhart Tolle, Steve Ross, and Rabbi Marc Schneier.

Thanks to:

Derrick Adams, Bill Adler, Chris Albrecht, Sal Albatellos, Aaliyah, Jacob Arabo, Peter Arnell, Clarence Avant, Ruby Azrak, Andre Balazs, Steve Bartels, Heidi Smith, Ingrid Newkirk, Vinnie Bell, Bill Bellamy, Gilles Bensimon, Kelly Bensimon, Troy Beyer, Jason Binn, Erik Blam, Mary J. Blige, Kendu Isaacs, Michael Bloomberg, Jon Bon Jovi, Stella Booze, Christopher Briggs, Bernie Brillstein, Sheldon Brody, Sherry B. Bronfman, Edgar Bronfman Jr., Marie Brown, Carol Brown, Mark Burg, Reverend Calvin Butts, Jan Cain, Jason Carbone, Mariah Carey, Shawn "Jay-Z" Carter, Ilene Chaiken, Rebecca Chaiklin, Young In Chung, Bill Clinton, Hillary Clinton, Lyor Cohen, Sean Combs, Michael Concepcion, Rhonda Cowan, Marilyn Crawford, Deana Cunningham, Andrew Cuomo, Chuck D, Heavy D, Sante D'Orazio, Solomon Dabah, Damon Dash, Sandra Davidson, Donny Deutsch, Michael Diamond, Tony DiSanto, Michele Dix, Peter Drakoulias, Dro DMX, Vida Dominguez, Peter Ezersky, Osman Eralp, Joshua Farrakhan, Mustafa Farrakhan, Steven Feiner, Flavor Flav, Harold Ford, Katie Ford, Robert Ford, Gary Foster, Tom Freston, Glen E. Friedman, LaShaun Fullerton, Larry Gagosian, Oz Garcia, Rebecca Gayheart, David Geffen, Nancy Geller, Nelson George, Irv Gotti, Brian Graden,

Earl Graves Sr., Brian Grazer, Julie Greenwald, Brad Grey, Allen Grubman, Ellen Haddigan, Mark Hall, Andre Harrell, Dr. Dorothy Heights, Tommy Hilfiger, Stephen Hill, Selwyn Hinds, Michael Hirschorn, Luke Hoverman, Zach Horowitz, Adam Horvitz, Reginald Hudlin, Cathy Hughes, DJ Hollywood, Arthur Indursky, Jimmy Iovine, Haqq Islam, Jesse Jackson Sr., Robert James, Jam Master Jay, Spuddy Jenkins, Jinx, Leilani Johnson, Robert Johnson, Eddie Bernice Johnson, Quincy Jones, Bishop Jordan, Ashley Judd, Kerry Kennedy, Nate Kestenman, Alicia Keys, Gayle King, Mia Kirshner, Barry Klarberg, Larry Kopp, Alan Hergott, Stan Lathan, Debra Lee, Kenny Lee, Ed Lewis, Chris Lighty, Kevin Liles, Peter Lowy, Madonna, Darryl McDaniels, Bill Maher, Al Malnik, Kim Manley, Craig Marshall, Chris Mathieson, Marshall Mathers, Victor Matthews, Wendell Mattison, Dave Mays, Kim Melo, Jack McCue, Judith McGrath, Lucia McLean, O'Neal McKnight, Jillian Manus, Gregory Meeks, Ron Meyer, Bill Milliken, Jody Miller, Scott Mills, Doug Morris, Tommy Mottola, Chris Morrow, Captain Dennis Muhammad, Akbar Muhammad, Sister Claudette Muhammad, Don Muhammad, Donna Muhammad, Elijah Muhammad, Ishmael Muhammad, Josh Muhammad, Kamal Muhammad, Kevin Muhammad, Lantanja Muhammad, Leo Muhammad, Leonard Muhammad, Leonard Muhammad Jr., Maria Muhammad, Mustapha Muhammad, Rashad Muhammad, Brother Sean Muhammad, Sharif Muhammad, Sherwood Muhammad, Mother Tynetta Muhammad, Wali Muhammad, Nas, Petra Nemcova, Vivi Nevo, Cynthia Nixon, Craig Nobles, Christina Norman, Guy Oseary, Jennifer Oppenheimer, Bert Padell, Tim Park, Rebecca Parker, Dolores Parker, John Pasmore, George E. Pataki, Alan Patricof, Jamie Patricof, Christina Paljusaj, Ronald Perelman, Richard Plepler, Dr. Primus, Brett Ratner, Benny Ratt, Scott Rauch, Antonio "LA" Reid, Morris Reid, Simone Reyes, Denise Rich, Steven Rifkind, Guy Ritchie, Ritchie Johnnie Roberts, Chris Rock, David Rosenberg, Paul Rosenber, Jane Rosenthal, Howard J. Rubenstein, Steven Rubenstein, Rick Rubin, Stephen Ruzow, Rose Salem, Steve Salem, Diane Sawyer, Paul Schindler, Chuck Schumer, Raj Shah, Tupac Shakur, Al Sharpton, Nina L. Shaw, Abe Shnay, Lara Shriftman, Bobby Shriver, Joel Silver, Anne Simmons, Sharon Simmons, Robert C. Skinner Jr., Biggie Smalls, Rich Slomovitz, Olivia Smashum, Will Smith, Todd "LL Cool J" Smith, Steve Smooke, Mary Catherine Sneed, Eliot Spitzer, Deborah St. Ange, Annie St. Louis, Jivamukti Staff, Lovebug Starski, Michael Steele, Bill Stephney, Carolyn Strauss, Arnold Schwarzenegger, Maria Shriver, John Sykes, Andre Leon Talley, Susan Taylor, Bill Thompson, Greg Thompson, Nena Thurman, Robert Thurman, Bonnie Tobias, Van Toffler, Donald Trump, Chris Tucker, Leyla Turkkan, Sandy Smallens, Bernt Ullmann, Hal Upbin, Gretchen Wagner, Jeff Wald, Maxine Waters, Susan Weaving, Jann Wenner, Sanford Wernick, Emil Wilbekin, Serena Williams, Bruce Willis, Jeannie Wilson, Oprah Winfrey, Anna Wintour, Adam Yauch, Andrew Young. My yoga teachers: Iyala Berley, Allison Bridges, Kelly Britton, Jeff Brown, Jeffrey Cohen, K. C. Cooley, Seane Corne, Jessie De La Rosa, Jules Febre, Paisley Fenyes, Faith Fennessey, Sandhi Ferreira, Jillian Friedman, David Gluck, Petros Haffenrichter, Monica Jaggi, Jennifer Johnson, Julie Kirkpatrick-Gueye, Beth Krafchik, Jessica Kung, Lakshmi (Shanna Lee), Heather Lilleston, Matthew Lombardo, Orly Mallin, Ruth Lauer-Manenti, Manorama, Maria Massana, Ganeshela, Carlos Menjivar, Ana Marie Muriel, Narayani (Nicole Nichols), Kristina Pao Cheng, Maria Preuster, Rima Rabbath, Shiva Rea, Cassandra Rigney, Liz Roberts, Cathrine Rolfe, Colleen Saidman, Uma Saraswati, Alyssa Scheunemann, Jeff Scios, Shivadasi (Felise Berman), Shri (Sarah Court), Eve Stahlberger, Dechen Thurman, Natalie Ullmann, Dana Van Woerden, Ana Maria Velasco, Esther Widjaja, Kriota Willberg, Katherine Worden, Yogeswari (Estelle Eichenberger). Everyone at Rush Communications, Kellwood, Hip-Hop Summit Action Network, Phat Farm, Baby Phat, Simmons Jewelry, Rush Philanthropic, Russell Simmons Music Group, Run Athletics, Rush Mobile, Uni-Rush, Def Jam Enterprises and Simmons Lathan Media Group: Victor Syng, Joanne Perkins, and Kyoko Perkins.

Chris Morrow would like to thank:

Russell Simmons and Nahshon Craig, my wife Peggy Cheng (for everything), Bill, Judi, and Suzie Morrow, the Cheng, Morrow, and Karabel families, Akasha Archer, Big Tigger and LITD, Carrie Davis, Jason Hernandez-Rosenblatt, Jennifer Leimgruber, Ira Robbins, Jillian Manus, Michelle Tessler, plus Bill Shinker, Lauren Marino, Hilary Terrell, Lisa Johnson, Ashwini Ramaswamy, and everyone at Gotham Books.